MEN'S WORK AND MALE LIVES

Men's Work and Male Lives

Men and work in Britain

JOHN GOODWIN
Centre for Labour Market Studies, University of Leicester

Ashgate

Aldershot • Brookfield USA • Singapore • Sydney

Published by
Ashgate Publishing Ltd
Gower House
Croft Road
Aldershot
Hants GU11 3HR
England

Ashgate Publishing Company
Old Post Road
Brookfield
Vermont 05036
USA

British Library Cataloguing in Publication Data
Goodwin, John
    Men's work and male lives: men and work in Britain
    1. Male employees - Great Britain 2. Sex role in the work
    environment - Great Britain 3. Men - Great Britain -
    Identity
    I. Title
    305.3'3

Library of Congress Catalog Card Number: 98-74132

ISBN 1 84014 577 3

Printed in **Great Britain**

Contents

List of tables

Introduction

Introduction

The present study focuses on the sociology of men[1] and work via an empirical case study of the lives of nearly 5,000 men in the UK. This group of men are members of the National Child Development Study (NCDS), and all completed the NCDS survey returns during the last sweep of this survey in 1991. Due to the nature of the data[2], the men were mainly 'white' and heterosexual. All the men were aged 33.

However, to study men, in whatever context or area of enquiry, for some will seem a novel act. For others it will (re)present a threat to their research, teaching and their existing beliefs about society. Yet, for those who work within the field of studying men, the research is more than a superficial challenge to an established gender enquiry. It is more about describing and analysing the attitudes, experiences and relationships that men encounter; its about their employment, their education and their experiences in the family. Finally, on a macro level, it is about how society perceives men and what men do.

As such, this current research addresses two related objectives. First, the book attempts to argue that an analysis of men has been largely absent in British gender based sociology. The point has to be made that a sociological study of men is not only required, but essential if a fuller understanding of 'gender' is to be gained. However by making such a point, it is essential that these sentiments are not taken as an apology or justification for the behaviour of some men. What it is an argument for is that men should be studied in their own right, and that men do not have to be appended to, or studied by accident in the study of women.[3]

Second, that men's experiences of the labour market, and labour market issues have become lost in the broader 'gender and work' based research. As such men's labour market experiences are not examined *per se*. This is highlighted by Collinson and Hearn (1994)

texts on organisations have appeared which fail to examine masculinity despite explicitly citing men in their title, e.g. Men Who Manage (Dalton 1959) Organisation Man (Whyte 1956) Men at the Top (Elliot 1960) and Man on the Assembly Line (Walker and Guest 1952). Alternatively some writers in industrial relations, industrial sociology have talked about 'managers', 'workers', 'shop stewards', 'the working class' and implicitly treated those categories interchangeable with men.

(Collinson and Hearn 1994: 3-4)

The importance of such sentiments are further enhanced when one considers the fact that work is inextricably linked to men's lives. Therefore, to study men and work is really to examine the very nature and content of male lives, with work as one of the defining features of men's lives.

Given these broad objectives and views it is possible to set out four main aims for this book:

(i)   To establish that there is a real absence of an empirical understanding of men in British gender based sociological research;

(ii) to explore how men and work are linked by examining and using existing accounts of gender theory and feminism;

(iii) to examine men's recent experiences of the British labour market; and finally

(iv) to provide an empirical account of men's work via an analysis of existing data. To do so using established hypotheses and notions of full-time and non-standard [4] work to illustrate the analysis.

General Themes and Debates

Men and Sociology

In classical sociology, a limited analysis of men and work appeared before any of the gender critique offered by academic feminists. For example, an analysis of gender roles can be seen very clearly in both the work of Marx, Durkheim, with both suggesting the sexual division of labour develops as society moves towards industrial based civilisation. For Marx

The division of labour offers us the first example of how...man's own act becomes an alien power, opposed to him, which enslaves him...as soon as the division of labour begins, each man has a particular exclusive sphere of activity forced upon him and from which he cannot escape.

(Marx cited in Bottomore and Rubel 1986: 110)

Durkheim's analysis reflected upon the sexual division of labour, offering an account of the growing increased differentiation of task and role that is characteristic of men and women in industrial society.

We are therefore led to consider the division of labour in a new light. In this case, indeed, the economic services that it can render are insignificant compared with the moral effect that it produces, and its true function is to create, between two or more people, a feeling of solidarity.

(Durkheim 1984: 17)

Yet for such classical sociologists, the focus on gender was not as important as their larger schemes of work. Later as the discipline of sociology developed, gender roles returned to the sociological enquiry (see Parsons 1956), and specific male groups became the focus for research (especially if their behaviour was deemed to be something of a social problem). A good illustration of this is juvenile delinquency, a common theme throughout the 1950s and 1960s, explaining male social ills by the absence of the father or mother (Bowlby 1946; Hacker 1957; Hartley 1959; Sexton 1969).

Such themes were of central importance to the American sociological debate. For example, Hartley (1959) discussed links between father absence and the over presence of the mother to increased levels of anxiety in young boys. Hartley's research produced a picture of boys who had very distant relationships with their fathers, and boys who had been taught to value everything feminine from an early age while living in a social environment dominated by women. Hartley suggested that the problem here was not father absence but masculine socialisation carried out primarily by women only. Hacker (1957), separately took these debates further by suggesting that

As a man, men are now expected to demonstrate the manipulative skill in interpersonal relations formerly reserved for women under the headings of charm, tact, coquetry, womanly wiles, et cetera. They are asked to bring patience, understanding, gentleness to their human dealings. Yet with regard to women they must still be sturdy oaks.

(Hacker 1957: 229)

Hacker points out that the man in a relationship was often necessarily absent from the family, yet criticised for the effect that this had on his children (Carrigan *et al* 1987).

A further conflict for men was the increasing dichotomy between the sexuality of some men and societal expectations. With the increasing visibility of male homosexuality Hacker also suggested the need to establish empirically arguing that 'a typology of men, perhaps according to family constellations or social class position, in terms of their interpretation of the demands of masculinity and their felt capacity to fulfil them (Hacker 1957: 232).

In terms of male work, Komarovsky (1964), in 'Blue Collar Marriage', portrayed a vivid picture of the interactions that constitute everyday life. Komarovsky showed a picture of masculinity that was harsh, and according to Tiger, such harshness could be explained. Lionel Tiger's (1969) 'Men in Groups' documented men's control of war, politics, production and sports arguing that this was linked to genetic pattern built in to men based on ancestral co-operative hunting.

Numerous other examples of the crisis of masculinity such as Thrasher's The Gang (1927) and Whyte's 'Street Corner Society' (1943). Yet the point here is that all this early work on men can be seen to have a common theme running through it. Fout identifies this well and links it to the male Protestant moral purity movement[5], which he suggests was the initial men's movement, in Germany. This men's movement focused on the growing anxiety about 'appropriate male behaviour' and such moral concerns underpinned aspects of the sociological enquiry.

The importance of such debates cannot be underestimated. Yet much of what has been discussed so far (with the exception of Bowlby) is mainly American both in pedigree and outlook. In terms of British work on men, it is possible to identify a more recent, and certainly more limited men's movement in a number of publications that examined the experiences of men such as *Achilles Heel*, and *Men's Anti-sexist Newsletter*. Men's groups started to appear in Britain from around 1972, with like-minded pro-feminist men getting together to become more non-sexist. According to Segal (1990) these men's movements were in a muddle. They did not know whether to organise a support group for women's liberation or a groups transforming male consciousness arguing for male liberation.

> By 1975 there were between twenty and thirty groups of such like minded men around Britain, who were predominantly heterosexual and involved in relationships with feminists. A decade later…almost all towns in Britain…had some men's groups.
>
> (Segal 1990: 284)

In an academic, sociological framework there have been a number of Men's Conferences in the UK, the last one occurring in 1980[6] (see Segal 1990). One can also find (limited) commentaries on men in contemporary sociological classics such as those offered by Goldthorpe *et al* (1968), Beynon (1973), and Jenkins (1983).

For example, Goldthorpe *et al* (1968) offered a research monograph, which explored the attitudes and behaviour of a sample of affluent workers in the context of their industrial employment (Goldthorpe 1968: 1). Alternatively, Jenkins (1983) in 'Lads Citizens and Ordinary Kids', examined the working class life-styles of youth in Belfast and included an

4

account of the experiences of numerous young men. Jenkins explores every aspect of these young men's lives from sexuality to education and the transition to employment.

Yet, such commentaries, contrary to the feminist critique, did not consider men *per se*, but did so more by accident.

Men, Work and Employment in Britain

Amongst the many changes that have occurred in the labour market over the past thirty years, one of the most drastic is the increase of women's participation in paid employment and the decrease in male employment (Blanchflower 1986; Beechey and Perkins 1987; Coyle 1988; Walby 1990; Witz 1992; Hakim 1996).

Again, the idea of the linkage between men and work is expressed in the fact that traditionally, it is the man that was perceived to be the breadwinner, and the individual concerned with production outside of the home. The role of men was/is often defined by full-time, permanent employment. However, as suggested, along with the increase in women's employment, there has been a decrease in men's employment and the belief in long-term full time employment (Burchell 1990; Dawes 1993).

It is now not clear what jobs men actually do, and in some instances, why men do similar jobs to women. For example, in the Labour Force Survey for 1993, it is demonstrated that between Winter 1992/3 and Spring 1993, the percentage of men working part-time, increased by 2.6 per cent, whilst the increase percentage for women was only 1.7 per cent. Indeed in all of the seasonally adjusted figures, male part-time employment was the fastest growing employment form. Yet traditionally, as previous research has shown, women were over represented in these non-standard forms (Green *et al* 1992; Beechey and Perkins 1987; Dale and Bamford; 1988), and that non-standard forms of employment are (but not exclusively) characterised by low pay, limited benefits, economic insecurity and often have limited skill requirements (Green 1992).

This change can be seen as a broader historical shift. For example, in the Spring of 1984, there were 549,000 men in part-time work, but by the Spring of 1992, this had increased to 828,000. For women the increase had been less dramatic, although women still constituted the largest group of part-time workers. However, the traditional ideas of gender distinction between core and periphery workers may now be, or may become blurred; thus employers may include some women (or some groups of women) amongst their core workers and some men amongst their peripheral workers.

Yet , that such transitions in the labour market and the impact that they have had on women have been explored fully at this juncture, full and critically (Hakim 1996). However, for the study of male work, it soon becomes evident that most existing analyses are limited. For example, very few commentators have reflected upon the impact of non-standard employment on men. The reason for this appears to be that most works only use men as a reference point against which to measure women's participation.

Linking Sociology, Men and Work

...full-time employment fell from 21 million in 1951 to 19 million in 1995. All of this net loss has been in male employment...The question is it changed to the detriment of men as well as to the advantage of women?...Most commentators...emphasise that the workforce now consists of almost equal numbers of men and women...This is one source of the fear that work is being demasculinised. The other is the all too visible decline...of male manual jobs. The fear is expressed in that young working class men whose energies are not harnessed by jobs will express these energies in more destructive ways, rioting and fighting the police.

(Hakim 1996: 74 -75)

As suggested previously, men and work are closely linked yet, as with much of existing research in this area, very few of the studies cited actually attempt to offer an explanation of the centrality of employment to men's lives. However, one could argue that just as the position of the women in the labour market, and in the family is structured by patriarchy, so are men's family and labour market positions.

For example, socialist feminism may offer something to a discussion such as this as it offers some explanation of men's roles. It is argued by Hartmann (1979) that men have organised around the division of labour to exclude women from paid work. For example, the division of labour enforces lower wages upon women in the jobs that are available as they are defined as secondary, household workers. Low pay keeps women dependant upon men for money, and it is men who benefit from the household work that women do. In turn the circle is completed in that the position of women in the domestic division of labour weakens her position in the labour market.

Literature

It's been thirty-five years since Simone de Beauvoir's 'The Second Sex', and twenty-five years since Betty Friedan's 'The Feminine Mystique', announced the rebirth of modern feminism, transforming the women problem into a problem of the systematic denial to women of equal rights...its been fifteen years since male

Anglophones became aware that we have gender roles.

(Kimmel 1990: 93)

This book draws its literature from three main sources. First the growing body of literature linked under the headings of 'men's studies' and 'feminist scholarship'. Second, the book makes use of literature that focuses on the labour market and related issues. Third, as will be outlined below, a range of relevant literature that relates to the issues which can (and do) affect male lives.

The nature and content of work based sociological literature has been outlined extensively elsewhere, with commentators reflecting well on both 'content' and 'context' (see Hakim 1996). However the range of sources for the study of men attracts less attention, and with the exception of Ford and Hearn (1991), receives little commentary. The remainder of this section will be spent offering such a reflection.

As outlined in the above discussion a more theoretical study of men (for men) has been attempted before (Tolson 1987), but an adequate empirically based sociology of men and employment has not been adequately developed. The existing academic study of men can be divided into four broad areas[7]. First, men's studies work can be characterised by its political assumptions. The political nature of men's studies can be broken down into three main areas, pro-feminist (such as Hearn 1988; 1989), neo-liberal traditionalism (see authors such as Dench 1994) and finally gay affirmative (Edwards 1994).

The political nature of writings about men turns mainly to an exploration of power. Here one can use the work of feminists to suggest that the overall relationship between men and women is one which involves domination and oppression regardless as to whether such a relationship exists in actual fact.

A second broad area can be grouped together as theoretical approaches. Much of the theoretical base of research on men stems from the feminist tradition and their critique of gender roles. For example, some men studies scholars take the unit of analysis of patriarchy, seeing men as the agents of patriarchal oppression.

A third category is 'mythopoetic' men's studies. This is largely a product of the USA, and this is the type of men's studies that has entered the popular imagination suggesting men's studies is about 'men going into the woods to beat drums' (although this movement does claim to have some grounds for doing so). For example, Bly (1992) argues that by re-visiting and re-interpolating the stories and legends and myths of an ancient past, one is not only discovering deep masculine identity, but also one is finding men's authentic self.

The final area (and to date the most limited), is empirical discoveries. Carrigan *et al* suggest that the empirical content of men's studies turns out to be slight and that good quality research on men is rare[8] . What is needed is an empirical analysis of men that provides an outline of their lives how they actually are, not how they should be or how ideologically we would like them to be. This is not to suggest that the analysis should be devoid of a theoretical base - far from it, one could use the work of feminism to understand the roles that men occupy. But what is very clear is that we have to acknowledge that a difference exists in sexual power - whether that is right or not is entirely a different matter and has to be answered elsewhere by researchers in more of a political enquiry.

The Structure of the Book

The book is split loosely into three thematic parts, Sociology Men and Employment; Investigating Men; the final part of the book is Conclusions: Moving Male Work Further. Within these broad headings, the book is organised as follows:

Sociology, Men and Employment

This section is split into three main chapters. Chapter one considers the further development of (and the need for) a sociology of men in British gender based research. This chapter also highlights two separate (but related) themes, namely an absence of an empirically based critique of men and second how existing feminist theory can be used when combined with more contemporary work on men, to understand men's positions in the labour market.

Chapter two builds on the first chapter by offering a brief review of existing approaches that link men and work. However, whilst all these approaches have something to offer and the importance of such an exercise acknowledged, it is not the intention here to provide a summary of all the theoretical works on men or masculinity. This would be to simply replicate work done elsewhere (Doyle 1989; Brod *et al* 1994; Edley and Wetherell 1995). Nor does this chapter attempt to provide a new, overarching and all comprehensive theory of men and masculinity (or masculinities) as this also seems to be the project of others (see Connell 1995)[9]. However, it will be argued that the best way to understand the linkages between men and work is by combining aspects of feminist theory with a 'men's role' approach, and contextualising this as a social, cultural and historical construct which in the West is organised around the division of labour.

The third chapter in this section provides an overview of the nature of male employment in different industries, occupations and regions and for employees of differing age, marital and parental status and ethnic origin. Trends in male employment in recent years (such as the growth on non-standard employment) are also to be analysed.

Investigating Men's Work

Part two of the book contains six main chapters based around the premise that explicit research on men is currently limited within British gender based sociology. The reasons for this are manifested in a number of ways. First there is the overt assumption that all research is about 'men' (a falsehood). Second because of the feminist traditions that have so influenced sociological research, researchers (and teachers) are all too careful to equate gender research with researching women. Finally, because of forward moves in gender analysis made by the feminist tradition, any analysis of men has to occur within that paradigm, and is usually, therefore, carried out by women.

The first chapter in this section attempts to introduce the general approach used in the study. This chapter will reflect on the nature of gender based research and introduce the data used in the empirical chapters.

The five remaining chapters in this section each address a separate theme related to men's working lives. The themes covered in this book are a general introduction to male work in NCDS5; Men's Attitudes and Work Orientation; Men, Households and Private Work; Men, Training and Skills; and finally Psychological Ill-Health and Men's Work. Each of these chapters have two common elements. The first is that each of the issues will be explored in the literature. Second, a theme suggested in the literature will then be used to guide the empirical analysis. In many ways the data will be used to test out certain 'received wisdom' relating to men and work.

Conclusions: Moving Male Work Further?

The final part of the book contains one chapter which will reflect on what the book has achieved under the heading of 'Moving Male Work Further ?'. This really represents the dual broad objectives of this book. First, to argue for a sound and empirically based exploration of men. Second, to reflect the concern relating to men's labour market experiences and the need for men to reflect on the changing nature of male roles. In essence the book concludes that the nature of male work needs to be re-considered and that the nature of gender research, particularly that relating to men, needs to be expanded and made more explicit.

Concluding Remarks

This introduction has provided an insight into the aims of the book, its structure and its content. However to conclude the contribution this book is making, along with its distinctive features, need to be highlighted. The contribution that this book is making to both gender and work debates is twofold.

- First, the book highlights and acknowledges the absence of an adequate, empirically based study of men in British gender and work based sociology. Where men are explored, such research largely focuses on the theoretical issues of studying men or men are treated as a homogeneous empirical grouping against which to compare women. The book suggests that this fact needs to be rectified if gender is to be fully understood.

- Second, much has been written about female workers however, male work has not been problematised for or by men, with authors such as Collinson and Hearn (1995) arguing that men's work has now become invisible. To rectify this, the book reflects upon the centrality of work to masculinity and uses a large-scale quantitative data set to explore issues relating to men's work experiences.

The distinctive features of this book are that

- The focus of the discussion will be on men explicitly.

- That men's experiences of work and work related issues are explored quantitatively, using the National Child Development Study, for the first time.

- The book takes account of a number of existing hypotheses on men which were not the result of studies of men *per se*. The book argues that it should be possible to further explore such findings on 'men' and that they can be broadened out to take account of the employment differences between groups of men. By engaging in such an exercise, this book offers an empirical study of men, where the focus is actually on the men themselves.

The discussion now turns to section one of the book. This section begins with a consideration of the need for a sociological study of men, based on empiricism, in British sociological research.

Notes

1   Work in this book means paid employment external to the household.
2   A full discussion of the data is provided in chapter 4.
3   In making such an assertion it must be pointed out that the study of men can only be successful if the position of women is understood and acknowledged. However, this has been done fully elsewhere.
4   Non-standard workers are employees who work part-time and/or have more than one job and/or are employed on a temporary, seasonal or casual basis and/or have short periods of continuous service with the same employer. They may also be former employees of an organisation whom that organisation now hires on a self-employed, or freelance, basis to carry out particular tasks.
5   According to the moral purity movement, he writes, to sin was to exhibit behaviour that transgressed traditional assumptions about suitable male gender roles (Fout 1992; Steackley 1975; Stümke 1989). Fout suggests that the moral purity groups evolved out of a context where the gains made by women brought into question the roles played by women - the protagonists sought to (re)educate boys and men about their proper male role and duties. The aim of the education was to re confirm the central position of men in society and also have men maintain their dominance in the family.
6   Although men's issues have been dealt with in other conference arenas such as the British Sociological Association
7   Within these four broad areas, the study of men can by sub-divided loosely into twelve research areas. These areas are not discrete and some represent more of a research interest than others and many of the concerns here are also the concerns of the feminist and women's studies movement. The twelve areas can be outlined as Bibliography; Sexuality, Health and Emotions; Violence and Competition; Boys, Child care and Fatherhood; Personality, Socialisation and Education; Paid Work; Power, Politics and Patriarchy; History and Imaginative Writing; Religion and Spirituality; Anti-Sexism; Studying Men and Masculinity; The Critique of Men. All twelve areas attract some attention by men's studies scholars and activists alike. Yet the extent to which these areas are explored academically or empirically is open to question.
8   In fairness they do acknowledge that this is with the exception of   research into homosexuality.
9   As suggested later, doing so would require the exploration of other fundamental issues such as sexuality and ethnicity.

1 The Sociological Gender Critique

Introduction

> It is difficult now, from the vantage point of the late 1980's to recall a time when gender relations were not regarded as a legitimate focus for sociological study.
>
> (Maynard 1990: 269)

Gender has become a primary focus for sociological research and teaching[1], due to the efforts of the feminist movement and women's studies that questioned the sexist base of academic sociology. In many ways the observation that Maynard (1990) makes is correct. The arrival of feminism, and the development of women's studies, has moved the analysis of gender from within the margins of the family, to the centre of sociological enquiry. However, a more recent contribution to the understanding of gender, stratification, oppression and inequality, the development of so called 'men's studies', has attracted criticism and debate amongst those who originally called for the gender critique.

Given these developments, this chapter has a number of aims. First the chapter will consider the development of men's studies and hopefully go some way to clarifying what men's studies entails. Throughout the discussion it will become apparent that a systematic study of men is needed within sociology (and other social sciences) as a necessary complement to the study of women. Secondly the chapter will consider those criticisms that have been developed by certain feminist scholars and reflect on some of the limitations with existing approaches to studying men. Finally, the discussion will conclude with an outline of how men are to be considered in this book.

The Gender Critique

It is now well documented that feminist scholarship has criticised sociology for containing a structural sexism (Stacey 1981), as well as stereotypes and distortions introduced through the common sense notions and methodological assumptions that sociologists have incorporated into their analyses (Oakley 1974; Morgan 1981; Stacey 1981; Dunning 1986; Hammersley 1992)[2].

> Sociology is sexist because it is male-oriented. By male-oriented I mean that it exhibits a focus on, or direction towards the interests and activities of men in a gender differentiated society.
>
> (Oakley 1974: 2)

Alternatively, as Seidler (1994) suggests, such a problem is more deeply rooted in sociology's origins.

> Sociology emerged as a child of the Enlightenment and it seeks its ancestry within the forms of thought and feeling that characterised the Enlightenment...It is common to rethink social theory in terms of the particular Enlightenment identification of masculinity with reason and the notion that society should be made an 'order of reason', with the idea that society should be recast and remade in the 'image of men'. This is to lay bare a particular relationship between masculinity and our inherited forms of social and political theory.
>
> (Seidler 1994: 1)

Yet as Leighton (1992) suggests, gender as an analytical concept within sociology was marginalised both within teaching and, until recently, research. As a consequence of this, at the outset of the gender critique, all feminist critiques of sociology were committed to addressing the discipline's inherent sexism both in terms of its social theory and social research. This was to be done by redressing the gender balance and describing the lives and experiences of women, who had been ignored for so long by existing academics. Indeed Kimmel (1987) suggests that the main rationale for women's studies rest upon the proposition that traditional scholarship has a *de facto* programme of men's studies and that a certain amount of re-definition was required. The '*stages of feminism*' reflect this, addressing what it is to be female and later with second wave feminism questioning the enforced masculine definitions of femininity and patriarchy. It would be time consuming here to reflect fully on the contributions of feminist (and other women) scholars, and such contributions have been largely explored elsewhere. Yet one main point needs to be made. Despite, (and possibly because of) the well intentioned feminist critique, men have become increasingly hidden in gender based research. Indeed on examination of much of the literature on gender and other areas central to sociological enquiry, such as gender and employment, men are often absent or marginal to the analyses made[3]. Hearn (1989) explains this by arguing that this invisibility of men is a reflection of men's taken for granted structural power and domination. To look at men critically and usefully, must involve a close

13

examination of patriarchy that will inevitably be a difficult task for (some) men. Yet such a critique of patriarchal practice is required.

Ford and Hearn (1991) note, patriarchy has many different meanings, and has produced a number of theories about the role of men and women [4], with some feminists rejecting patriarchy (see Hakim 1996) whereas others suggest it is central to any understanding of women's (and men's) oppression. Such points have been acknowledged and the consideration of patriarchy has lead generally to an increase in the amount of writings on men and masculinity, and the development of the so-called 'new men's studies' mainly in the United States and in a very limited way in the UK. What also needs to be noted, therefore is, in the absence or the increasingly marginal consideration of men in gender research, a new trend or 'new revival' in the writings on men

In recent years, there has been something of an explosion...in the production of sociological texts by men writing about masculinity.

(Pringle 1995: 2)

As Pringle (1995) suggests, recently within sociology, and across social scientific research in general, a new approach to the study of gender has emerged. Work is being undertaken in areas such as men's sexuality, fatherhood and childhood experiences, not as a movement against feminist analysis, but as an attempt to examine the roles of men, and to redress the sociological scale of gender analyses. This area of enquiry has become known as 'The New Men's Studies' and (like women's studies), takes patriarchy as being central to its own analysis drawing attention to changes in the male role and now differing definitions of masculinity. However, what is men's studies ? At first glance this may seem like a very simplistic and straight forward question to answer as Brod suggests :

While seemingly about men, traditional scholarship's treatment of generic man as the human norm in fact systematically excludes from consideration what is unique to men qua men. The overgeneralization from male to generic human experience not only distorts our understanding of what, if anything, is truly generic to humanity but also precludes the study of masculinity as a specific male experience, rather than a universal paradigm for human experience. The most general definition of men's studies is that it is the study of masculinities and male experiences as specific and varying social - historical - cultural formulations.

(Brod 1987:2)

As Brod argues, at it simplest, men's studies is the study of men, bringing men back towards critical purview rather than equation with the

14

generic. However, as with the variety and diversity that is found within feminism and women's studies, men's studies and the critique of men has different meanings and implications for those who are working with and within it. Another useful definition of men's studies comes from Hearn (1987, 1989) who emphasises the centrality of patriarchy and the forward moves made by feminism. In general, Hearn identifies three basic components of men's studies. Firstly, it is the need for men concerned with gender, feminism and working against sexism and patriarchy to examine men and masculinities our/themselves.

Secondly, there is a need to do this critically. Hearn (1987) suggests that men's (patriarchal) practice exists both in public and private worlds , and if men and gender relations are to change, this public/private male domination needs to be questioned. In many respects this argument is not new, but simply more apparent than it was previously. As Seidler notes:

> So 'sexism' isn't simply an abstract ideology that has to be challenged in people's heads, but is a complex set of social relationships that we live out in our everyday lives...Somehow we need a way of recognising the power that we, as men, have in relation to women, while not being paralysed or silenced about masculinity. It means recognising that sexual politics deeply challenges the ways we are allowed to be, as men and the kind of power that we take for granted.
>
> (Seidler 1991: 65)

Thirdly, the need for such an undertaking to be located in terms of a standpoint - the standpoint being anti-patriarchal. For Hearn (1989), men's studies is located at the 'anti-patriarchal' praxis, where all pro-feminist men challenge existing notions of masculinity. However, this standpoint has only come about because of the forward moves made by feminism, feminist sociology and to some extent, gay liberation. Men's studies merely reflects a positive response to these forward moves. The central theme of the response seems to be a critical assessment of what it is to be male and the politics of masculinity. As Hearn (1989) notes, it is no longer possible to take for granted maleness or masculinity. Indeed this seems to be a logical extension of the feminist arguments that a re-definition of what it is to be feminine is required, and that this must have a certain effect on the culturally accepted notions of what it is to be male, and accepted notions of masculinity.

These shifting definitions of maleness and masculinity are what men's studies are a response to. Feminism was (and still is), important for the introduction of men's studies as it questioned existing notions of masculinity.

... it is the case that women and femininity cannot be understood without reference to men and masculinity also .

(Maynard 1990: 283)

However, as well as defining what men's studies constitutes, Ford and Hearn (1991) also offer a note of caution, suggesting the following ground rules for men's involvement in the critique of men. Firstly, they suggest that men should not seek to appropriate feminism or feminist theory. Men must respect the autonomy of feminism/women's studies, whilst not seeking to establish a critical study of men as an autonomous discipline. Secondly, the study of men and masculinities should be open to all. Thirdly, the major task of such a discipline is the development of a critique of men's (patriarchal) practice, not a critique of feminism or women.[5] The basic concern is to see what implications feminist theory has for both men and male practices.

Fourth, the critique of men should span traditional academic divides and should include disciplines such as psychology, economics and politics. Finally, men doing research, learning, teaching, study, theorising and academic discourse about men and masculinities need to subject their own practice to scrutiny (Ford and Hearn 1991).

As authors such as Brod (1987), Kimmel (1987) and Hearn (1988) note, a critique of feminism is not the remit of men's studies and it would be a mistake to view men's studies as such a critique. Scholars who work within the men's studies paradigm wish to create an academic discourse that addresses the totality of patriarchy and oppression, and raise consciousness, whilst remaining objective with regards to gender. In doing so the exponents of men's studies do not want to set the study of men apart from the study of women, in fact quite the reverse is true. Indeed, Brod (1987) argues that the best case for men's studies can be made by making the point that men's studies are not only compatible with, but are essential to the academic and political projects of the feminist reconstruction of knowledge.

He backs up his claim by stating that, firstly feminist scholarship set itself the task of reconstituting knowledge by supplementing existing ideas with information about and by women. This he points out, is the same as the objectives of men's studies as it too attempts to emasculate patriarchal ideologies that masquerade as knowledge (Brod 1987). Secondly, he argues that an objective of feminist scholarship was to explore and correct the effects on women of their exclusion from traditional learning. Men's studies wants also to address this fallacy.

Carrigan *et al* (1985, 1987), Kimmel (1987) and Hearn (1989) make similar points to Brod. Men's studies, Kimmel (1986, 1987) argues, was inspired by the academic breakthroughs made by women's studies, and whilst it does not wish to replace women's studies, it addresses similar

16

issues completing the radical picture of gender which feminist scholarship started to paint.

> If men are changing at all however, it is not because they have stumbled upon the limits of traditional masculinity all by themselves. For at least two decades the women's movements has suggested that the traditional enactments of masculinity were in desperate need of an overhaul.
>
> (Kimmel 1987: 9)

Yet such an approach has not been accepted wholly by some feminist academics.

Feminist Responses and the Case for Men's Studies

> What do we think and feel about the men's movement ? Is it a movement toward a society of mutual respect and safety for all, or just propaganda for a 'kinder, gentler patriarchy' - or both ?...For Feminists, the phenomenon of men organising on behalf of themselves as men in a society that is - for the most part - defined and controlled by men, holds a certain curious irony.
>
> (Hagan 1992: xi-xii)

Many feminists are hostile to men's studies as it is seen as an attempt to 'muscle in' on gender analysis, intruding into a space that is jealously guarded by women (Goodwin 1993). For example, Maynard (1990) argues that feminist scholars are worried that these 'new' researchers will take up research grants that would have normally gone to women's studies. She even goes as far as to suggest that claims for men's studies

> ...seem to represent a sectarian and isolationist position from which sociology has little to gain .
>
> (Maynard 1990: 285)

Maynard (1990) argues that what work has been produced, is theoretically unsophisticated, patchy and varied in quality. Indeed the central tenets of men's studies have also come under considerable scrutiny, with the claims of such scholars as Hearn (1989) that men have been ignored by sociology being criticised. Maynard (1990) points out that even though men have not been studied in sociology recently, men have been examined in the writings of women's scholarship and that this claim is just not true.

In this sense, feminism and women's studies may have achieved a considerable amount more than redressing the sociological scale. A discourse may have been created where women are over examined in relation to gendered activity. It is possible that women have monopolised writings, and have come to dominate the theoretical discourse on gender.

The very thing that feminist scholars accused (male) sociologists of doing in sociology's past. The study of gender is often more aptly described as the study of women, with (women) scholars dominating gender analysis both in terms of researchers and the researched. As Brod (1987) notes:

> We might ask why women are seen as 'working mothers' even though they work in the workforce, while statistics on levels of fatherhood in the workforce remain uncollected.
>
> (Brod 1987: 265)

It is here that Maynard's initial observation outlined at the start of this paper, can be questioned. It is hard to imagine a time when the *feminine* gender was not regarded as a legitimate focus for sociological enquiry. Masculinity and men, however, are different matters. Even though the academic pursuit of (female) scholars in trying to make the 'invisible' visible was correct, it has to some extent made the partially visible analysis of the male disappear. I am sure that feminist scholars would (and do) argue that enough attention was paid to men in the 'bad old days' of sociology when theory was dominated by men, and that concerns such as these are unfounded.

> It may seem strange to describe the study of men as a new area. This is particularly so when the current interest in gender arose partly in response to the fact that sociology had been previously concerned with the study of men.
>
> (Maynard 1990: 282)

This may not be the case. It may be true that throughout the history of sociology the focus has been on certain men in certain situations (for example in employment), and that men have wrongly been equated with humankind, but men *per se* have been ignored and untheorised about as a specific gender. Men have either been seen as members of a class, employment group or the perpetrators of inequality, but not as an academic project in their own right (Kimmel 1987, Brod 1987, Hearn 1988).

> ...men may be talked of as fathers, workers, bosses, medics, brothers, mates, or more colloquially as 'buggers', 'sods' and 'fuckers'...but rarely as men.
>
> (Hearn 1989: 8)

Superficially, the views offered by some feminists or women's studies scholars, seem to reflect a certain horror at the very concept of men's studies. However these ideas may cover up a series of underlying philosophical dilemmas. Perhaps the hostility shown towards men's studies is an attempt by (certain) women scholars to protect their own research interests. However the point cannot be escaped that two genders exist, and neither has the right to monopolise gender research to the exclusion of the other. Certain (feminist) scholars do not seem to share this idea. A dilemma occurs in that feminism and women's studies are quite prepared to offer an analysis of men and masculinity, but do not want to tolerate any such academic pursuit coming from the area of men's studies. This echoes a criticism that feminists have levelled at the (masculine) sociology of the past. Feminism was horrified by the mere suggestion of a man describing and defining a women's reality. Yet, years later feminist scholarship seems quite prepared to describe and define a man's reality and experience.

One must also question how men are actually dealt with in much of existing feminist literature. Following on from the above statement by Maynard (1990), who continues

> They are presented as subjects; as agents of sexist behaviour, as perpetrators of violence and as the creators of a norm of compulsory heterosexuality...
>
> (Maynard 1990: 284)

Maynard is quite right, a good deal has been written already about men, but it looks at men only in the context of women's lives, not in light of their own lives or experience. Hearn (1989) is correct, men are seen as anything but 'men'.

Some Other Problems with Existing Accounts of Men and Men's Studies

Alongside the feminist critique of a study of men it is also possible to identify a number of limitations within this developing paradigm. Indeed, returning to Maynard's retrospective assertion that 'from the vantage point of the late 1980s it was difficult to recall a time when gender relations were not regarded as a legitimate focus for sociological study' a number of these problems can be identified.

Carrigan, Connell and Lee (1985 and 1987) in one of the early 'landmark' texts on masculinities (see Brod 1987; Hearn 1996), raised their concerns about the limited availability of good empirically based research on men. They suggest :

19

Approaching the recent literature, we were concerned with three things: its empirical discoveries, its political assumptions and its theoretical framework. Its empirical content turns out to be slight. Though most social science is indeed about men, good quality research that brings masculinity into focus is rare.

(Carrigan, Connell and Lee 1987: 64)

Using an analysis of sociological abstracts between 1963 and 1978 they outlined two things. First, the relative number of articles that appeared in the sociological abstracts that appeared on men and women under the 'sex-role' banner. Second, they offered some commentary on the limited number of empirically based work. Such an approach is replicated here and the results are presented in Table 1.1. This table gives the actual number of articles published on gender in the ten year intervening period between 1993 and 1983. The table then gives an indication of how many of these articles were about men explicitly, of which in turn were from British academics and finally of which were empirical.

Table 1.1
Retrospective Analysis of Men in 'Sociology of Gender' Articles in the International Bibliography of Sociology 1983-1993

Year	Articles on Gender	Of Which Were on Men	Of Which Were British	Empirical
1993	294	26	0	0
1992	223	11	3	0
1991	328	6	3	0
1990	334	16	4	0
1989	255	8	1	0
1988	110	3	1	1
1987	252	10	5	1
1986	111	4	0	0
1985	163	2	1	0
1984	76	0	0	0
1983	73	3	0	0

Source: Own calculations from analysis of the International Bibliography of Sociology 1983-1993.

Three main points can be made about these findings. First, as with the results reported by Carrigan *et al* (1987) the vast majority of gender based research actually looks at the role of women and does not consider the role of men explicitly. This confirms the views of scholars such as Hearn (1987) but also highlights the still current trend to equate the study of women with the study of gender (for examples of this see Felstead 1993, 1994).

> Until recently masculinity has tended to be absent from mainstream academic research. Earlier studies of gender relations, in which a unitary notion of masculinity was often employed, largely concentrated on women and girls.
>
> (Mac an Ghaill 1996: 1)

The optimistic view of Máirtín Mac an Ghaill that the situation has changed is open to question and debate. Despite some increase in the publication of material which reflects on men critically, the gender debate is still centred around the experiences of women.

Second, that the vast majority of those articles published on men were in fact mainly from outside Britain. As such it seems that British sociologists only have a limited interest in the issue of masculinity and the nature of men's lives.

Finally, reflecting the sentiments of Carrigan *et al*, the vast majority of the work on men is either theoretical or political, with very few empirical articles being published 'about men'. For example, the work of Hearn, one of the main exponents of men's studies, is largely located within a theoretical discourse (this is also true of a number of others such as Connell 1995). Yet it seems amazing to note that such a trend still exists. The data from this most recent analysis of sociological abstracts suggests that of those articles on men written by British academics, only two were empirically based. As Pringle later notes:

> ...it is possible that the emphasis on theoretical and methodological considerations may betray an over-concentration on issues that are relatively abstract and 'safe' in emotional terms.
>
> (Pringle 1995: 2)

Such findings still mean that much needs to be done in developing a study of men.

Concluding Remarks: Studying Men

The above debates have far reaching implications, not only for the study of gender, but for sociology and the social sciences as a whole. The chapter has highlighted the arguments for a study of men and the responses that this has generated. The concern now is that men's studies, may become a discrete topic (through no fault of its own) within the sociological enquiry.

Considerations of men may continue to be appended to studies of women, which will ultimately contribute very little to our understanding of men's experiences in Britain. Where considerations are offered they should attempt to move away from the purely theoretical. What is required is a more integrated approach where the forward moves made in the analysis of women is applied to men and men's issues in an empirical as well as theoretical analysis. Only when this is done will the sociologist avoid the isolationist or sectarians' dilemma. As such this study of men will pursue the following schema.

First, consider men and male work experiences from within the sociological paradigm making men more visible. In this sense, this research follows the concern of Hearn (1989). It recognises that men are seen as anything but men. If one is to avoid the isolationist sociological study of gender then men need to be studied, and second brought back into gender research 'in their own right'.

Second, the book considers the need to reflect critically on the impact on the forward moves made by feminism and the concept of patriarchy. Within this work there is quite a difficult task of developing a critical framework with which to understand men and on which to base further empirical work. Perhaps it is here that the discussion starts to diverge for other men's studies scholars (such as Brod 1987; Hearn 1989; Morgan 1992). My framework begins with the fact that for any gender analysis one has to start with the assumption that men and women occupy very different roles. These roles have been largely defined by tradition, historical development and cultural practice. If one wants to understand this and consider one has to ask 'why do men end up in the traditional roles that they do ?' To do this, men have to use and reflect on feminist sociology. I intend to argue that the best initial approach to understanding men is to combine feminist theory, with other sociological approaches and inturn with a concern for studying men and the cultural relativity of gender practice. Then apply this framework to empirical accounts of men. This is not meant as an appropriation of feminist theory, but merely reflects the moves forward that feminist scholarship has made in our theoretical understanding of men. Although this is acknowledged by other authors (Kimmel, 1987) feminists start by developing a different and often inadequate framework for studying men.

Third, that there is a need to explore men's work experiences empirically as well as theoretically. The theoretical forward moves that have been established are beneficial however there is a need to move on from the theoretical calls for men's roles to change (see Hearn 1987) to a sociological define, describe the realities of male lives with real data.

In order to explore men's lives, in such a way, a location of enquiry is required. Work and employment provide one site for an empirically based sociological consideration of men. The reason for this is that men and work are inextricably linked in most Western societies. The theoretical basis of such an assertion will be explored more fully in the next chapter, and that chapter will aid an understanding of men and work generally.

The theories concerning the opportunity and inequality faced by women in relation to work, have historically been presented in many differing formats. However all seem to imply there is little merit in studying work as a gendered activity for men, as for men work is the norm and men are the total of their labour. The theory relating to the positions that men take in work or the labour market is even less visible in labour market research and very little is explicitly written about men's work or male experiences in the labour market.

> A critical analysis of men and masculinities is particularly important in the study of work, organisations and management. Yet an examination of the available literature reveals a recurring paradox. The categories of men and masculinity are frequently central to analyses, yet they remain taken for granted, hidden and unexamined. Men are both talked about and ignored.
>
> (Collinson and Hearn 1994: 3)

However, further to the paradox that Collinson and Hearn (1994) suggest, a further dilemma for male workers exists. There is a traditional assumption which men have to aspire that suggests they will work full-time in a 'breadwinner role' for the duration of their working lives and that anything else would not be fitting for a man and not in keeping with some notions of 'masculinity'. Indeed, despite increasing labour market de-regulation since the first Thatcher government at the end of the 1970s, and the fact that for many this ideal situation of full-male employment has become socially and economically impossible, coupled with the now established feminist discourse to the contrary, the traditional beliefs about full-time male employment remain, and are held by both men and women alike (for a consideration of women's employment see Hakim 1996). Finally, unlike in other 'gender' based research, men must not be treated as a homogeneous grouping.

In the following chapter, this process will begin. First, chapter two will outline why men and work are closely associated by examining existing accounts of gender. Second, in chapter three, male labour market trends will be explored.

Notes

1   This trend is well documented elsewhere and needs little expansion. (see Stacey 1981; Mitchell and Oakley 1986)
2   It also has to be noted that Black women writers have pointed out that the study of gender is often limited by the structural racism and assumptions made by (white) writers. Gender contains and ethnic dimension and that women nor men *per se* do not share the same experiences. For those interested in these issues see Hull 1982 and Westwood and Bhachu 1988.
3   Ford and Hearn (1991) do provide a list of studies that examine men in relation to paid employment.
4   For example, see such works as Eisenstein (1979) 'Developing a theory of Capitalist Patriarchy and Socialist Feminism', Hartmann (1979) 'Capitalism, patriarchy and job segregation by sex'.
5   Regrettably in some instances this may be unavoidable due to the way that gender analysis has progressed, taking men as the object of criticism and ridicule without offering an understanding.

2 Linking Men and Paid Employment

Introduction

> For every man, the outcome of his socialisation is his entry into work. His first day at work signifies his 'initiation' into the secretive conspiratorial solidarity of working men...
>
> (Tolson 1987: 47-48)

The previous chapter presented an argument that suggests men's lives are not fully explored within British gender based sociology. Further, if gender roles are to be fully understood, more empirical (and theoretical) investigations into men are required. As suggested above, the reason for this is that men, to date, have been largely ignored in a great deal of existing gender analysis.

Traditionally, scholars from both the feminist traditions and from men's studies approaches have already spent considerable time developing their own theoretical positions on men and the inequality that Lenski (1966) refers to. For example, scholars have developed psychoanalytical approaches to men, gender and inequality (Fromm 1962; Stoller 1985; Hudson 1991; Coward 1983), Marxist and historical materialist approaches (Tolson 1977; Clatterbaugh 1990; Seidler 1991; Pollert 1996), dramaturgical approaches (Goffman 1959; Hargreaves 1986); cultural approaches (Hoch 1979; Hofstede 1980; Thomas 1995; Connell 1995), and so on. All these approaches have something to offer any discussion of men's lives and as such the importance of these works must be acknowledged. However, valuable as they may be, it is not the intention here to provide a summary of all such theoretical works on men or masculinity as this would be to simply replicate work done elsewhere (see Doyle 1989; Brod *et al* 1994; Edley *et al* 1995). Nor is the aim to attempt to provide a new, overarching and 'all comprehensive' theory of 'men and masculinity' (or masculinities) as this again seems to be the project of others (see Seidler 1994; Connell 1995; MacInnes 1997).[1] Rather, and perhaps more simply, this chapter aims to explore those theoretical approaches which can aid an understanding as to why work (or more precisely paid public work) is of central importance to men's lives and one aspect of masculinity. For example, as Carrigan *et al* (1987) suggests

> The starting point for any understanding of masculinity...must be men's involvement in the social relations that constitute a gender order...Two aspects of its organisation [are]...the division of labour and the structure of power.
>
> (Carrigan 1987: 89)

As Carrigan notes, the starting point must include a consideration of the division of labour, but why ? What is the origin of the linkage between men and work ? For many in our current epoch, the position that men occupy in the labour market is very clear, they are either employed or they are seeking employment. As for women they can be workers, homemakers and/or mothers[2]. Yet unlike fatherhood, motherhood has a clearly defined role that is mainly 'private' (but also 'public' if required). Fatherhood, by comparison does not actually exist in the 'private' beyond its links to the public realm, as unlike motherhood the main function of fatherhood, historically, has been 'economic provision' and very little else. As Daly (1994), in exploring the gendered nature of the welfare[3], suggests

> Men are defined as workers/breadwinners, either as current workers, former workers, temporary worker non workers or potential workers. The criteria under which they receive state support refers in the main to their labour market characteristics...
>
> (Daly 1994: 788)

Daly argues that the construction of women's eligibility is different.

> Flowing primarily from either their relationship to men or the family, women's resource to income maintenance has been and is mediated by their marital and family situation...The access of other women to income maintenance is largely determined by whether they are perceived to have a man who would support them...
>
> (Daly 1994: 789)

To explore such issues further, this chapter draws upon two fundamental principles. First, that the linkage of men to in the West must be the product of long-term social, historical, relational and cultural [4] processes. As such, any understanding of men's current identification with work must be set within a developmental context. As Connell (1995) notes:

> To understand the current pattern of masculinities we need to look back over the period in which it came into being. Since masculinity exists only in the context of a whole structure of gender relations, we need to locate it in the formation of the

modern gender order as a whole - a process that has taken about four centuries.
(Connell 1995: 185)

One has to acknowledge the historical and its cultural relativity of male roles and the historical process through which they develop. The second principle is the suggestion that work role develop from the historical interrelationship between patriarchy (a set of social relations based on gender) and capital (a set of social relations based on production). [5]
In the remainder of this chapter these two fundamental principles will be explored, first through a brief examination of the history of masculinity based mainly on the analysis of Connell, but also on the work of Elias (1995) and Lenski (1966). The book will also reflect on how active men have been in developing the links between men and work. Second, three broad theoretical perspectives are discussed, all of which identify the gendering of work from within a historical framework and locate male work roles at the capital patriarchy axis. The theories which are covered a are a brief examination of aspects of the Marxist and Durkheimian approaches. Second an exploration of the 'gender roles' paradigm. Finally a consideration socialist feminism.

The History of Men and Work 'Revisited'

Any discussion of the origins of the modern male work role is subject to speculation and one has to ask 'why do men end up in the traditional roles that they do ?' To do this, men have to use and reflect on feminist sociology. I intend to argue that the best initial approach to understanding men is to combine feminist theory, with other sociological approaches and inturn with a concern for studying men and the cultural relativity of gender practice. Then apply this framework to empirical accounts of men. This is not meant as an appropriation of feminist theory, but merely reflects the moves forward that feminist scholarship has made in our theoretical understanding of men. Although this is acknowledged by other authors (Kimmel, 1987) feminists start by developing a different and often inadequate framework for studying men. Third, that there is a need to explore men's work experiences empirically as well as theoretically. The theoretical forward moves that have been established are beneficial however there is a need to move on from the theoretical calls for men's roles to change (see Hearn 1987) to a sociological define, describe the realities of male lives *with real data*.
One commentator who has reflected on the historical origins of modern masculinity and is Connell (1995). In a wide ranging discussion of the nature of masculinities, Connell provides a complex but brief sketch of the

history of masculinity in order to develop a set of 'rough bearings' for his discussion (Connell 1995: 186).

> In the period from about 1450 to about 1605...the modern capitalist economy came into being around the North Atlantic, and the modern gender order also began to take shape in that region. Four developments seem particularly important for the making of those configurations of social practice that we now call 'masculinity'.
>
> (Connell 1995: 186)

The four developments that Connell refers to are 'the cultural change that produced new understandings of sexuality and personhood in metropolitan Europe'; 'the creation of empires by the Atlantic seaboard states'; 'the growth of the cities that were centres of commercial capitalism; and finally 'the onset of large-scale European civil war' (Connell 1995: 186-189).

Connell locates the first of these developments in the rise of secular culture and the declining power of the Catholic church and the monasteries, with marital heterosexuality replacing monasticism. Such changes can be linked to the Protestant reformation. The power and influence of religion began to decline. Religion could no longer control the intellectual world nor could it totally to regulate everyday lives of people (Connell 1995). Within such changes, rationality replaced spirituality, belief is replaced by science and the once public relationships become privatised and secret.

> The Church certainly fought early for monogamous marriage. But marriage takes on this strict form as a social institution binding on both sexes only at a late stage, when drives and impulses come under firmer an stricter control. For only then are extramarital relationships for men really ostracised socially, or subject to absolute secrecy...Like many other drives, sexuality is confined more and more exclusively, for both man and women, to a particular enclave, socially legitimised marriage. Social tolerance of other relationships, for both husband and wife...is suppressed increasingly...Every violation of these restrictions, and everything conductive to one, is therefore relegated to the realm of secrecy, of what may not be mentioned without loss of prestige or social position.
>
> (Elias 1994: 150- 154)

The second was the growth of 'empire', and the development of the first 'culturally defined' male type - that of the soldier and the trader.

> Empire was a gendered enterprise from the start, initially an outcome of the segregated men's occupations of soldiering and sea trading. When European women went to the colonies it was mainly as wives and servants within households controlled by men...Apart from a few monarchs, the imperial states

created to rule the new empires were entirely staffed by men, and developed a statecraft based on the force supplied by the organised bodies of men.

(Connell 1995: 187)

Elias also refers to the development of a modern society being characterised by a certain level of monopolisation. He argued that free use of military weapons was denied the ordinary individual, but reserved for a central authority of what ever kind. Likewise the taxation of the property or income of individuals is concentrated in the hands of a central social authority. The financial means thus flowing into this central authority maintain its monopoly of military force, while this in turn maintains the monopoly of taxation (Elias 1995: 346).

The third development, is the rise of commercial capitalism in cities, with the entrepreneurial culture and workplaces of commercial capitalism creating and legitimating a new form of gendered work and power in the counting-house, the warehouse and the exchange (Connell 1995; 188). Such a theme is raised elsewhere (for example, Weber 1976; Lenski 1966), but perhaps not explicitly in a way that links men to working life. However, Ashton and Goodwin (1995), in a brief exploration of the development of the medical profession in the UK, clearly identify the gendered nature of male (medical) work. The rise of the professions in urban localities signifies the increased specialisation of workers and the location of money and power. For example, originally physicians, surgeons and apothecaries were trades people, whose status in society was largely determined by that of the clients they served. Surgeons were part of the Barber-Surgeons company in London. By the mid 18th century, however, they separated to form their own company (Campbell, 1747) and by the 19th century there was the transformation of the trade professions into a medical profession. There are a number of reasons why this should happen in the nineteenth century (for further discussion see Johnson, 1972). As Ashton and Goodwin suggest :

...urbanisation and industrialisation created large hospitals which facilitated the study of diseases. This in turn created major advances in our knowledge of the human body and the causes of illness and disease. The same processes concentrated the practitioners and facilitated their organisation. Their organisation in mediaeval companies provided the model for the modern form of organisation and enabled them to impose the apprenticeship system as the normal mode of entry, thereby controlling access to the occupation. Success in controlling access made them powerful bodies to which the government had to respond and did so by granting them the licence to operate. This gave the 'traditional' British professions their distinctive position which can be characterised as follows: professional organisation licensed by the state to control practice; single professional body; control over entry; control over the curriculum and a well established body of knowledge; body of professional ethics to govern conduct; autonomous institution - makes its own rules, accountable to itself and its members.

(Ashton and Goodwin 1995: 3)

Thus the nineteenth century witnessed the creation of a series of professional bodies which had the legal right to control access to a set of occupational activities and determine the conditions under which they practised. It is within this historical processes such as this that work in general, and the medical profession in particular, becomes deemed to be 'male'. This creates a whole area of employment where women become disadvantaged. That's to say in medicine, the reason for low levels of female participation in medicine is that the medical profession itself, (which is still largely controlled by men), made it difficult for women to gain access to specialist training. This can be coupled with the belief that certain specialities are too difficult for women (such as surgery). [6]

...we have evidence of the rise of male professions and the elimination of female ones during the sixteenth and seventeenth centuries. The medical profession, male from its inception, established itself through hierarchical organisation, the monopolisation of new, 'scientific' skills, and the assistance of the state.

(Hartmann 1976: 151)

Within this framework, only men are seen to be able become fully 'competent' professionals as it is they who control entry and control the body of knowledge.

The final issue in Connell's argument is the onset of civil war, and whether religious or dynastic in origin, Connell argues, this disrupted the legitimacy of the gender order. For example, Connell suggests that the Quakers, emerging from the English civil war, who argued publicly for religious equality for women. Yet the real impact of such a war was the consolidation of the patriarchal order via the strong centralised state (Connell 1995: 189), with the state institutionalising men's power in the form of professional armies.

With the eighteenth century, in seaboard Europe and North America at least, we can speak of a gender order in which masculinity in the modern sense - gendered individual character, defined through an opposition to femininity and institutionalised in economy and state - had been stabilised.

(Connell 1995: 190)

Here Connell also suggests that the idea of 'gentry' as a type of masculinity associated with the development of the state. Men from the gentry became the local administration, staffed the military apparatus and controlled violence, whether over workers, men, the lower classes or women. Such 'gentrified' local administrators also employed other men.

Male workers on behalf of the state to do work for the state. For example, whilst it goes without question that wealthy individuals or estates, along with the development of a male 'business class' financed and administered the state, it was other men whole actually built it. The role that other, 'non-gentry' working men played, and the services they provided to the state, can be seen in works such as Sullivan's (1983) history of Navying men.

> Navvies built canals, railways, dams and their pipe tracks, the big nineteenth century sea-port docks...Navying began suddenly in 1760...it ended around 1940...They were perpetual outsiders: a people apart. Sub-working class. Sub the bottom most heap of English working society...[but] with the muck he created new landscapes and changed old societies. It was mass transformation by muscle and shovel.
>
> (Sullivan 1983; 54)

The services that these men provided was their own physical labour. Navvies performed the hard, dirty and physical work required in the development of the state. They mainly did so in geographical isolation, and were characterised as drinking, rioting itinerant men. They were invented as the Industrial Revolution required men to build canals, docks and railways and once invented stayed on to provide labour for the 'great schemes of public work' (Sullivan 1983).

Duplicitous Men: Men and Work as a Social Construction

One problem with these approaches (with the exception of Elias) is that they imply, and outline, a seemingly 'passive' historical process in which men 'just become' linked with work and paid employment. However, there is evidence to suggest that historically men have been very 'active' in developing an artificial social construction that legitimises men's own working lives vis-à-vis the working lives of women. That is to say the link between men and work cannot be taken for granted as it may be a 'socially constructed ideology' which men have actively pursued. For example, Roberts (1988) highlights the response of male potters who, in 1845 fearing the loss of work as women were minding the machines, wrote a petition full of 'concern' for these women (Roberts 1988: 13)

> To maidens mothers and wives, we say machinery is your deadliest enemy...it will destroy your natural claims to home and domestic duties and will immure you and your toiling little ones in overheated and dirty shops, there to weep and toil and pine and die.
>
> (Roberts 1988: 13)

Roberts also quotes Lord Shaftesbury who, when passing the Ten Hours Bill in the House of Commons, suggested

> They meet together to drink, sing and smoke; they use, it is stated, the lowest, most brutal and most disgusting language imaginable...What is the ground on which the woman says she will pay no attention to her domestic duties, nor give the obedience which is owing her husband ? Because on her devolves the labour which ought to fall to his share, and she throws out the taunt, 'If I have the labour, I will also have the amusement.
>
> (Roberts 1988: 13)

What these two quotations are actually pointing to is the long struggle that men have engaged in (often implicitly as well as explicitly) to exclude women from work to legitimise their own working 'rights'. As such, what they also suggest is that as men were engaging in such a struggle there must/could have been a time in history when men were not so explicitly associated with paid public work and that such a linkage could be a relatively recent phenomenon. Authors such as Engels (1845), Hartmann (1976), Pinchbeck (1981) Walby (1986) and Roberts (1988) have reflected on this very point.

Hartmann clearly identifies a time in which women were also associated with work. Indeed, what Hartmann also implies is that, not only was there less division in the public working lives of men and women (in that it was less clearly prescribed who should work and who should not), but that women and children were also sought in the early capital process as they were an available source of labour.

Despite the differing perceptions of skill, both men and women were central to the work and production process with women not being defined as 'housewives' but as workers also. Yet this situation only continued until the family industry system and the guilds broke down under the need for large scale production. As the nature of capital production began to change two parallel processes (in which men were active rather than passive) began to emerge which established and solidified men's linkage with paid work. The processes were, first, the workplace organisation of men in response to their labour market 'displacement'. As Engels notes:

> Of 419,560 factory operatives of the British Empire in 1839, 192,887, or nearly half, were under eighteen years of age, and 242,296 of the female sex, of whom 112,192 ere less than eighteen years old...in the flax-spinning mills, 70.5 per cent of all operatives are of the female sex. These numbers suffice to prove the crowding out of adult males. But you only have to go into the nearest mill to see

the fact confirmed.

(Engels 1845: 165)

Second, the emergence of 'moral concern' for family life and child care provision and the need for a family wage.

Men believed that a limited amount of work was available and suspected that allowing women to share work would cause some families to go without pay as a consequence of other families taking more than their fair share.

(Hunt 1981: 24)

In all directions the family is being dissolved by the labour of the wife and children, or inverted by the husband's being thrown out of employment and made dependent upon them for bread...

(Engels 1845: 219)

Men's workplace organisation ranged from the development of strong trade unions with exclusionary practices, to state legislation in the form of the Factory Acts.[7] For example, Hartmann (1976) argues that men had been better able to organise themselves as wage workers and that such 'organisational ability' is linked to the development of patriarchal relations in the family that in turn were reinforced by the state and religion. This Hartmann suggests made it 'likely that men would develop more organisational structures beyond the household' (Hartmann 1976: 152) However, why should male wage workers organise themselves against women? There seems to be two explanations for this. First, that men viewed women's employment as a threat. The economic system had changed and had become more competitive and women were competitive due to their traditionally low wages. Walby (1986) takes this discussion further by considering the most lucrative jobs in cotton and textiles. She argues that men organised within their union to exclude women by denying them entry to the union and therefore training and therefore access to the most lucrative positions. The second reason was so women could continue to do household work.

Women's jobs were lower paid, considered less skilled, and often involved less exercise of control. Men acted to enforce job segregation in the labour market: they utilised trade-union associations and strengthened the domestic division of labour which required women to do housework, child care and related chores.

(Hartmann 1976: 153)

This links to the second process of 'moral concern' for family life and child care, and represents what Walby (1986) calls the 'intersection between patriarchy and capitalism'. This 'domestic ideology' located women firmly within the home whilst men earn a 'family wage' to support his family .

Hartmann argues that the Victorian upper classes were 'outraged' by the working conditions of women. The consequence of this outrage was the development of (and support for) separate spheres for men and women. Men went out to work to earn money to support their families and women stayed at home and supported those families with unpaid housework.

> ...the industrial revolution marked a real advance, since it led to the assumption that men's wages should be paid on a family basis, and prepared the way for the more modern conception that in the rearing of children and in homemaking, the married women makes an adequate economic contribution.
>
> (Pinchbeck 1981: 312-13)

Whether one agrees with Pinchbeck's analysis in total, what this refers to is a period of time when paid work for women was less appropriate and their financial dependency on men increased.

The works of Hartmann (1976) and others, suggest indeed that men have actually been active in developing a 'legitimate' link between their own gender and public paid employment. However it is important to note that the 'rights and wrongs' of these processes are not in question, nor is the fact that they occurred. What is important is that first, these writers demonstrate historically men have acted in their own interests with regards work and second that this socially constructed ideology exists in this current historical epoch. The discussion now turns to examine three 'broader' existing theoretical perspectives that consider the gendering of work from within a historical framework.

Locating Men and Work in Sociological Theory

As suggested above, male roles and men's identification with work is the result of long-term historical processes. Two key factors in this process are the privatisation of certain acts and the development of commercial capitalism. Willot and Griffin (1996) suggest that the ideological separation between men and women into public spheres and private spheres remains central to the construction of 'male roles' in the west (Willot and Griffin 1996: 82) . Such separation suggests that men experience the labour market in very different ways to women, and that the origins of such separation can be traced back to the industrial revolution and beyond, for example, the restoration (see Kimmel 1987), or roman civilisation (see Elias 1987).

As suggested above, the development of such interrelationships have been approached in a number of theoretical perspectives. For example, in, Marxist theory as the moving sites of production (Engels, 1845); in the Durkheimian tradition as the development of conjugal gender roles (Durkheim, 1893; Parsons and Bales, 1953); and in the socialist feminist tradition (Eisenstein 1979; Hartmann 1976).

Marx and Durkheim

In a Marxist framework, the sexual division of labour develops as society moves towards industrial based civilisation, as the site of production shifts from the home to the market.

> ...consciousness receives its further development and extension through increased productivity, the multiplication of needs, and what underlies both these needs is the increase of population. Along with these changes, there is a development in the division of labour which was at first nothing but the division of labour in the sexual act, and then...(it) emerges spontaneously, or naturally, by virtue of natural abilities (e.g. physical strength).
>
> (Marx 1986: 86-7)

For example, Engels argued that male roles and power were derived from the ownership of private property, and the origins of this power form the rests in the ownership, control and domestication of animals. As such the oppression of women could only end with the equal distribution of such private property. Scholars such as Engels, from the Marxist camp, have explained the patterns of gender employment as being determined by capitalist relations. That is to say as the site of production changes so does the sexual division of labour, marking the development of gender roles.

> On what foundations is the present family based? On Capital, on private gain...The family will vanish as a matter of course when its compliment vanishes....both will vanish with the vanishing of capital...the abolition of the present system of production must bring with it the abolition of...prostitution, both public and private.
>
> (Marx 1848: 501 - 502)

Women's lower pay and lower levels of labour market participation, and men's higher pay and higher participation are shaped by capital and labour relations. Women are seen as subordinate and a marginal category of workers whilst men are defined as primary workers. Such a withdrawal of women from the labour market enables the family to raise its standard of living, ensuring the non-alienated care of the young, to control the supply of labour so as to raise its price and produce male workers and a solidary working class.[8] Similar views and historical dynamics can also be found within a Durkheimian perspective.

For Durkheim, as society moves towards civilisation, inequality emerges between the sexes. Such changes occur due to the changing morphology of society and as people have more contact there is a greater need to specialise in order to survive, so women move to the home to provide affectual functions and men move towards a public arena and a work role.

> We are therefore led to consider the division of labour in a new light. In this case, indeed, the economic services that it can render are insignificant compared with the moral effect that it produces, and its true function is to create, between two or more people, a feeling of solidarity.
>
> (Durkheim 1893/1987: 17)

As suggested, the true 'function' of the division of labour is to create a feeling of solidarity between two or more individuals, and the development of the conjugal society is the most striking example of this. He argues that it is precisely because men and women are different that they seek each other as part of the same universal. They have a mutual need to which 'the other' is the natural complement.

In such an analysis the further we look back into the past, towards the segmental society, the differences between men and women become less obvious. Indeed in primitive society, the sexual division of labour was reduced to the sexual organs and the respective parts played in the reproductive process. Attraction, cohesion and solidarity are based on similarities. Durkheim reports that inequality only emerges between the sexes in proportion with the growth of civilisation. Indeed, in contrast to primitive society, the division of labour brings about organic solidarity. The social division of labour increases the sexual division of labour. For example, in primitive society, men and women were involved in politics and warfare. In the society based on organic solidarity, women have retired from these areas. Her role has become more specialised and women today lead very different lives to men, concerned with effectual functions, not the intellectual functions of men.

Parsonian Functionalism and the Development of Gender Roles

One of the most well established and influential approaches is the 'gender roles' paradigm (Carrigan *et al* 1985; Edley, 1995). Role theory has at its core the notion that gender identities or gender roles develop as a consequence of socially defined rules and norms that prescribe and control behaviour. Such normative values are transmitted to men (and women) throughout their lives via a multitude of socialising agents such as family, church, state, and work. As Harris (1995) suggests a key part of any person's identity

...concerns his or her understanding of gender, comprehending social notions of gender, and applying these concerns accurately to the self. A man's gender identity enables him to identify himself as a man within a specific culture.

(Harris 1995: 37)

Moving away from the biological tradition which locates masculinity only in genetics (Goldberg, 1973) or the more prosaic accounts such as psychoanalysis which locate gender socialisation *only* within 'particular' familial relationships (Coward, 1983), gender-role theory suggests that men actually learn to be male and behave in a way that is socially prescribed (Hargreaves, 1986).

The notion of 'role' is now a 'standard' in both sociological and psychological research and theorising, however, as Carrigan *et al* (1985) and Edley *et al* (1995) note, the precise antecedents of 'role' constituting a theory is subject to conjecture. However, the 'gender role' approach to gender relations was at its peak between the 1930s and the 1970s (Pleck, 1981; Carrigan *et al* 1985; Edley *et al* 1995), with most scholars returning to (and citing) Parsons as the main exponent of this paradigm (Oakley 1974; Chestermann, 1979; Carrigan *et al* 1985).

A key part of this sex-role theory was the Parsonian analysis of the nuclear family. Parsons, argued that the nuclear family provided the 'best' family form for industrialised society. With modernisation the family became a specialised unit with the primary task of socialising children. Parsons (1956) suggests that for it to be adequate, parents must have structurally different roles - instrumental and expressive roles.

The area of instrumental function concerns relations of the system to its situation outside the system... 'instrumentally' establishing the desired relations to external goal-objects. The expressive area concerns the 'internal' affairs of the system, the maintenance of integrative relations between the members, and regulation of the patterns and tension levels of its component units.

(Parsons 1956: 47)

Men are involved with occupational structures, develop instrumental roles and struggle with wider society. Women develop expressive functions from their role in the family, nurturing and providing a supportive framework for child development. Women then socialise their children into these functions. To explain this aspect of the process, Parsons' turns to the psychoanalytical tradition and suggests that masculinity results from the resolution of the Oedipus complex.

Parsons (1966), later combined this analysis with an account of the occupational system, as being the primary or main determinant of social status. Industrialisation required a mobile workforce and the conjugal family developed as the most efficient unit to achieve this mobility. Strain within this unit would arise in the event of competition for employment opportunities between husband and wife. Parsons locates the differentiation of sex roles as crucial in avoiding this.

Such a conception is developed more fully in an earlier work of Parsons (1956). Here along with Bales, he suggests that childhood socialisation requires the differentiation of sex-roles caused by the demands of the occupational structure. Parsons argues that adequate socialisation requires parents to have structurally different roles - instrumental and expressive. In this sense it is the man who is engaged in occupational structures, develop instrumental structures and struggle with wider society. Women develop expressive functions from their role in the family, nurturing and providing a supportive framework for child development. Men are socialised by many social agents, such as family, school and media into a sexual division of labour which sees men as being thrust into work, as Tolson (1987) suggests

> The foundations of masculinity are laid down in boyhood, in a boy's experience of family, school and his peers. The family provides the basic emotional orientation, which is extended - institutionally in the education system and formally in the culture of peer groups - through to adolescence and manhood.
>
> (Tolson 1987: 22)

Tolson (1987) argues that within the internal world of the family, there is a development specific to boys and in this sense, the family provides a 'frame' of manhood as being the future for boys - the father figure represents what the boy will (and should aspire to) become. The fathers presence seems to contain a promise of fulfilment and affirmation of masculine power. Images of masculinity are maintained via family reminiscences and in this way the boys gender identity is also formed by these historical accounts within the family.

Like Tolson (1987), those who are concerned with gender roles and the social learning tradition cite (and have explored) a number of the important socialising agents that encourage sex appropriate behaviour. Studies have explored the impact of parents on sex-specific behaviour (Alan *et al* 1981; Snow *et al* 1983; Booth *et al* 1994; Rindfuss *et al*, 1992; Simons *et al*, 1992; Martin *et al* 1995), the role of the school in reproducing gender stereotypes (Fagot, 1977; Dart *et al* 1988; Connolly, 1995), the media such as television and magazines (Lysonski, 1985; Mort, 1988; Criag, 1992; Rapping, 1994). Yet regardless of the socialising agent, or the provider of the sex-role ideology, the gender specific messages are the same, that male-female differences are based around a sexual division of labour.

Linking Men and Work in Socialist Feminism[9]

One of the most important theoretical approaches to gender roles is socialist feminism. Socialist feminism developed within the second wave of feminism and the movements calling for women's liberation in society, in 1960s (Rowbotham, 1989).

> The term 'second wave', applied as a prefix to feminism, implies that it describes a specific moment in history, and signifies a discernible transformation in this body of knowledge - specifically a shifting of boundaries towards a new wave of radicalism.
>
> (Whelehan 1995: 1)

Socialist feminism argues that gender and class (patriarchy and capitalism) both have an equal part to play in determining the position of men and women in society. Two of the main exponents of such an approach are Eisenstein and Hartmann.

For Walby (1986) Eisenstein's (1979), work was a synthesis of Marxist (thesis) and Radical feminism (antithesis) and the argument that the two systems were essentially one (Walby 1986; p31). Eisenstein (1979) considers the two systems so closely related that they can be analysed in terms of one concept, arguing that the power that derives from Capitalist Patriarchy.

> (Capitalist Patriarchy)...is the mutually reinforcing dialectical relationship between capitalist class structure and the hierarchical sexual structuring.
>
> (Eisenstein 1979: 5)

This indicates that capitalism and patriarchy are not autonomous power systems (nor are they identical), but have a mutual dependence upon each other. They exist together, and if a full account of the gendered division of society is provided, they cannot be isolated in analysis as their interdependence is so great. Indeed, moving away from traditional Marxist analysis, that argues that patriarchy arose with capitalism, Eisenstein locates the roots of patriarchy in pre-capitalist history. It pre-dates capitalism she argues that men interpret and politically use the fact that women are reproducers and this results in differing relations to reproduction and the development of a sexual hierarchy. The sexual hierarchy is carried over from one historical epoch to another to ensure male dominance. In the current epoch, she argues that the sexual division of labour is based in reality due to years of ideological pressure based around the notions that women are reproducers. History has set this up as a necessity and that the idea that women are mothers is determined by her biology. This in turn determines her social and economic purpose. That's to say such a division of labour predates capitalism, divides men and women up into respective hierarchical sex-roles and structures their duties in the family and economy. This assertion further points to the dependency of capitalism and patriarchy. That is capitalism needs patriarchy to operate efficiently and patriarchy needs capitalism. Patriarchy provides the sexual ordering of society for political control, whilst capitalism, in the pursuit of profit, feeds off this patriarchal order.

A good illustration of this is that although women work and serve the needs of capital, they are defined, not as workers, but as mothers. This allows capital to pay women less as work is not their primary role in society. Being defined as mothers, locates women in the domestic arena, where they serve the needs of men through the provision of unpaid services. Men, conversely are defined workers (and not fathers) and regardless of their class benefit from the sexual structuring of society in the rewards they obtain.

The dual-system approach argues that capitalism and patriarchy are two distinct forms of social relations, that must be examined separately, but which are dialectically related to each other. Hartmann (1979, 1981), for example, sees gender and class as working together at all levels, and to understand sexual divisions and gender relations we must examine all micro and macro phenomenon. She argues that many traditional (Marxist) approaches have concentrated on capitalism alone in explaining the oppression of women. In contemporary society capitalism and patriarchy operate in partnership. Hartmann (1981) defines patriarchy as being:

> A set of social relations between men which have a material base, and which, though hierarchical, establish and create interdependence and solidarity among men that establish them to dominate women.
>
> (Hartmann 1976b: 11)

She argues that patriarchy is based in men's control of women's labour

> The material base upon which patriarchy rests, lies most fundamentally in men's control over women's labour power.
>
> (Hartmann 1976b: 11)

Hartmann (1976) argues that patriarchy pre-dates capitalism, and points to the division of labour by sex as being one of histories' universals. She cites a number of anthropological studies to explain how patriarchy emerged and concludes that women suffered a decrease in social status when they lost the control of her subsistence through changes in production methods that devalued her labour, confining her to the home. In this respect she asserts that the roots of women's present position lie in the sex-ordered division of labour and that it is the division of labour that is the main mechanism for maintaining the superiority of men over women.

It is argued by Hartmann (1979) that men have organised around this division of labour to exclude women from paid work. For example, the division of labour enforces lower wages upon women in the jobs that are available as they are defined as secondary, household workers. Low pay keeps women dependant upon men for money, and it is men who benefit from the household work that women do. In turn the circle is completed in that the position of women in the domestic division of labour weakens her position in the labour market. She argues that both capitalism and patriarchy benefit from this arrangement, the former with the gaining of unpaid services, the latter in that women provide an unskilled workforce that can be used to undercut male workers (Hartmann 1976: 168).

Hartmann concludes that the hierarchy of the domestic division of labour perpetuates the hierarchy in the labour market. This in effect, interlocks the independent but interacting, systems of patriarchy and capitalism.

In a more recent consideration of socialist feminism Walby also adopts a similar perspective. Walby argues that there is not one but essentially six patriarchal structures that are all interdependent[10]. However, in a similar fashion to the dualists, Walby argues that patriarchy and capitalism are analytically independent but argues that tensions exist between the two systems. For example, she argues that employers seek to employ women when seeking cheap labour, but such a move has been resisted by men as it undermines their control and domination within the household. She argues that conflict between the two systems is endemic of the history of the interaction between the two, and that without an analytical distinction it would not be possible to understand the changing nature of paid work. On the basis of the relative interaction of the six structures, she argues that in recent Western history, patriarchy has taken mainly two forms, namely public patriarchy is the exclusion of women from social life and her location in the home, and patriarchy which is the subordination of women in all social sites.

The Appropriateness of Existing Theory

There are of course limitations with all the approaches that have been identified, such as Marx's economic determinism and Durkheim's inherent conservatism. There are also important limitations with the gender roles approach. However, it is not necessary here to replicate all the criticisms of Parsons and the gender role paradigm[11] (see Oakley 1974; Poster 1978; Thorne 1982; Segal 1983: Carrigan *et al*, 1985; Myers, 1988; Edley 1995), suffice to say that there three main criticisms worthy of reflection. These are, a lack of a consideration of power differences, the notion of multiple roles, and the reasons for roles and role sanctions. As suggested one of the main problems with sex-role approaches is that gender-role theorists create an artificial division between men and women and reduce the importance of 'power' that men have over women. Yet not all men are advantaged as there is a power differential between groups of men and between individual men. There is not one masculinity but a range of masculinities. This point is taken up by Carrigan *et al* (1987), who suggests that gender role approaches have great deal of appeal to social theorists, but suggest that such role theory does not actually describe the concrete reality of peoples lives, in that not all men conform to these roles. Most men's lives depart form the traditional or accepted 'male role'. The way that sex-role deals with this difference is to define it as deviant or as a failure of socialisation.

The very idea of a 'role' implies a recognisable and accepted standard, and sex-role theorists posit just such a norm to explain sexual differentiation. Society is organised around a pervasive differentiation between men's roles and women's roles, and these roles are internalised by all individuals...Conflict arises when society demands that men live up to an impossible standard...The male role is unduly restrictive because hegemonic masculinity does not reflect the true nature of men.

(Carrigan, Connell and Lee 1987: 77-78)

According to Carrigan *et al*, the starting point for any understanding of masculinity must be men's involvement in social relations that constitute a gender order. Such relationships are historical and are characterised by a rigid division of labour based on sex and differentials in power (or patriarchy).

There are also important limitations with Socialist feminism. For example, Walby (1986) argues that the work of Eisenstein is very ambiguous and that the theory is not fully thought out. Walby argues Eisenstein's work suggests that the system of patriarchy and capitalism both contribute to the 'whole' (patriarchy provides law and order, capitalism provides the economic system). However in this sense it is still possible to talk of separate systems and not the unified system that she wanted. Although the work of Eisenstein is an improvement on the previous capital or patriarchy only approaches, her work requires some clarification and reformation (see also Pollert 1996).

Further problems occur for the dualist position, in it's over concentration on capitalism as the only economic system that produces exploitation and oppresses women. Such an analysis cannot account for the exploitation of women in pre-capitalist and non-capitalist societies.

Despite the amount (and type) of criticism of that has been offered against Socialist feminism and Dual systems analysis, by Walby (1990), and others, the theory should not be dismissed unreservedly and can be effectively used to understand men's roles, even if it is, as Pollert (1996) suggests, as a tool for description rather than explanation.

Likewise the criticisms of general theorists such as Parsons are acknowledged. However gender theorists should not be too hasty in rejecting the general principles that underpin the gender-roles approach, as such principles do have value as a tool for understanding the links between men and working life. The reasons for this are, first, it is a truly social account of the way that men's roles develop and avoids the worst excess of other approaches such as the biological or psychoanalytical. As an approach it locates behaviour in social expectations and the relationships between individuals and society (Edley *et al* 1995).

Concluding Remarks: Men and Work in Late Twentieth Century Britain

As suggested at the beginning of this chapter it was not the intention to provide a summary of all such theoretical works on men and work or on masculinity, nor did it aim to develop a new, overarching and 'all comprehensive' theory of masculinity (or masculinities). The discussion aimed to explore (and outline) those theoretical approaches which can aid an understanding as to why work (or more precisely paid public work) is of central importance to men's lives. Indeed the question was posed - '*What is the origin of the linkage between men and work ?*' In exploring this question two fundamental principles drawn upon. First, that it is the product of long-term social, historical, relational and cultural processes (in which men have been active in) Second that a key issue in this historical development is interrelationship between patriarchy (a set of social relations based on gender) and capital (a set of social relations based on production).

All three general theoretical approaches outlined here have something to offer a discussion of how work becomes associated with men's lives. In the Marxist and Durkheimian models from example a general approach of how the division of labour and attendant roles are developed. Gender role theory suggests how individuals are socialised into such roles. Socialist feminism suggests how the system is the current epoch leads to a situation where traditional gender divisions are maintained. All three approaches seem to suggest that men become associated with work through the historical interplay between productive relations, the development of capitalism and the shifting sites of production. Linking back to Connell (1994) all also seem to acknowledge that gender relationships do not just exist, but develop over time. A man's identity, personality and experience derive from his place in society (Edley *et al* 1995), and that place has been defined socially and historically.

The review of the most useful theories, alongside an explicit historical analysis, points to the conclusion that men's identification with work in western society, has become a function of [12] (and is maintained by) a social sex-ordered division resulting from both capitalist and patriarchal relationships as develop in Western civilisation. As the capitalist division of labour develops through increased specialisation, men become associated with a public labour market role, and women associated with low wages as they are defined, primarily, as household workers. Low pay keeps women dependent on men for support and in the home where men benefit from their labour. In turn this position weakens the position of women in the market. Such positions are supported by developments in areas such as capitalism, urban growth, violence monopolisation, religion and so on. For example, as religion declines relationships become private, men's public role develop as soldiers alongside the needs of empire and as workers to support the needs of industry. As industry develops and movement occurs between country and town with men's (and women's) roles becoming increasingly specialised. The normative values of this social division of labour are transmitted to men (and women) throughout their lives via a multitude of socialising agents such as family, church, state, and professions, guilds trades and unions develop to protect such specialisation and men's position in public work.

In any epoch, of which the current is only one momentary phase (Elias 1987b), the modern capitalist economy and the development of male working roles occurs as a consequence of a number of long term historical processes. The way that these developments emerge and change aspects of masculinity over time influences the form that men's lives take today.

The chapter has attempted to establish theoretically why a linkage between men and work exists. Work remains of central importance to men in Britain as such, the next chapter moves the debate on from the 'theoretical' to examine men's work experiences in Britain as outlined in existing data.

Notes

1 Indeed to do so would require and exploration of issues such as sexuality and ethnicity which are not the focus here.

2 Authors such as Hakim (1996) acknowledge this point when considering women's positions is society. Hakim suggests that a woman's position is determined by their access to role and status in paid employment and their status accorded to their reproductive and domestic role (Hakim 1996: p5).

3 The role of the state in the reinforcement aspects of masculinity can be seen in other areas. For example, the state regulates sexuality via the criminalisation of homosexuality for certain ages. One can also cite other areas legislation that maintain masculinity. For example, the stigmatisation of single parenthood, the nature of state formed family policy generally, men's unemployment benefits and widows pensions vis-à-vis women all support the construction of modern masculinity and its linkage to work.

4 Indeed, if one examines the development of patriarchy and capitalism in any one culture, at anyone time or over a period of time, it is also possible to argue that men's roles, like women's, vary historically and culturally. The form that they take in one culture cannot be easily applied to men in another culture. However, at this juncture this is beyond the scope of this book. For example, Tolson suggests that '...masculinity is a culturally specific and socially functional 'gender identity', with peculiar (often negative) consequences for men themselves' (Tolson 1987: 13).

5 Such an assertion is similar to Marx's idea that 'Capital is not a thing, but a social relation between persons and a relation determined by things' (Marx 1957: 849).

6 A similar analysis can be found away from medicine. Mansfield (1997) has also reflected on similar themes in relation to 'mystery' and the development of the Livery Companies of London. He argues that men are socialised or trained into the 'art and mystery' of certain trades and therefore such work becomes associated with men.

7 Walby (1986) cites the Factory Acts of 1844, 1847, 1864, 1867, 1874, 1878, 1891, 1895, and 1901 as being 'patriarchal strategies of exclusion' (Walby 1986: 100).

8 For example, the work of Dalla Costa (1973) suggests that housework creates value and surplus value and that women are central to capitalism. The work women do in the household was necessary for workers to be able to go to and do their jobs in the factories and offices. Capitalism could not function without women cooking, cleaning and 'keeping house'. Domestic labour must create value, so women must be central capital.

9 Clarification needs to be offered here. What needs to be acknowledged here (unlike in some recent commentaries such as Pollert 1996), is the way in which this is conceptualised differs between two identifiable sub-divisions within socialist feminism. The divisions are 'Unified-systems' approaches and 'Dual-systems' approaches. The former is characteristic of the analyses made by

Eisenstein (1979), and the later is characteristic of the work conducted by Hartmann (1976) and Mitchell (1975). The dual system approach can be further sub-divided, in that there are those theorists who describe capitalism and patriarchy as being determined at different levels of society (Walby 1986). For example, there are those scholars who argue that patriarchy is confined to reproduction and capitalism is confined to production. For others such as Mitchell (1975), patriarchy is confined to non-material areas such as ideology, the unconscious, culture and sexuality, and capitalism to the economy. Secondly, there are those that argue patriarchal and capitalist relations are articulated at all levels of society (Hartmann 1979).

10 The six patriarchal structures that Walby identifies are; the patriarchal mode of production; patriarchal relations in paid work; the patriarchal state, male violence; patriarchal relations in sexuality and patriarchal culture. The relative influence of any of the six structures will vary historically and will affect the gender relations for that period.

11 Such a critique is completely within the public domain, for example, it is well established that Parson's work on roles can be questioned as it sees no possibility of instrumental functions in the household (such as cooking, cleaning etc.) changing, it fails to consider the family as a potential source of inequality and that the relationship between men and women is one of domination and subordination a good critique. For a useful summary of the criticism see Carrigan *et al* 1987.

12 Clarification of this concept is required. This is not meant as the reified term 'function' developed by Durkheim (and abused by Parsons), but one based on Elias, who argues '...the concept of function must be understood as a concept of relationship. We can only speak of social functions when referring to interdependencies which constrain people to a greater or lesser extent. This element of coercion can be clearly seen in the function performed by each tribal group as the enemy of the other...It is impossible to understand the function that A performs for B without taking into account the function that B performs for A. This is what is meant when it is said that the concept of function is a concept of relationship' (Elias 1970: 78).

3 Men, Work and Employment in Britain

Introduction

> The structure of the workforce has changed over the last 25 years. One of the most striking changes has been the significant rise in female economic activity while the proportion of males who are economically active has fallen.
>
> (Central Statistical Office, Regional Trends, 1996: 72)

Chapter one suggested, and chapter two developed further the theme that work is central to the masculine experience and the very nature of men's lives. Whilst it goes without question here that masculinity is closely linked with working[1], such a view could imply that there is no need to study work as a gendered activity for men. For men, work is a very important factor, very little is explicitly written about male experiences in the labour market *per se*. Indeed, research which has problematised work as a gendered activity has largely focused on the position(s) of women in the labour market (see Hakim 1996 for an excellent review of women's work). Yet as Collinson, *et al* note :

> A critical analysis of men and masculinities is particularly important in the study of work, organisations and management. Yet an examination of the available literature reveals a recurring paradox. The categories of men and masculinity are frequently central to analyses, yet they remain taken for granted, hidden and unexamined. Men are both talked about and ignored.
>
> (Collinson and Hearn 1994: 3)

The invisibility of men in work needs to be explored, and as such, this chapter moves away from the largely theoretical to begin to examine the actuality of men's work experiences in Britain. In doing so, this chapter highlights two important trends in male employment. The first trend the chapter examines is the decline in male labour market participation and the decline in male full-time employment. The second trend the chapter examines is the growth in male non-standard employment forms, providing an analysis of the trends in male part-time working, male temporary working, male self-employment and male homeworking.

This is done in a discussion of general labour market trends, and through an examination of male working forms and male employment trends between the early to mid 1980s and 1996[2] .To do this effectively, this chapter draws on some data and analyses that have been offered elsewhere both in academic (see Felstead *et al* 1996; Joeman, 1993; Campbell, *et al*, 1992) and government or official publications (see for examples, OECD 1991,1996; Labour Force Survey Historical Supplement, 1993)[3].

Economic Recession and the Declining Numbers of Male Full-Time Workers

The history of male employment has been characterised by a series of historical shifts. For example, the movement from the agrarian state to the industrial one. Further, within the industrial epoch, male work has been characterised by movements between industries and occupations, and movement 'in' and 'out' of employment altogether, as Orwell famously notes:

> I first became aware of the unemployment problem in 1928. At that time I had just come back from Burma, where unemployment was only a word, and I had gone to Burma when I was still a boy and the post-war boom was not quite over. When I first saw unemployed men at close quarters, the thing that horrified and amazed me was to find that many of them were ashamed of being unemployed. I was very ignorant, but not so ignorant as to imagine that the loss of foreign markets pushes two million men out of work...
>
> (Orwell 1937: 155)

In the current epoch, the period between the first Thatcher government of 1979 and this present research, has been characterised by a series of radical changes in male labour market participation. For example, there has, for the first time since the depression in the 1930s, been uncertainty about the availability and stability of work. There has been an economy that has been directed by neo-liberal policies leading to inevitable cycles of 'boom and boost' and economic recession. However, such issues can be linked together to suggests that one of the main features of the period 1980 to 1996 is a slowing down of economic growth. This trend is shown in Table 3.1.

This table suggests that Britain at the end of the 1980s and the early to mid 1990s, and again in the early 1990s experienced economic recession and periods of high and low economic as a consequence of those periods of recession. The first recession of this period has been well documented elsewhere and was subject to much academic as well as political conjecture. The economic recession of the 1990s was experienced in a number of OECD countries with slowed economic growth (for example, Australia, New Zealand, Finland, Sweden and the United Kingdom).

Table 3.1
Employment Growth for Selected OECD Countries - 1989 to 1996
(thousands and percentage change)

Country	Level 1994(000s)	1989	1994	1996*
Japan	64,536	1.9	0.0	-0.1
North America#	151,066	2.0	2.2	1.2
Central , Western and Southern Europe				
Austria	3,452	1.8	0.2	-0.6
Czech Republic	5,049	-	1.2	1.6
France	22,295	1.3	0.3	-0.3
Germany	34,957	1.3	-0.7	-0.9
Greece	3,790	0.4	1.9	0.7
Ireland	1,225	-0.1	3.5	2.3
Italy	20,120	0.1	-0.6	0.2
Netherlands	5,290	1.7	1.5	1.2
Spain	11,730	4.1	-0.9	0.7
Switzerland	3,775	1.1	-0.2	0.2
Turkey	19,664	1.3	2.5	1.8
UK	**25,567**	**3.1**	**0.7**	**0.3**
Labour Force				
UK		**-0.4**	**-0.5**	**0.0**

*Estimate # USA, Canada, Mexico.
Source: Adapted from OECD (1996) Employment Outlook, page 3. 1989 and 1991 data from OECD (1991) Employment Outlook, page 6.

The OECD (1991) reported that GDP/GNP in the whole of the OECD area grew by only 2.6 per cent in 1990 compared to 3.3 per cent in 1989. In the United Kingdom GDP/GNP for the same two years was 0.6 per cent and 1.9 per cent respectively. In 1991 and the recession is evidenced with GDP/GNP at -1.8 per cent. As a result of this economic slowdown employment growth in the OECD (see Table 3.1) area also slowed to around 1.3 per cent which may be compared to 1.8 per cent in 1989 (OECD 1991: 4). In the UK the figures for the same period were 3.1 and -3.4 per cent respectively. In the years 1994 and 1995 the level of the labour force also fell by a further -0.4 and -0.4 per cent respectively.

This lack of employment growth affected living standards and welfare of many, adding to the problems of poverty and social exclusion (OECD 1991: ix). These figures also point to another consequence of such economic slowdown at both the end of the 1970s and at the start of the 1990s was a drastic increase in unemployment, especially in the UK and particularly for men. In the recession of the 1980s unemployment rose to a peak of three million one hundred and fifty thousand in the spring of 1984. The dramatic nature of this rise in unemployment is demonstrated in Table 3.2. This shows that in the four years between 1979 and 1983 unemployment jumped from eight hundred and eighty eight thousand to over two million.

Table 3.2
Male Unemployment for Selected OECD Countries - 1973 to 1993 (thousands)

	1973	1979	1989	1990	1993
Japan	440	740	830	770	950
USA	2,275	3,120	1,257	1,155	4,932
Central , Western and Southern Europe					
Austria	13	28	58	63	88
Belgium	48	113	149	-	232
France	224	581	970	935	1,384
Germany	150	417	1,070	968	1,508
Greece	39	31	296	308	164
Ireland	53	66	157	-	138
Italy	603	724	1,220	1,102	1,188
Netherlands	88	781	558	494	271
Portugal	42	122	233	220	125
Spain	267	759	2,561	2,441	1,837
Switzerland	0	5	17	20	74
UK	**476**	**888**	**1,802**	**1,908**	**2,209**
UK Women	**81**	**346**	**487**	**400**	**656**

Source: Adapted from OECD (1996) Employment Outlook, page 199.1989 and 1990 data from OECD (1991) Employment Outlook, page 257.

A peak in the recession of the 1990s led male unemployment rise to 2,837,000 by August of 1992. Along with the fact that male unemployment was gradually rising between 1989 and 1992, women's unemployment fell in 1990 by eighty seven thousand on the previous year. To some extent the fluctuations in male (and female) unemployment figures were mirrored in the actual levels of male full-time employment.

> The decline of manufacturing industry has not been completely balanced by the growth of service industries, so that full-time employment fell from 21 million in 1951 to 19 million in 1995. All of the net loss has been in male employment...Clearly the nature of work has changed since 1951. The question is, has it changed to the detriment of men as well as to the advantage of women ?
>
> (Hakim 1996: 74)

As Hakim suggests, in terms of male and female experiences of the labour market, one noticeable feature of the British labour market is that there has been a decline in the numbers of men working, and particularly men working full-time. Such a trend has also been noted by Beechey and Perkins (1987), who point out that

> Although men's activity rates in Britain have remained consistently higher than women's throughout this century, they have fallen in recent years. The activity rate for men was 65 per cent in 1901, 69 per cent in 1931 and 67 per cent in 1951, but since then it has fallen steadily and in 1981 it was just 60 per cent.
>
> (Beechey and Perkins 1987: 11)

Continuous full-time work that involves working for others, receiving a wage, being based in an employer's premises for an indefinite period is seen as the 'standard' employment form (see Felstead *et al*) and one that is closely linked with men (Beechey *et al* 1987; Collinson and Hearn 1994; Hakim 1996). Table 3.3 presents the data of labour force participation by gender for all those aged 16 or over for the period 1971-2006, and from this table three main general trends can be seen. First, the number of those who are 16 or over who are eligible to work has increased over this period from 24,900,000 to a projected 30,092,000 in the year 2006.

Second, that alongside this increase in the overall number of 16 year olds available for work, there has been a ten per cent decrease in the numbers of men working. There has been a decline from 80.5 per cent in 1971 to 72.6 per cent in 1995 and down to a projected 70.0 per cent by the year 2006. Third, the data suggests that over the same period there will be an increase of around 13 per cent in the numbers of women working.

To summarise, this data seems to suggest that whilst the overall number of working age individuals is increasing, and the number of women participating in the labour market is increasing, men's participation is decreasing.

Table 3.3
Labour Force by Gender of All Aged 16 and Over (Great Britain percentages) - 1971 to 2006

Year	Males	Females	All 16+ (000s)
1971	80.5	43.9	24,900
1976	78.9	46.8	25,700
1981	76.5	47.6	26,200
1984	75.9	49.2	27,172
1986	75.2	50.0	27,566
1991	73.4	53.1	28,185
1992	73.9	52.8	28,582
1993	72.9	53.0	28,454
1994	72.6	53.0	28,421
1996	72.2	53.7	28, 717
2001	71.5	55.5	29,469
2006	70.0	56.7	30,092

Source: Adapted from Social Trends 1996, Central Statistical Office, HMSO, p84, and Social Trends 1989, page 70.

However, it needs to be acknowledged that these are general participation rates and do not differentiate between male full-time work and non-standard work, nor do they suggests that the increase in women's participation is largely located in the full-time sector. As Hakim (1996) is at pains to point out

> There is no evidence...that women have been taking full-time jobs from men or that changes in female work rates could account for the loss of men's jobs. All the increase in employment in Britain in the post-war period, from 22 million jobs in 1951 to 25 million in 1995, consisted of growth in female part-time jobs.
> (Hakim 1996: 62-63)

Yet Hakim's concern is with refuting the displacement thesis and that women's gains in employment have been as a consequence of stealing work from men. Displacement or otherwise is not the issue for men, but the fact that change has occurred is. Hakim (1996) hides the fact that employment has changed for men within a consideration of women's employment but such changes need to be highlighted.

Table 3.4
Employees in Employment by Gender and Standard Industrial Classification* (Percentages) - 1981 and 1995

	1	2	3	4	5	6	7	8	9	10	11
Males 1981	2.4	4.8	32.5	-	8.1	15.9	9.1	10.4	6.8	7.3	2.8
Males 1995	2.3	0.6	25.1	1.2	6.5	20.3	8.4	16.5	6.4	8.7	4.2
Females 1981	1.1	0.9	18.0	-	1.4	23.4	3.0	12.2	7.5	26.4	4.8
Females 1995	0.8	0.1	10.8	0.3	1.2	23.4	3.2	17.0	6.2	30.7	5.0

* 1=Agriculture, hunting, forestry and fishing, 2=Mining, quarrying, 3=Manufacturing, 4=Electricity, Gas, Water, 5=Construction, 6=Distribution, Hotels, Catering and Repairs, 7=Transport, Storage and Communication, 8=Financial and Business Services, 9=Public Administration and Defence, 10=Education, Social Work and Health, 11=Other.
Source: Adapted from Regional Trends, 1996, Central Statistical Office, HMSO, p80-81.

The changes in male employment over time are further emphasised by the figures presented in tables 3.4 and 3.5. For example, table 3.4 shows the employment of men (and women) by standard industrial classification for 1981 and 1995 respectively. Such a table points to the changing nature (and content) of male employment over this fourteen year period. The table suggests that for men there has been a drastic decrease in working in industries such as mining, manufacturing and construction whilst working in areas such as distribution, hotels, catering and repairs, or financial and business services, has increased.

Table 3.5 further illustrates the decline of male full-time employment. In 1951, male full-time employment stood at 15,262 thousand, yet by 1995 this had fallen to 12,954 thousand. Conversely women's full-time employment had increased from 784 thousands to 6,302 thousand in the same period. Given this trend, it may now be more appropriate to re-conceptualise what work men do. Instead of conceptualising all male workers as full-time workers and women as part-time or marginal workers it may be possible that there has been a blurring of the edges of what is men's work and women's work and men's working roles have changed.

Table 3.5
All Full-Time Employees by Gender 1951-1995 (in thousands)

Spring	Men	Women
1951	15,262	784
1971	15,574	1,892
1984	13, 308	5,340
1985	13,113	5,418
1986	13,048	5,480
1987	13,071	5,587
1988	13,450	5,840
1989	13,829	6,230
1990	13,878	6,366
1991	13,461	6,235
1992	12,858	6,099
1993	12,737	6,236
1995	12,954	6,302

Source: Labour Force Survey Historical Supplement (1993), Government Statistical Office, page 5. 1951, 1971, 1993 and 1995 data from Hakim, C., (1996) Female Heterogeneity and the Polarisation of Women's Employment, Athlone.

The arguments that the future of work lies in the viable alternatives to wage labour have been put forward on a of variety grounds. Governments advocate self employment, small scale enterprise…in the belief that they are alternatives and will improve the economy.

(Allen 1994: 115)

The Growth of Male Non-Standard Forms of Employment

For many men, the general absence of work has meant that some men have had to spend more time within the household (although it may not be by choice). Other men, are also experiencing (for the first time) a situation where it is the female partner who is the major wage earner, and where it is women who have notions of career. Men now also need to be conceptualised as part-time workers, homeworkers, temporary workers, casual workers, self-employed workers or as job-sharers, as well as full-time workers. Men perhaps also need to be now considered as 'non-workers'. As Felstead and Powell (1996) note

There is an almost unshakeable belief that the trend in the industrialised economies of the world is towards greater labour market flexibility. The growth of 'non-standard' forms of employment is taken as one indicator of this trend.

(Felstead and Powell 1996: 1)

Green *et al* (1992) and Felstead *et al* (1996) confirm the view that 'non-standard work' has been increasing in many industrialised nations, and attempt to explain this as a consequence of the changing nature of employment in such industrial economies. The growing reliance of industry and employers on non-standard workers is to provide numerical and pay flexibility. The whole nature of non-standard work is tied up with the desire to have a temporary and therefore flexible workforce. As far as the employers were concerned, the most common reasons for employing non-standard workers are: to provide short-term cover while other staff were away; to match manning levels to peaks in demand; to adjust manning levels; to provide specialist skills.

Atkinson (1985) introduced the term 'flexible firm' to describe an emerging type of work organisation that can respond quickly to labour market demands and technological advances. This adaptability is achieved via: functional flexibility - employing workers that can do a number of tasks; numerical flexibility - being able to alter workforce size through the hiring of non-standard workers; and pay flexibility - the ability of the employer to reduce pay and benefits. Green *et al* (1992), suggest that the growth of non-standard work derives from the growth of flexible firms and the emphasis that they place on numerical flexibility.

Green *et al* (1992) and Felstead *et al* (1996), focus on four basic types of non-standard work: part-time work, temporary (contract or casual) work, multiple-job holding, and own account self-employment. They use the label 'non-standard', with full-time, permanent, paid work as the benchmark (page 1). For example, Felstead *et al* (1996) suggests that the 'standard' or 'typical' for of employment involves working for 'another', for a wage and working in a subordinate role. This is indicative of full-time employment and the expectation of indefinite full-time work.

Green *et al* (1992) suggest that most researchers have evaluated non-standard work negatively, referring to it as 'precarious employment'. However they suggest that while some non-standard jobs may be poorly paid because of their limited skill requirements, and that they are undervalued because these jobs are held by women, it must be recognised that some non-standard jobs are well rewarded and no more precarious than standard jobs (for example, those non-standard jobs held by business consultants, doctors and lawyers). They also suggest that some workers may prefer the non-standard forms, such as young parents.

The non-standard working form that this current research will examine are, part-time work, self-employment, temporary working and, more briefly homeworking[4].

Men and Part-time Working

This has long been the most common form of non-standard working. Indeed, now part-time employment is the most common type of non-standard work in Britain and in many other Western European countries. Some authors go as far to suggest that about one in five British jobs are part-time and that whole sectors of the economy are now organised almost exclusively on a part-time basis (see Blanchflower 1986; Beechey *et al* 1987; Green *et al* 1992; Felstead and Powell 1996). Research suggests that the post-war period has been marked by an increase in the use of part-time workers by employers. In Britain, full-time employment only grew by 4 per cent between 1983 and 1988, compared to an increase in part-time work of 28 per cent (Employment Gazette 1988; Green *et al* 1992). For both sexes, full-time work is declining in it's importance, both absolutely and relative to part-time work (Blanchflower 1986).

> What is so significant about part-time work is not merely its vast numerical increase. It is that over the past 30 years or so in Britain we have witnessed the development of a new form of work which is highly exploitative and heavily gender-specific.
>
> (Beechey and Perkins 1987: 1)

Beechey and Perkins suggest that there were three reasons for the growth of part-time work between the 1950s and the 1960s, it was a ploy used by employers to attract women to work, who did not want to work full-time; to increase production, with women workers taking jobs in twilight shifts; to use women in catering or cleaning jobs[5]. By 1986, almost half of the women employed in the labour market were employed in part-time jobs and half the growth of women's employment has been linked to the availability of part-time work (Coyle 1988). Felstead and Powell (1996) in a more contemporary account suggest that there is a strong association between women and part-time work, showing in their analysis of the labour force survey for 1989 and 1994, 85 per cent of those working part-time were women.

Further to this point it seems that those industries and occupations where women had traditionally, also had a high incidence of part-time workers. Blanchflower *et al* (1986), argue that part-time work is most noticeable in four industry groups - education, business services, miscellaneous services, and hotels and pubs. In these industries, part-time employment accounted for over 50 per cent of all female employment. Martin and Roberts (1984) point out that a high proportion of female part-time workers can be found in lower level occupations as compared to the women that work full-time in such occupations. Such views are supported elsewhere (see Green *et al* 1992; Felstead and Powell; 1996).

However, despite an obvious and historical identification of part-time work with women (see Myrdal and Klein, 1968), the incidence of part-time work amongst men has also increased. Indeed, in many instances since the end of the 1980s it is possible to find more men undertaking part-time work than in any other time in history a fact which past and more contemporary literature does not comprehend nor examine in any detail.

Table 3.6
Male Part-Time Work for Selected OECD Countries as a Proportion of Employment - 1973 to 1995

Country	1973	1979	1983	1993	1994	1995	Change
Austria	1.4	1.5	1.5	1.7	3.0	4.0	+2.6
Belgium	1.0	1.0	2.0	2.3	2.5	2.8	+1.8
Canada	4.7	6.5	8.7	11.0	10.7	10.6	+5.9
France	1.7	2.4	2.5	4.1	4.6	5.0	+3.3
Germany	1.8	1.5	1.7	2.9	3.2	3.6	+1.8
Ireland	-	2.1	2.7	4.8	5.1	-	+3.0
Italy	3.7	3.0	2.4	2.5	2.8	2.9	-0.8
Japan	6.8	7.5	7.3	11.4	11.7	10.1	+3.3
Netherlands	-	5.5	6.9	15.3	16.1	16.8	+11.3
New Zealand	4.6	4.9	5.0	9.7	9.7	9.3	+4.6
Spain	-	-	-	19.7	16.2	11.4	-8.3
Switzerland	-	-	-	6.6	7.1	7.7	+1.1
USA	8.6	9.0	10.8	11.0	11.5	11.0	+2.4
UK Men	2.3	1.9	3.3	6.6	7.1	7.7	+5.4
UK Women	39.1	39.0	42.4	43.9	44.4	44.3	+5.2

Source: Adapted from OECD (1996) Employment Outlook, page 192.

Data relating to male part-time employment is presented in tables 3.6 to 3.9. To summarise, Table 3.6 shows that over the period between 1973 and 1995 there has been a 5.4 per cent increase in the incidence of male part-time working in the UK. This is in line with male part-time working in other selected OECD countries apart from two main exceptions. Both Spain and Japan have seen a decrease in the numbers of male part-time workers. The Netherlands on the other hand has seen an 11 per cent rise in male part-time employment. Similar UK trends are presented in table 3.7.

Table 3.7
All Part-Time Employees by Gender (in thousands and hours) - LFS
Spring 1984 - 1991

| Spring | Men | Women | Average Hours of Work | |
			Men	Women
1984	416	3,968	15.9	17.0
1985	426	4,056	15.1	17.0
1986	440	4,156	15.3	17.2
1987	483	4,226	16.1	16.9
1988	557	4,324	14.9	17.2
1989	535	4,458	15.1	16.9
1990	583	4,468	15.6	17.3
1991	618	4,496	14.5	15.2
1992	646	4,493	13.8	15.2
1993	667	4,559	-	-
1994	726	4,658	-	-

Source: Labour Force Survey Historical Supplement (1993), Government Statistical Office, p5. Labour Force Survey QB (1994) No.9 page 17. Labour Force Survey Historical Supplement (1993), Government Statistical Office, p12.

Table 3.8 presents information on the age of male part-time workers for the periods 1989 and 199. The data suggests an interesting trend. Whereas most age groupings have seen an effective increase in part-time working, the incidence of part-time work for those men aged 45-54 has effectively doubled in this five year period. Table 3.9 shows that part-time work has also increased in all the regions of the UK in the four years between 1991 and 1995.

Table 3.8
Age and Working Part-Time by Gender - 1989 and 1994 (thousands)

Age	Men		Women	
	1989	1994	1989	1994
15-24	294	377	557	589
25-34	82	117	1,003	1,107
35-44	73	93	1,383	1,342
45-54	54	108	1,027	1,155
55-64	102	147	611	638
Total	**604**	**842**	**4,581**	**4,829**
% of Employment	4.1	6.2	40.7	43.1

Source: Adapted from Felstead, A and Powell, M., (1996) Contrasting Fortunes in Time and Space: Non-Standard Work in Canada and in the United Kingdom, mimeo. page 11b/c.

Table 3.9
Part-Time Labour Force by Gender and Region (percentage of All Employees) - 1991 and 1995

	1991	1995
Males		
UK	5.3	7.0
North	4.7	6.3
Yorkshire and Humber	4.8	7.0
East Midlands	4.8	6.7
East Anglia	5.0	8.3

Table 3.9 Continued

South East	6.0	7.4
South West	6.6	7.7
West Midlands	4.5	6.6
North West	5.1	6.4
Scotland	5.2	7.1
Wales	5.4	6.6
Females		
UK	43.0	43.8
North	48.0	46.6
Yorkshire and Humber	48.0	49.6
East Midlands	43.7	45.2
East Anglia	49.0	47.0
South East	39.8	39.4
South West	48.6	49.2
West Midlands	44.1	44.4
North West	43.0	43.6
Scotland	39.9	42.8
Wales	43.2	47.7

Source: Adapted from Regional Trends, 1996, Central Statistical Office, HMSO, page 82.

Temporary Working

There has been a growing debate on the growth on temporary employment as providing flexibility (Atkinson, 1987; Green, 1992; Heather *et al* 1996) or developing marginal groups within the labour market (Casey *et al*, 1989; Nätti, 1993).

A temporary worker is an individual who is occupying a job which is available only on a temporary basis and Casey (1989) identifies a number of categories of temporary workers as: Consultants or freelancers; Labour only sub-contractors; Casual Workers; Seasonal Workers; Fixed-term Contract Workers; Workers with a contract dischargeable by performance; Workers on Training Contracts; Temporary Workers on Indefinite Contracts; Agency Workers; Employees of works contractors; Participants in Special Training Programmes. Heather *et al* (1996) define temporary workers as :

...those whose employment is seen by both employer and employee as being for a limited period only. They include casual employees, seasonal employees and employees on contracts that run for a fixed term, or until a particular task has been completed. They also include agency temporaries...freelancers, external consultants and self-employed workers.

(Heather *et al* 1996: 404)

Temporary working has been rising for both men and women in recent history. For example, table 3.10 presents information on temporary working in a selected number of OECD countries between 1983 and 1993. It can be seen that the use of temporary working has generally increased across all the OECD countries. With the exception of Denmark and Portugal there has also be a general increase in the use of male temporary workers. In the UK male temporary working increased by 2.2 per cent between 1983 and 1994, whereas women's temporary employment remained largely static for the same period.

Table 3.10
Incidence of Temporary Working by Selected OECD Country - 1983 and 1994 (percentages)

	1983/87	1994	Men 1983	1994	Women 1983	1994
Australia	15.6	23.5	9.0	17.9	26.2	30.6
Belgium	5.4	5.1	3.8	3.5	8.5	7.5
Canada	7.5	8.8	6.9	9.2	8.2	8.5
Denmark	12.5	12.0	12.2	11.1	12.7	12.9
Finland	11.3	13.5	9.3	12.3	13.3	14.7
France	3.3	11.0	3.3	9.7	3.4	12.4
Germany	10.0	10.3	9.0	9.8	11.5	11.0
Ireland	6.1	9.4	4.7	7.4	8.8	12.1
Italy	6.6	7.3	5.2	6.1	9.4	9.3
Japan	10.3	10.4	5.3	5.4	19.5	18.3
Netherlands	5.8	10.9	3.5	7.9	9.3	15.0
Spain	15.6	33.7	13.3	31.4	18.4	37.9
Sweden	12.0	13.5	9.7	12.3	13.9	14.6
UK	5.5	6.6	3.3	5.5	7.3	7.5
USA	-	2.2	-	2.0	-	2.4

Source: Adapted from OECD (1996) Employment Outlook, page 8.

Table 3.11
Temporary Working by Industry - 1989 and 1994 (thousands)

Industry	1989	1994
Agriculture	31	22
Natural Resource-Based	30	25
Manufacturing	202	194
Construction	116	85
Distributive Services	88	70
Business Services	121	171
Education, Health and Welfare	369	590
Public Administration	82	108
Retail Trade	232	108
Other	265	142
Total	**1,556**	**1,592**
% of Total Employment	6.8	7.3

Source: Adapted from Felstead, A and Powell, M., (1996) Contrasting Fortunes in Time and Space: Non-Standard Work in Canada and in the United Kingdom, mimeo. page 11b/c.

Table 3.12
Main Employment of Men and Women; UK - 1994 and 1995 (percentages)

	Men	Women
1994		
Part-time Temporary	2	5
Full-time Temporary	5	3
Part-time Permanent	5	40
Full-time Permanent	88	52
1995		
Part-time Temporary	2	5
Full-time Temporary	2	4
Part-time Permanent	5	39
Full-time Permanent	88	53

Source: Adapted from Employment Gazette Jan. 1995, Jan. 1996.

Table 3.13
Employees in Temporary Work and as a Percentage of Employees; UK 1986 - 1995

	All	Men	Women
1986	1,300	500	800
% of All Employees	-	-	-
1993	1,697	801	806
% of All Employees	7.7	6.9	8.5
1994	1,611	750	861
% of All Employees	7.4	6.6	8.3
1995	1,451	676	776
% of All Employees	6.8	6.0	7.6

Source: Adapted from Employment Gazette Jan. 1995, Jan. 1996. Data for 1986 adapted from Employment Gazette, April 1988, page 245.

Table 3.14
Age and Temporary Working by Gender - 1989 and 1994 (thousands)

Age	Men		Women	
	1989	1994	1989	1994
15-24	408	316	377	275
25-34	108	172	179	201
35-44	70	115	189	198
45-54	34	80	89	120
55-64	38	57	63	58
Total	**659**	**741**	**897**	**852**
% of Employment	5.4	6.5	8.6	8.2

Source: Adapted from Felstead, A and Powell, M., (1996) Contrasting Fortunes in Time and Space: Non-Standard Work in Canada and in the United Kingdom, mimeo. page 11b/c.

Table 3.15
Reasons Why People Take Part in Temporary Work;
UK - Spring 1984 - 1995

	1984	1987	1990	1994	1995
All Employees in Temporary Jobs					
	1,236	1,181	1,188	1,396	-
Reasons for taking temporary work:					
Job included contract of training	6	4	4	7	7
Could not find a permanent job	35	30	24	43	47
Did not want a permanent job	32	31	38	27	24
Other reasons	28	34	35	24	22

* Figures are for Great Britain
Source: Adapted from Employment Gazette (1995), page 57, 1995 data from
Employment Gazette, Jan. 1996 LFS7.

Tables 3.11 to 3.15 provide a range of other statistics on the incidence of temporary working. Table 3.11 demonstrates that between 1989 and 1994 the use of temporary working has either increased or decreased depending upon industry. For example, agriculture has seen a decline in temporary working, whereas education, health and welfare have been marked by a clear increase in the use of temporary workers.

Table 3.14 provides information on the incidence of male temporary working by age for the period 1989 to 1994. This shows that for male workers aged between 15-24 there has been a decrease in temporary working. However, for all other male age groups (from 25 to 64) male temporary work has increased.

Men and Self-Employment

Research in industrial sociology and the sociology of work has generally proceeded on the assumption that employment in large organisations is either more pervasive or more important than activities in small workplace settings...In recent years, however, small business and self-employment have become a topic of considerable debate in academic and public-policy circles.

(Bögenhold and Staber 1991: 223)

This assertion of Bögenhold and Staber (1991) is indeed the case of industrial sociology and economics. The focus on self-employment has taken many forms with a variety of subject areas, for example; self-employment, franchising and the small firm, (Felstead 1990, 1991, 1992; O'Connell-Davidson 1994); self-employment, class and its cyclical nature (Bögenhold and Staber 1991 1993; Meager 1992b). One common theme is that the numbers involved in self-employment, franchising and subcontracting are increasing (see Bögenhold and Staber 1991; Felstead 1991; Fevre 1987; O'Connell-Davidson 1991, 1994; Hakim 1988; Dale and Bamford 1988; Casey and Creigh 1988; Campbell and Daly 1992; Bryson and White 1996a, 1996b). For example, Campbell and Daly (1992) summarise the self-employment labour market trends between 1981 and 1991 as having the following characteristics :

Self employment increased by 1.1 million (52%) between 1981 and 1991, to a total of 3.3 million; Of this growth men accounted for 0.8 million and women 0.4 million; Over two-thirds of the self-employed have no employees;The number of employees with a second job in self-employment doubled form 0.1 million in 1981 to over 0.2 million in 1991.

(Campbell and Daly 1992: 269)

However, according to Felstead *et al* (1992) measures of the levels of self-employment can vary greatly and that a difficulty also arises in the fact that data on self-employment relies on self reporting and therefore subjective definitions. Indeed as Leighton (1983) reports when these classifications are examined they are incorrect - the apparently self-employed are in fact in many instances employees.

Most social class characterisations of the self-employed or 'the petty bourgeoisie' assign them to more or less homogeneous category on the basis of their employment status...*[one definition could be]* the self employed as persons who own their own means of production...

(Bögenhold and Staber 1991: 224)

This definition is also problematic in that it simply rests on the ownership of the means of production. Felstead (1992) also suggests that the allocation of the self-employment with autonomy needs to be challenged.

The self-employed and small business owners cannot be treated as belonging to a single, homogeneous group. On the contrary, such a group comprises a wide variety of working relationships set along a continuum ranging from the stereotypical view of 'being one's own boss' to those entirely dependent on large capital for their work.

(Felstead 1992: 32)

This common sense notion of self-employment is one based on autonomy, power control, and one largely free of alienation. The common-sense approach sees the self-employed as being in control of their own pace of work, the quality of their work and its timing. They are working on their own account and are not subordinate to any employer. As research suggests (Burchell *et al*, 1992; Felstead *et al* 1992) point out, one problem with this is that it has never really been challenged or tested against the reality of self-employment.

Burchell *et al* (1992) highlight a number of factors that may be considered direct or indirect indicators of dependency, Does the respondent work at home?; Why did the respondent enter self-employment?; Do they control the price of their labour/product?; Do they work for an employer?; Do they bear all the economic risk? Just as many of the nominally self-employed find themselves in a subordinate market position by virtue of the fact that they are dependent on a small number of clients or on others for a product (Felstead 1991). This form of self-employment, Felstead identifies as franchising[6].

How can the rise in self-employment be accounted for? According to some, when an economy goes into rapid decline, as the British economy did during the late 1970s and the early 1980s, a dilemma occurs for neo-liberals in the decline of the economy, the desire for employment (to generate wealth) and the undesirability of state involvement in leading the labour market. Such a situation is increasingly difficult for governments to maintain, no wealth is created and recession goes on. One possible solution to this is to encourage increased levels of self-employment, workers for whom the state has no direct responsibility, but from whom that state can reap the benefits of the wealth that they create. Links have been established between unemployment and the rise of self-employment (see Meager *et al* 1994; Campbell and Daly 1992; Bryson and White 1996b).

In terms of actual data, Tables 3.16 to 3.20 provide information of self employment in the UK. Table 3.16 suggests that self-employment actually varies by geographical region and over time with the south eastern regional economy having the highest incidence of part-time working between 1981 and 1991.

Table 3.17 explores the distribution of male and female, part-time and full-time self-employed workers. This data suggests that in the ten years between 1984 and 1994, male self-employment has been much higher than women's. The data also shows there was a peak in self employment, for both men and women and full and part-time, in the years 1989 and 1990 and again for part-time self-employed women in 1993 and 1994.

Table 3.16
Self-Employment by Region - LFS 1981 to 1991 (thousands)

	1981	1990	1991
South East	747	1,288	1,173
East Anglia	90	151	138
South West	272	381	399
West Midlands	175	322	273
East Midlands	150	234	245
York. and Humberside	168	274	258
North West	228	328	329
North	92	119	118
Wales	119	166	161
Scotland	135	208	223
GREAT BRITAIN	2,177	3,471	3,316

Source: Campbell, M. and Daly, M. (1992) 'Self-Employment in the 1990's' Employment Gazette, June 1992, page 271.

Table 3.17
All Full-Time and Part-Time Self-Employment for Men and Women (in thousands) - LFS Spring 1984 - 1991

Spring	FT Men	PT Men	FT Women	PT Women
1984	1,847	133	328	318
1985	1,900	132	355	336
1986	1,933	122	363	322
1987	2,092	154	397	366
1988	2,224	148	412	371
1989	2,440	180	441	372
1990	2,455	186	460	376
1991	2,362	164	439	357
1992	2,188	180	402	368
1993	2,109	199	400	381
1994	2,179	211	407	395

*Figures are for Great Britain.
Source: Labour Force Survey Historical Supplement (1993), Government Statistical Office, p5. Labour Force Survey QB (1994) No.9 page 17.

Table 3.18
Own Account Self Employment by Industry - 1989 and 1994
(thousands)

	1989	1994
Agriculture	177	152
Natural Resource-Based	23	20
Manufacturing	228	189
Construction	687	675
Distributive Services	183	179
Business Services	223	334
Education, Health and Welfare	108	283
Public Administration	41	10
Retail Trade	309	309
Other	324	165
Total	**2,306**	**2,320**
% of Total Employment	8.8	9.3

Source: Adapted from Felstead, A and Powell, M., (1996) Contrasting Fortunes in Time and Space: Non-Standard Work in Canada and in the United Kingdom, mimeo. page 11b/c.

Table 3.19
All Self Employed and Average Hours by Gender (in thousands and hours) - LFS Spring 1984 - 1991

Spring	All	Men	Women	Average Hours of Work Men	Women
1981	2,177	1,726	451	-	-
1983	2,295	1,747	549	-	-
1984	2,615	1,976	639	52.9	51.7
1985	2,714	2,029	685	51.4	50.3
1986	2,726	2,046	680	51.5	49.9
1987	2,996	2,234	762	51.8	49.9
1988	3,142	2,358	785	51.4	49.3
1989	3,425	2,607	819	50.4	47.8
1990	3,471	2,627	844	45.0	47.0
1991	3,316	2,511	805	47.5	46.1

Source: Campbell, M. and Daly, M. (1992) 'Self-Employment in the 1990's' Employment Gazette, June 1992, p 270. Labour Force Survey Historical Supplement (1993), Government Statistical Office, page 12.

Table 3.20
Numbers of Self-Employed by Age- LFS 1981 to 1991

Age	1981 All	Men	Women	1991 All	Men	Women
16-24	134	108	26	246	198	48
25-44	1,120	884	236	1,773	1,291	441
45-54	491	387	103	786	591	195
55-59	187	149	38	260	201	59
60-64	131	107	24	160	130	30
65+	114	90	24	131	100	31

Source: Campbell, M. and Daly, M. (1992) 'Self-Employment in the 1990's Employment Gazette, June 1992, page 277.

Table 3.18 shows the distribution of self-employment by industry, while table 3.19 explores the distribution of self-employment by hours of work. As with other forms of non-standard working, self-employment appears to have an age dimension. The data in Table 3.20 suggests that the prime age for self-employment is 25-44.

Men and Homeworking

Homeworking is the supply of work to be performed in domestic premises, usually for piecework payment. Known also as outwork, it is a global phenomenon...women working at home produce everything from clothes, shoes and quilts to windscreen wipers and industrial transmission belts.

(Allen and Wolkowitz 1987: 1)

There has recently been a renewal of interest in homeworking in Britain (see Felstead *et al* 1994; Felstead and Jewson 1995; Felstead *et al* 1996; Phizacklea *et al* 1995). The reasons for this renewed interest, Felstead (1996a) suggests, centres around issues of tax and National Insurance equity, issues of low pay and the introduction of homeworker protection by the International Labour Office (ILO).

Such issues suggests that more information is required on homeworking, both nationally and regionally. However, as research suggests (see Allen *et al* 1987; Felstead, 1996a; Felstead and Jewson 1995; Felstead *et al* 1996; Phizacklea *et al* 1995) the definition that is adopted will affect the estimates of homeworking that are produced, and no one single definition exists. Allen *et al* (1987) argue that in Britain two dominant images exist of homeworkers. One image is characterised by the declining manufacturing industries or traditional sectors of employment at the margins of industrial production. Attention, for example, is given to the garment industry where small profits and a fluctuating market force the use of homeworkers - it is also linked (stereotypically) with ethnic groups. The second image that Allen and Wolkowitz (1987) identify, portrays homework as being located in the new technology industry where many kinds of work can be decentralised[7] into the workers home. Other research suggests greater diversity than this typology presented by Allen *et al* (see Felstead *et al* 1996). Felstead (1996a) suggests the use of the definition contained within the 'Homeworkers Bill 1991', that is

> an individual who contracts with a person not being a professional client of his (sic) for the purpose of that person's business, for the execution of any work (other than the production or creation of any literary, dramatic, artistic or musical work) to be done in domestic premises not under the control or management of the person with whom he (sic) contracts, and who does not normally make use of the services of more than two individuals in carrying out that work.

> (Felstead 1996a: 226)

The development of Homeworking as a production method is also subject to conjecture (see Allen *et al* 1987). A range of circumstances which are likely to lead firms in industrial societies to adopt homeworking have also been identified within academic literature (Hakim, 1984b: Wray 1985; Felstead 1996a; Felstead *et al* 1996). Technical and numerical flexibility are obvious considerations. For example, homeworking can be adopted when the production process is already highly fragmented. However, it is also feasible in many other circumstances, even when production (through technical necessity) is highly centralised, homeworking may be used for ancillary processes like packing, packaging, maintenance etc. Regardless, homeworking is an old form of production and saves the employer on fixed costs, overheads, management, labour, recruitment, supervision.

Such (although more recent) trends are presented in Tables 3.21 to 3.24. The two most useful tables presented here are adapted from Felstead (1996) as he explores the biographical characteristics of male homeworkers using the Labour Force Survey. He suggests that the vast majority of male homeworkers are white and married and that they are more likely to be aged between 40-49 and based in the south east of England. He also suggests that men tend to see themselves as being self-employed and are more than likely to be working for a private firm or business in the motor trade.

Concluding Remarks

This chapter aimed to provide a general review of male labour market participation of a period of around sixteen years in our current stage of history. This chapter began by suggesting that the invisibility of men in work needs to be explored, and as such, the chapter moved away from the 'theoretical' to examine data relating to men's work experiences in Britain.

To do this the chapter drew upon existing and published labour market reports (that previously have perhaps not focused on men *per se*) to illustrate the discussion. Within this project, this chapter highlighted two main trends in male employment; the decline in male labour market participation and the decline in male full-time employment; and second, the growth in male non-standard employment forms, providing an analysis of the trends in male part-time working, male temporary working, male self-employment and male homeworking.

From the data and the exploration of these trends, three general conclusions can be offered, first, that the evidence considered in this chapter supports the view that the nature and content of male work have changed and are continually changing. It was demonstrated that male employment has been characterised by a series of historical shifts, such as the fact that for the first time since the depression in the 1930s there has been uncertainty about the availability and stability of work. These historical shifts in the availability have led to fluctuations in the nature, type and amount of work available for men. For example, the data showed that there has been a ten per cent decrease in the numbers of men working. There has been a decline from 80.5 per cent in 1971 to 72.6 per cent in 1995 and down to a projected 70.0 per cent by the year 2006. The figures presented in tables 3.4 and 3.5. For example, table 3.4 shows the employment of men (and women) by standard industrial classification for 1981 and 1995 respectively. Such a table points to the changing nature (and content) of male employment over this fourteen year period. The table suggests that for men there has been a drastic decrease in working in industries such as mining, manufacturing and construction whilst working in areas such as distribution, hotels, catering and repairs, or financial and business services, have increased.

Second, it was suggested that continuous full-time work that involves working for others, receiving a wage, being based in an employer's premises for an indefinite period is seen as the 'standard' employment form and is closely linked with men. However it was demonstrated that male full-time work has been declining despite such an association with men's lives. For example, table 3.5 suggested that in 1951, male full-time employment stood at 15,262 thousand, yet by 1995 this had fallen to 12,954 thousand. Conversely women's full-time employment had increased from 784 thousands to 6,302 thousand in the same period. Given this trend, it may now be more appropriate to re-conceptualise what work men do.

Third, given the decline of full-time work it was also argued that instead of conceptualising all male workers as full-time workers and women as part-time or marginal workers it may be possible that there has been a blurring of the edges of what is men's work and women's work and men's working roles have changed. Men now also need to be conceptualised as part-time workers, homeworkers, temporary workers, casual workers, self-employed workers or as job-sharers, as well as full-time workers. For example, in terms of part-time work, table 3.6 shows that over the period between 1973 and 1995 there has been a 5.4 per cent increase in the incidence of male part-time working in the UK. Male temporary working increased by 2.2 per cent between 1983 and 1994, whereas women's temporary employment remained largely static for the same period.

In terms of self-employment, the data demonstrated that there was a peak in self employment, for both men and women and full and part-time, in the years 1989 and 1990 and again for part-time self-employed women in 1993 and 1994.

Finally, in terms of homeworking authors such as from Felstead (1996) suggest that homeworking is becoming important for men, with the vast majority of male homeworkers are white and married and are likely to be aged between 40 -49 and based in the south east of England.

These general conclusions perhaps disguise the importance of such trends in employment for men. The changing nature of work is important as work is of central importance to men's lives. Any changes in employment will affect the mature of men's lives. For example, employment was traditionally the source of men's power and status in society. The impact of such trends need to examined in more detail and this leads to the second section of the book. The research now turns to focus on the life experiences of a sample of male workers from the National Child Development Study, carried out in 1991.

Notes

1   Although not exclusively influenced by work as other factors such as sexuality remain central.

2   The period 1980 to 1996 is one of the most interesting and important periods of (male) work in Britain. This is due to the social and political changes experienced during this time. Yet this must be understood within the context of the previous chapter. By doing this, it only provides a 'snapshot' of male work at one moment in history and that such trends exist now only as a part of larger historical process in working trends.

3   As such and given the fact that data is presented from between 1971 and 2006 there is some variation in accounts or estimates on the same variable or issue. This should not detract from the discussion as the data for discussion is presented in tabular form with origin clearly stated.

4   The discussion will not consider Multiple-job holding. This form has received much less attention. Suffice to say, in the UK the proportion of all workers holding at least two jobs rose from 2.4 per cent in 1977, to 4.1 per cent in 1984 (Green *et al* 1992) and on to 4.6 per cent in 1994 (Felstead *et al* 1996). The LFS also collected information on people who are economically active who also have a second job. The information revealed that nearly a third of second jobs were in self-employment compared with one in eight of main jobs. It is reported that people who were self-employed in their main job were more likely to be employed in a second job as well. It was also found that the number of people with a second job had been rising since 1984.

5   The period 1970 to 1980, they argue, provides a contrast to this. It was a time of economic recession for British manufacturing and this was marked with a decline in part-time employment, with women disappearing from the production lines.

6   Felstead (1991) goes on to identify the four common features as being, the franchisor is the owner of a name, idea, process or product and the goodwill associated with it; the issuing of a franchise permits (subject to contract) the franchisee to use whatever it is the franchisor has; inclusion of regulations in the contract that controls the way in which the franchisee operates; the payment by the franchisee of a royalty. A further distinction that Felstead offers is between two forms of franchising; Product or Trade Mark franchising.

7   Computer programming, typing and other clerical work.

Table 3.21

Occupational Distribution of Homeworkers - LFS 1981 and 1992

	1981	1992
Professional/Managerial	44	49
Clerical/secretarial	15	22
Craft and Related	21	11
Personal Services	12	11
Sales	5	4
Other occupations	*	3

* Less than 30

Source: Joeman, L. (1993) cited in Felstead, A., *et al* (1994) Homeworkers in Britain: An Analysis of Large Scale Data Sets, Interim Report to The Employment Department.

Table 3.22

Homeworkers: Composition of Occupational Categories by Gender - LFS Spring 1992

	Men	Women
Professional/Managerial	69	39
Clerical/secretarial	4	30
Craft and Related	12	10
Personal Services	2	15
Sales	9	2
Other occupations	3	3

Source: Joeman, L. (1993) cited in Felstead, A., *et al* (1994) Homeworkers in Britain: An Analysis of Large Scale Data Sets, Interim Report to The Employment Department.

Table 3.23
Homeworkers: Personal Characteristics - QLFS Spring 1994

	Men	Women
Marital Status		
Married	73.5	89.3
Living Together	9.3	2.0
Single	7.6	3.6
Widowed	3.0	1.7
Divorced		2.1
Separated	1.8	1.3
Ethnicity		
White	97.4	96.3
Other	2.6	3.7
Age		
16-19	1.6	0.6
20-29	7.6	10.0
30-39	17.3	29.5
40-49	34.4	29.2
50-59	19.3	18.6
60-64	10.2	7.1
65+	9.7	5.1
Region		
North	2.5	4.1
Yorkshire+H	7.8	7.6
East Midlands	3.3	7.6
East Anglia	2.6	4.3
London	9.1	10.3
Rest of SE.	25.9	28.3
South West	14.0	10.9
West Midlands	8.5	9.5
North West	16.4	6.6
Wales	8.1	5.1
Scotland	1.7	5.8

Source: Adapted from Felstead, A (1996) Homeworking in Britain: The National Picture in the Mid-1990s. Industrial Relations Journal, Vol.27 No.3 pp. 231-232.

Table 3.24
Homeworkers: Employment Characteristics - QLFS Spring 1994

Employment Status	Men	Women
Employee	29.9	58.4
Self-Employed	70.1	41.6
Type of Work Supplier		
Private Firm or Business	95.1	94.8
Other	4.9	5.2
Hours Usually Worked		
0-7	8.4	28.0
8-15	9.3	30.9
16-30	19.2	24.1
31-40	23.9	7.8
41-48	8.2	1.6
49-60	20.8	2.2
61-97	9.4	2.5
Industry		
Agriculture,		
Hunting and Forestry	3.8	5.4
Fishing	0.7	0.4
Mining	-	0.1
Manufacturing	18.9	23.5
Electricity, Gas, Water	-	-
Construction	11.0	14.4
Motor Sales	30.9	14.5
Hotels and Restaurants	2.6	1.6
Transport and Storage	4.3	3.5
Financial	3.1	2.5
Real Estate	18.1	17.8
Public Admin	1.9	0.8
Education	-	0.6
Health and Social Work	1.7	7.9
Other Social	2.1	4.9
Private Households with		
Employed Persons	0.9	2.0

Source: Adapted from Felstead, A (1996) Homeworking in Britain: The National Picture in the Mid-1990s. Industrial Relations Journal, Vol.27 No.3 pp. 234-235.

4 Researching Men: Outlining a Quantitative Case Study of Men

Introduction

> Sociological concepts and terms...were devised by men about the male world of the public domain and about the family as it was seen by the male world.
>
> (Stacey 1983: 9)

> Feminist science, then, is presently concerned with two tasks: first, to point out the various ways in which currently accepted scientific methods and theories are, in fact, sexist, and thereby distorting, and second to try to devise new methods and theories which will not have the weakness that non-feminist science has.
>
> (Eichler 1980: 119)

What Stacey (1983) suggests, and what Eichler (1980) attempted to rectify, and develop was the point that social science (particularly sociology) was (is) sexist and that previous discourse and concepts were by men and about men. As discussed in previous chapters, however, we have seen that this was only partially the case. Sociological research and concepts were developed by certain men about other men in certain situations. The argument here is that as well as this being inadequate, a position now exists where in gender based research, women conceptualise about gender and research women. As such, explicit empirically based research on men does not now occur in British 'gender based' sociology. Yet as argued earlier in this book and elsewhere in order to understand gender fully, the position of men needs to explored.

This chapter seeks to introduce the methods that are used in this present research and the attendant epistemological issues. The first part of the discussion will deal with the development of the methodology and the research. The second part will consider further the concept of a quantitative case study, and the nature of the research data. Finally, an outline of the limitations of this approach will be provided.

Background to The Research: A Dearth of Data

As suggested in chapter one, one of the main limitations of gender based research is a neglect of men. In much of the literature central to the sociological enquiry, such as gender and employment, men are absent or marginal to the empirical analyses offered (whether quantitative or qualitative). Where men are explored further limitations are evidenced, namely that such 'research' largely focuses on the theoretical issues of studying men or men are treated as a homogeneous grouping not affected by difference.

The importance of this cannot be underestimated. Debates on men in Britain have not really been pushed forward at an empirical level and now seem limited to an almost exclusively theoretical discourse. As such, if this research is to contribute anything, it was clear that this research would needed to be an empirical as well as theoretical exploration of men. It would also be essential not to treat 'men' as a single grouping.

Once such decisions are made, a further difficulty is encountered. This was that in researching men (or indeed gender) there are very few tangible guidelines for carrying out such research. As such, and indeed in common with much research into the social arena, the present book has gone through a number of methodological stages in exploring the most appropriate approach. These are summarised here.

In its early stages, the research process began with the development of a self-administered questionnaire. This covered a range of aspects and included attitudinal statements and a work history diary. This questionnaire was piloted in early 1992 in a Midlands city, with respondents being identified from an industrial directory. This proved to be a very unsuccessful approach. Out of a pilot sample of fifty, only two questionnaires were returned with differing levels of completion. This suggested that an original and highly quantitative survey approach would not be the most suitable method for this kind of research. One can speculate as to the reasons for this. For example, it is difficult to convey the idea that masculinity research is important and in turn, this suggests that such a research methodology would not generate the desired response.

The second stage of the research drew heavily on the feminist tradition. Feminist research has made progress in researching women, and so it was considered that such a paradigm would offer a useful second starting point. For example, in confirming the initial experience with questionnaires, previous feminist research has indicated the limitations of using highly quantitative methods for researching gender (Oakley 1974; Morgan 1981; Graham 1983). The epistemology that underpins the traditional sociological approach to studying gender and work, would be one that is highly quantitative and born out of a positivist tradition.

One could therefore assume that a more qualitative approach would be beneficial and the methods developed through feminist research and feminist discourse may also be useful for researching the lives of men and masculinity[1].

To explore the applicability of a more 'feminist methodology', an unstructured interview method was also considered and developed. An initial sample of men were identified and asked to attend an interview. The men were identified through personal contacts and relationships established between the researcher and respondents during teaching sessions. Again the response to the requests for interview were not that encouraging and the breadth of data required for this current research was evidently not going to be available or collectable via this particular methodology.

Third, given the limitations experienced with an original quantitative approach or the more feminised qualitative approach, the decision was made to combine the political issue of gender research with the notion of a quantitative study on men, posing the question could men and work be fully explored using existing quantitative data ? The initial rationale here was that it should be possible to test empirically certain *existing* ideas or 'received wisdom' on or about men's lives and work using data that had been already collected. As such research was to be exploratory the term 'quantitative case study' was used. A more detailed discussion of this is provided below.

Developing a Quantitative Case Study Approach[2]

The discussion so far has suggested that, first there is the overt assumption that all research is about 'men', but that this is not totally true as men are not examined *per se*. Second that because of certain feminist traditions that have influenced the sociological tradition, researchers are all too careful to equate gender research with researching women. Finally, where men are explored it is usually from a theoretical perspective rather than an empirical one or men are treated as a homogeneous grouping.

Such assertions and practices are useful as they can provided a set of empirical hypotheses for this research. That is to say, it may be possible to further explore those findings on 'men' which were not the result of a study of men *per se*. That such findings could be broadened out to take account of the employment differences between groups of men, and finally, by doing so the research offers an empirical study of men where the focus is actually on the men themselves. A review of literature suggests that there are a number of hypotheses or issues that may be suitable for this kind of research. They are :

i) Collinson and Hearn (1994) suggest there is a certain invisibility of men's work. Further to this they argue there is a traditional assumption to which men have to aspire that suggests they will work full-time in a 'breadwinner role' for the duration of their working lives and that anything else would not be fitting for a man and not in keeping with notions of masculinity. Yet for many this ideal situation of full-male employment has become socially and economically impossible but such traditional beliefs about full-time male employment remain, and are held by both men and women alike. Given these two points, men's experiences of work need to be further documented to avoid the invisibility of male work. This will be done in chapter five.

ii) Willinger (1993) argues that existing research that is directed to what men say about their work and family roles generates less interest than what men do in the family. Further to this, studies examining attitudes toward the changing roles of women and men have focused almost exclusively on women's roles or included only women as respondents. The point the Willinger makes will be explored further in chapter six.

iii) Authors such as Felstead (1994) using the Quarterly Labour Force Survey, Gibbins (1994) using an analysis of the Labour Force Survey; Green (1994) using the General Household Survey, and Ashton and Green (1996) assert that there are gender differences in training. These are revealed in the following ways : Men are more likely to get job-related training; Men are more likely to get their training paid for; Men are advantaged in the acquisition of skills; and finally, Men in unskilled manual occupations have relatively long training hours. Yet such statements can act as little more than a guide in researching men's participation in work related training. These findings are generated from research which compares women's with men's participation and does not consider a comparison of training differences in between different groups of men. These issues will be explored further in chapter seven.

iv) There has been a great deal of research undertaken which identifies the low participation of 'men' in household work. However very few researchers have explored the differences between men (such as men with different employment patterns) in participation. One author who acknowledges this is Coverman. Coverman's (1985) Hypothesis can be summarised as, first, *the more resources* (i.e. education, earnings and status in occupational position) a husband has, both in absolute terms and relative to his wife, *the less domestic labour* the man does. Second the *more traditional* the husband's *sex role attitudes*, the *less domestic labour* he does. Finally, the *more time available* the more likely the husband is to do housework. This will be further explored in chapter eight.

v)   Existing literature clearly identifies men as a vulnerable group in terms of mental ill health (Robins 1977; Beskow 1979; Wasserman 1984; Kposowa 1995; Canetto, 1995). It is possible to suggest an explanation for such a trend. The yardstick against which men in Britain is traditionally measured (work) has changed, but perceptions have not. Men are still expected to work full-time throughout their lives although the   possibilities of doing have greatly diminished. For men's self-identity this fact alone could have a catastrophic impact. Such a view is supported by Simon (1995) who suggests that men still perceive that the ability to provide economically is an essential part of the male role. This set of issues will be explored in chapter nine.

To explore such hypotheses further, an existing and wide ranging set of data was required and the National Child Development Study was identified as a useful source of data for this research.

The National Child Development Study Sweep 5

Britain has a unique tradition in conducting longitudinal birth cohort studies. Three continuing studies have been embarked upon …Each was launched as a perinatal mortality survey of the 16,000 to 18,000 births occurring nationwide in the target week in 1946, 1958 and 1970 respectively. Each survey has subsequently comprised further sweeps at different stages. The studies present, both individually and in combination, an unprecedented opportunity to investigate the forces and patterns that have shaped and continue to shape the lives of three overlapping generations of people in this country today.

(NCDS User Support Group 1991: 1)

As suggested, British academic and government based social research has available to it a rich history of large scale data sets, collected for a variety of reasons and used for many others. To supplement this British social research also has an established history of large scale longitudinal research, the two most famous being 'The National Child Development Study'(NCDS) and the 'British Cohort Study' (BCS). Both data sets collect information periodically from the same group of individuals who were all born during a specified week. It was considered that the main source of data for the empirical component of this research project should be National Child Development Study Sweep 5 (NCDS5). NCDS5 is a continuing longitudinal study of all those living in Great Britain (England, Scotland and Wales), who were born between the 3rd and 9th of March 1958.

The origins of the study lie in the Perinatal Mortality Study (PMS), which was sponsored by the National Birthday Trust Fund and was designed to examine obstetric factors that were associated with stillbirth and death in early infancy among the 17,000 children born in the chosen week[3]. The aims of the study were to explore 'the educational, behavioural, emotional social and physical development of a large and representative group of British children' (NCDS User Group 1991). In the long term the aim was to follow the progress of these individuals over a long period of time.

There have been four previous major attempts to trace all the original members of the original cohort and any immigrants to Britain who were also born during the control week. The aims of these subsequent phases of data collection have been to monitor the physical, social and educational development of the cohort members. The previous sweeps were carried out by the National Children's Bureau in 1965 (at the age of 7), in 1969 (at the age of 11), in 1974 (at the age of 16) and in 1981 (at the cohort age of 23) (the types of information collected in previous sweeps is presented in Table 4.1).

Table 4.1
Instruments Used in National Child Development Study- NCDS 1958 to 1991

	PMS	NCDS1	NCDS2	NCDS3	NCDS4	NCDS5
	17,414	15,468	15,503	14,761	12,537	11,363
	1958	1965	1969	1974	1981	1991
	Birth	7	11	16	23	33
Subject Interview			Yes	Yes	Yes	Yes
Parent Interview	Yes	Yes	Yes	Yes		
Medical Tests	Yes	Yes	Yes	Yes		
School		Yes	Yes	Yes		
Tests		Yes	Yes	Yes		
Census					Yes	Yes
Partner Interviews						Yes
Children						Yes

Source: Developed form NCDS Materials SSRU, City University 1993.

Although the original focus for the research was mainly medical and development, as Table 4.1 suggests there has been a gradual change in emphasis on which data should be collected (and from whom) between the first survey in 1958 and the latest survey in 1991. For example, the first survey collected information from the mother and the midwife from medical records. In the second survey the data was still only collected from the parents and focused on health issues and school performance. From the age of 11 the respondents themselves were interviewed. Data collection for the fifth wave of NCDS (NCDS5) was carried out in the summer and autumn of 1991 when the cohort sample was aged 33 years old.

> The final preparatory task before the fieldwork took place was an extensive programme of interviewer briefing. Altogether, 40 briefing meetings…involving a total of 600 interviewers, were organised by the fieldwork agencies in different parts of the country…The highly satisfactory outcome of these briefing meetings provided a reassuring pointer to the success of the main fieldwork programme, which took place between May and December 1991.
>
> (Ferri 1993: 11)

This sweep obtained information not only from the cohort member themselves but also from their partners (where appropriate), and for one third of the cohort members, from their children. The survey was carried out by a series of interviews, self-completion questionnaires and child development assessments[4] that gathered information on a wide range of social, behavioural and medical topics (information on the range of instruments used in NCDS5 is presented in Table 4.2). The NCDS team[5] particularly wanted NCDS5 to contain data on industries and occupations; employment and economic status; actual (and usual) weekly hours of employees; on length of service; on seasonal, casual, fixed-term contract, agency and other temporary employment; on second jobs and on reason for leaving last job; and on situation twelve months' previously in terms of occupation, employment status and whether working for same firm or organisation. Not only does this allow the work experiences of such men to be explored, but it also suits the purpose of the research here in that it provides a way of differentiating between 'groups of men'.

Table 4.2
Survey Instruments in the National Child Development Study - NCDS5
1991

Instrument	*Subject*
Your Life Since 1974 (C)	A self completion questionnaire covering marriages, partnerships, children, jobs, unemployment and housing
What Do You Think ?	A self completion questionnaire covering attitudinal information on marriage, women's roles, politics, work, skills, sexism, children and family, racism.
Cohort Member Interview	An interview that was divided into a number of sections covering in detail employment, education, family, income, health, citizenship, self-concept
Your Life Since 1974 (P)	A self completion questionnaire given to partners currently living with the cohort member which covered marriages, partnerships, children , jobs, unemployment and housing
Mother Interview	This instrument gained information for mothers including family life, pregnancies and birth, health history and child care.
Your Child	A self-completion questionnaire on children, completed by the mother
Child Assessment	This included measure to assess the development of the cohort members children

Source: ESRC NCDS5 User Guide 1993 and Ferri, E ed. (1993) Life at 33: The Fifth Follow-Up of the National Child Development Study, National Children's Bureau.

As such, the data contained within NCDS5 is useful for the present research for four main reasons. First, as the same wide ranging data is collected for all the men in the survey, such a data set contributes well to the idea of a quantitative 'case study'. Second, the collection of data for the BCS only began in 1970, compared to a starting data of 1958 for the NCDS sweeps. On a pragmatic level this would mean that far more data should be available for the individuals in NCDS, over a longer period of time. Third, the NCDS longitudinal survey collected a wide variety of data on all aspects of the individuals lives compared to other datasets such as 'The Labour Force Survey' (LFS) or the 'Work and Industrial Relations Survey' (WIRS). Indeed NCDS is one of the few datasets available in Britain that contains information on every aspect of an individuals life, from health and welfare, employment, housing to social attitudes and political affiliation. Finally, the size of NCDS must be a consideration as the full sample comprised of roughly 15,600 cohort members[6]. Of the 11,295 responses obtained in 1991, 5593 were men.

To explore the experiences of men in relation to the existing hypotheses outlined above, NCDS would prove useful as samples of male workers could derived from the 5593 male respondents using the NCDS5 variable 'Current Status at 33'. These sample groups were 'All Male Workers' (5091) which could then be broken down further into 'Male Full-Time Workers' (4109) and 'Male Non-Standard Workers' (982)[7].

For comparative purposes four corresponding women worker samples were also identified in NCDS5. 'All Women Workers' (4762), which broke down into 'Women Full-Time Workers' (1843) and Women Non-Standard Workers' (2919).

Limitations with NCDS [8]

The strengths of NCDS data have been well established elsewhere (see Shepard 1986; Ferri 1993), as well as above, however such data does contain a number of crucial limitations, for a research project such as this, which need to be acknowledged. Most fundamental of these limitations with the data is that it was not designed for the exploration of men's lives or masculinity explicitly. Indeed whilst the NDCS data does allow the exploration the relationship between men and various types of employment and unemployment and their relationship to work, training, domestic labour and health some crucial limitations need to be acknowledged.

One of the main limitations with longitudinal research, such as NCDS, is that of attrition, both through wastage and through an inability of the researchers to trace their respondents.

The very high original response rate is testament to the support and co-operation of the vast health service network that undertook the original perinatal mortality survey...At each subsequent sweep, an attempt was made to trace all surviving respondents. In the first three follow-ups, this was done through schools, and if that failed, by writing to the last known address, contacting health and social services and by making public appeals. At age twenty three, an attempt was made to follow up all respondents who still lived in Britain and who had taken part in at least one earlier sweep...Wastage of course occurred, and inevitably occurred as time went by.

(Marsh 1988: 59)

The data presented in Table 4.3 provides two important pieces of information. Firstly it is possible to see the overall decrease in the number of those targeted by the survey and the decline of the amount of data collected between the birth sweep and NCDS4. Likewise the table presents information on those targeted for NCDS5 and those actually traced.

Despite finding 75 per cent of the sample before the fifth sweep , the actual overall response rate for NCDS5 was 11,407. This represents an attrition of 6236 respondents. In other words 35 per cent of the original sample have been lost. Such a rate of attrition poses two main concerns. First and foremost, what are the characteristics of those being lost? To some extent this is dealt with below, but what it suggests is that there is a danger that the sample becomes homogeneous over time. Secondly, one could also be concerned as to why it is those individuals did not respond. For example, is such a research methodology actively discriminating against groups (such as those with lower educational attainment)? Alternatively are the tracing methods adequate?

Whatever the reasons for the decline in the overall number of respondents in the NCDS, one must consider it when analysing the data.

Table 4.3
Response Rates- NCDS5 1991 and NCDS1-4

Instrument	Target	Traced	Obtained	%
Cohort Member Interview	15,666	13,444	11,407	85
Cohort Member 'Your Life'	15,666	13,444	11,175	83
Cohort Member 'WDYT'	15,666	13,444	10,898	81
Partner 'Your Life'		9,138	7,126	82
Mother Interview		2,556	2,524	99
Mother 'Your Child'		5,067	5,012	99
Children Interviews (Tests)		3,575	3,467	97

Cohort	Target	Some Data %	Refused %	Other No Data %
Birth	17,733	98	-	2
NCDS1	16,883	91	1	8
NCDS2	16,835	91	5	4
NCDS3	16,915	87	7	6
NCDS4	16,457	76	7	17

Source: Ferri, E. (1993) Life at 33: page 12 and Marsh, C (1988) Exploring Data: An Introduction to Data Analysis for Social Sciences, Polity, London page 59.

Sexuality is one crucial component of men's identity. However it is an issue that is difficult to problematise within NCDS5. Indeed, within the fifth sweep of NCDS it was only possible to identify a small number of individuals who could be said to be living is same sex relationships based on the answers provide for a single question. The respondents were asked to identify a maximum of four 'marriages or similar relationships', the length of relationship and whether or not it was with an individual of the same sex. The interviewer notes suggested that a relationship was defined as such if it lasted for one month or more and commenced after the age of sixteen. The data relating to this part of the survey is presented in Table 4.4.

Table 4.4
Frequency of Respondents with Same Sex Partners by Number of Relationships and Sex for Whole NCDS5 Sample - NCDS5 1991

Same Sex Partner	Number of Relationships			
	1	2	3	4
Yes	160	35	9	3
Of which were male	87	20	5	1
Of which were female	73	15	4	2
No	10,164	2249	429	93
N	10,324	2284	438	96

Source: Own calculations from NCDS5 1991 data supplied by ESRC Data Archive.

From this table it is possible to see that for all respondents in NCDS5 there have been a total of 207 same sex relationships taking place over the 17 years since the respondents were aged sixteen. The vast majority of same sex relationships were a single relationship (79 per cent) - that's to say 70 per cent of those in a same sex relationship have had only one partner.

If one looks at the figures broken down by gender, it is possible to see that of those having only one same sex relationship in the identified 17 year period, 87 were male and 73 were female (0.7 and 0.6 per cent of the total sample respectively).

This data suggests that the vast majority of the sample were engaged in different sex relationships and that any analysis of sexuality would be heavily skewed in that direction. Since the figures relating to same sex relationships are so small, such relationships cannot be explored in any meaningful way.

Ethnicity

The membership in NCDS of different ethnic groups is also a cause for concern. As Marsh (1988) notes:

> In the sweeps at age sixteen and twenty-three, there is some evidence that the coverage among disadvantaged groups of various types declined. These biases are small, except with regard to ethnic status...

> (Marsh 1988: 59)

Table 4.5
Ethnicity Response Bias - Comparison Between NCDS5, Previous Sweeps and Other Surveys

Ethnic Group	GHS 1989-1991 (Ages 25-44)	NCDS5 (Age 33)
White	94	98
Indian	1	1
Pakistani/Bangladeshi	1	<1
Black/Caribbean	1	1
Other	2	<1

Source		Target %	Achieved %	%Bias
Mother born in West Indies	NCDS2	1.00	0.50	-50.00
Father Born in West Indies	NCDS2	1.10	0.60	-45.45
Child's Ethnicity is Afro-Caribbean	NCDS3	1.10	0.60	-45.45

* Percentage Bias is calculated as follows: ((NCDS5 achieved%)-(Target%)/(Target%))x100.
Source: Based on Shepard, P (1993) 'Analysis of Response Bias - Tables A1.1 A1.2' in Ferri, E. (1993) Life at 33: The Fifth Follow-Up of the National Child Development Study, National Children's Bureau, pages 185 and 188.

Table 4.5 provides information on ethnicity response bias and the numbers of particular ethnic groups in the NCDS survey. As one can see the survey is almost entirely made up of 'white' individuals. Although this does not differ greatly from the General Household Survey, it causes concern in that the employment experiences of Black, Indian and Pakistani men cannot be explored.

A further cause for concern is highlighted by the data in the second half of the table. It is possible to see from this that between NCDS5 and NCDS2 there has been a decline by almost half of the responses obtained from those with West Indian parents. Again this has implications for how representative the survey is.

Social Class

Along with the decline in the responses obtained from particular ethnic groups, there has also been a decline in the number of respondents with their origins in particular social class groups and those whose families had limited access to financial resources. This information is presented in Table 4.6.

Table 4.6
Social Class Response Bias - Comparison Between NCDS5 and Previous Sweeps

	Source	Target %	Achieved %	Bias%
Fathers Social Class 1965-Manual	NCDS1	66.50	65.00	-2.26
Fathers Social Class 1969-Manual	NCDS2	64.80	63.00	-2.78
Fathers Social Class 1974-Manual	NCDS3	63.10	61.00	-3.33
Father Stayed on at School	NCDS2	22.10	21.70	-1.81
Family in Financial Hardship 1969	NCDS2	11.00	9.90	-10.00
Family in Financial Hardship 1974	NCDS3	10.40	9.10	-12.50

*Percentage Bias is calculated as follows: ((NCDS5 achieved%)-(Target%)/(Target%))x100.
Source: Based on Shepard, P (1993) 'Analysis of Response Bias - Tables A1.1 ' in Ferri, E. (1993) Life at 33, page 185.

The final and more general limitation with NCDS5 its that it is limited in the extent to which it can take account of the life cycle. Without question, if one is interested in men's employment experiences over an individual life cycle this can be operationalised. However it does not really allow for inter-generational comparisons. For example, the experiences of these men may be peculiar to those born in the 1950s, but radically different to those born before or after this time.

Concluding Remarks

The genesis of this research took place over three years between 1991 and 1994, developing first from a project using original primary data onto one which explored the nature of masculinity and work within an existing data set. However despite the differences in the nature of the data collected, the main underlying aim remained - that was to document the lives of male workers in Britain empirically. It goes unquestioned that there are limitations with such an approach. For example, the discussion here is unable to use the richly contextual data that others have used (see Christian 1994). Likewise, one must acknowledge that the raw data for this exercise comes from largely heterosexual and white respondents and as such many aspects of 'real' diversity cannot be explored. However, what this research can do is reflect on work related issues that face men using the board spectrum of data contained within NCDS5. It allows a contribution to be made to the understanding of work and related issues for one group of 33 year old men and in doing so such a project should move the partially visible subject of men back into sight.

The discussion now turns to examine the work experiences of the male research samples from NCDS5.

Notes

1 This would then suggest that there is no such thing as 'feminist methodology' at all, and the whole debate is an ideological construct to differentiate between the research done on women by women, and the research done by men on women and men. The notion of feminist methodology is a very 'political' issue. This is because it implies that there is an objective method for researching gender (women), hence the absence of men from post 1970 gender based social research and theorising. However, one could assume that many of the methodologies used by gender researchers, that come from the feminist

tradition, should work well for researching men's lives. The argument being that a feminist method only represents a methodology that is more suitable for studying 'gender', and is therefore not about a woman's way of research or about accessing a women's way of knowing.

2   Critical reflections on this approach will be offered in the concluding chapter.

3   For a further discussion of these issues see Butler, N.R. and Bonham, D.G (1963) *'Perinatal Mortality'*, Edinburgh.

4   The assessments that were used were developed in the USA and adapted for the British context. The measures had previously been used in 1986, 1988 and 1990 on the children of the American Longitudinal Study (NLSY) (Erkinsmyth *et al* 1992).

5   In conjunction with the NCDS5 advisory groups who met between 1988 and 1991. They considered three critical principles: Scope that meant updating to the maximum extent the record of transition in education occupation, housing and family life, while covering in addition the broadest spectrum of cohort members current circumstances and characteristics. Cost, the cost of tracing and collecting data from individuals who are located completely randomly across the country brought with it cash limits. This is a major consideration in any research, especially survey research of this size. The funding for the fifth sweep was sought initially from the ESRC and the Medical Research Council (MRC). After their decisions left a shortfall, with the MRC offering no money at all, a proposal was put to the National Institute for Child Health development (NICHD) in the USA. This bid was successful and the total sum of money for the project from all sources was £3.1 million, with $500,000 coming from the USA. Acceptability is also very important. Minimising the burden on respondents and ensuring that the data collection exercise was acceptable to them was at a premium to encourage their continued participation in the study. This sets limits on the kinds, and amount of data to be collected.

6   This is compared to a target sample of 17,733 in 1958 and 16,457 in 1981, and achieved samples of 17,414 in 1958 and 12, 537 in 1981.

7   To enhance the analysis, throughout the research it was also possible to 'cluster' these groups into more homogeneous male worker samples based on the characteristics that they displayed (such as social class etc.)

8   A general outline of the limitations with the book are offered in the conclusions.

5 Men and Employment in the National Child Development Study

Introduction

> Men also do a great variety of informal and unrecorded work, sometimes displaying the same level and patterns of activity as women...sometimes doing more than women...sometimes doing less than women...
>
> (Hakim 1996: 203)

This chapter, in some ways explores the general themes suggested by Hakim (1996) and provides information on the characteristics and employment conditions of male workers in NCDS5. Such an enterprise is very important when one considers the central nature of work to masculinity meaning that men's experiences of work need to be further documented to avoid the invisibility of male work. As such this chapter has two broad aims. First, this chapter outlines the characteristics and employment conditions of male workers in NCDS5, with particular emphasis being placed on the characteristics of male full-time and male non-standard workers and their labour market participation. This by its very nature will mean that some of the discussion will be descriptive. However, this should not detract from the value of this discussion as the nature of male work *per se* and the nature of male work as presented by this data remains largely undocumented. Alongside this, broader themes can also be tested. For example, do men who work in non-standard forms have different employment experiences than those men who work in full time employment? Second, do those men who work in non-standard-forms have different employment experiences to those of women?

Given the longitudinal nature of NCDS, the second main aim of this chapter is to introduce a multivariate model to explore whether male non-standard workers specifically, and all male workers generally, have some particular pattern in their previous employment. For example, is it possible to predict men's current occupational status from other sociodemographic variables from earlier in their lives and careers?

Male Workers in The National Child Development Study

The National Child Development Study provides a very rich source of employment data. For example, job-duration, nature of work and employment status, and whether the work was full or part-time can be determined for every job held since March 1974. Indeed the depth and quality of this data has meant that historically, the work and employment status of members of the NCDS cohort has been the focus of a number of works, since the NCDS members entered the labour market in mid 1970s (Elias and Blanchflower 1989; Ward *et al* 1993). However, as suggested elsewhere in this book, the extent to which the gender and work analyses focus only on women, providing little exploration of men's work, is open to question. For the purpose of this research, NCDS5 can be used to explore the characteristics of male workers by explicitly providing a 'baseline' analysis of men's work.

Identifying Male Worker Samples

In NCDS5 there was a total sample of 11,293 with 5593 men and 5700 women. When these figures are broken down by the variable 'Current Employment Status at 33' it became obvious that men in this data, were more than twice as likely to be working full-time than women, but women were much more likely to work part-time.

Table 5.1 provides an outline of the distribution of current status for the whole sample. It also contains information developed by Ward *et al* (1993) which compares employment characteristics with employment data in the General Household Survey (1991), and the Labour Force Survey (1991).

For this research four main sub-groupings can be identified, male full-time workers, male non-standard workers, female full-time workers and female non-standard workers. The later are being used for comparison with the former.

The identification of male and female full-time workers is relatively straightforward using the variable 'Current Employment Status at 33'. There are 4109 male and 1843 female full-time workers. The sub-samples of non-standard workers were defined by using the same variable. These sub-samples included those workers who reported that they were either part-time employees, full or part-time self-employed. For these, the work role differs to that of the traditionally full-time and permanent work role. The sample of male non-standard workers also included those men who suggested their main role was looking after the home and family. The reason for this is that these men are also engaged in work, all be it 'unpaid and private production', and that this role diverges for that which may be perceived as 'traditionally' male.

Table 5.1
Gender of all Sample by Current Status at 33 and Employment Status by Gender at age 33 - NCDS5 1991

Status	Men	Women
Full-Time Employee	73.5	32.4
Part-Time Employee	0.9	28.8
Full-Time Self-Employed	15.6	3.5
Part-Time Self-Employed	0.3	3.2
Unemployed	5.9	2.1
Full-Time Education	0.4	0.8
Temp Sick/Disabled	0.4	0.3
Perm Sick/Disabled	1.6	0.8
Home and Family	0.7	26.5
Other	0.6	0.6

Status	NCDS		GHS 1991		LFS 1991	
	Men %	Women %	Men %	Women %	Men %	Women %
Economically Active	**96**	**70**	**97**	**70**	**95**	**70**
Paid Employment	90	68	87	64	86	64
Full-Time	89	36	-	38	85	39
Part-Time	1	32	-	25	1	25
Unemployed	6	2	10	6	9	6
Economically Inactive	**4**	**30**	**3**	**30**	**5**	**30**

Source: Own calculations from NCDS5 1991 data supplied by ESRC Data Archive. and Ward, C. *et al* (1993) 'Participation in the Labour Market' in Ferri, E. (1993) Life at 33: The Fifth Follow-Up of the National Child Development Study, National Children's Bureau, page 63.

The 982 male non-standard workers represented 8.6 per cent of the total sample in NCDS5 and only 16.5 per cent of the population of men in NCDS5. For women the figures were much higher, with 2919 female non-

94

standard workers, representing 26 per cent of the total population and 51 per cent of the sample of women.

Within the non-standard worker sub-samples, a number of points should be made. Men have higher participation rates in full-time self-employment than women (15.6 per cent and 3.5 per cent respectively). However, more women worked self-employed on a part-time basis than men (3.2 per cent of women compared with 0.3 per cent of men). Indeed, full-time self employment is the largest non-standard work form for men, with part-time employment being the second largest accounting for 5.4 per cent of the non-standard male sample and only 1 per cent of the full male population. For women, a different picture of economic status can be seen. Firstly, part-time work amongst women in the non-standard sample is 56.2 per cent, and of the total population it is 28.8 per cent. The second largest is full-time self employment, accounting for 37 per cent of the female non-standard sample.

Characteristics of Men's Work

Having identified the research sub-samples it is possible to take this baseline analysis further and outline their work related characteristics. Here characteristics of social class and standard occupational classification, organisation and place of work, pay, hours of work, partner's employment characteristics and finally previous job characteristics of the male workers are considered. Information of class and standard occupational classification is presented in Table 5.2. Table 5.3 provides information on activity in the labour market vis-à-vis the presence of children, based on Ward *et al's* (1993) analysis. Table 5.4 gives an outline of the range of job-titles by SOC.

Social Class and Standard Occupational Classification

Table 5.2 provides information on the Social Class of the respondents. Social Classes II Managerial and Technical and III Skilled Manual were the largest class groupings for male non-standard workers and this possibly represents the social class of those self-employed men within this category. Class II accounted for 26 per cent of the male non-standard workers, whilst III Skilled Manual accounted for 40.3 per cent. This differs from the population of males who work full-time, where class III Skilled Non-Manual was the largest class grouping at 46.6 per cent.

For women who work in non-standard forms there was more of an even spread amongst class groupings II to IV. The class position for those women who work full-time is different as classes III Skilled Non Manual and III Skilled Manual were the highest.

The distribution of non-standard work by the Standard Occupational Classification and gender also provides some interesting results. Table 5.2 suggests that men in the non-standard group are represented in SOC 5 - Craft and Related, more than any other SOC grouping at 36.4 per cent. The second largest grouping for male non-standard workers is SOC 1 at 28.8 per cent. There is more of an even distribution for male full-time workers, however, men are still more likely to be in SOCs 1 to 5 than any other. Women non-standard workers are split more or less evenly between SOC 1 - Managers (14.4 per cent), SOC 4 - Clerical (15.5 per cent), SOC 6 - Personal Services (14.4 per cent). Thirteen and a half per cent of women non-standard workers appear in SOC 5 -Craft and Related. Forty eight per cent of women full time workers are accounted for in just two SOCs, SOC 1 and SOC 4. Only 3.4 per cent of full-time women appear in the craft and related group.

Table 5.2
Characteristics of Non-Standard Workers and all Full-Time Workers by Gender - NCDS4 1981

	Men	Women	All F/T Men	All F/T Women
Social Class				
Professional Occupations	6.2	3.7	6.5	1.0
Managerial and Technical	26.0	24.0	34.1	3.9
Skilled Non-manual	9.2	25.4	12.8	46.6
Skilled Non-manual	40.3	19.2	28.9	28.8
Partly Skilled	10.8	19.8	13.3	6.2
Unskilled	2.7	5.4	1.8	0.7
SOC				
10 - Managers	28.8	14.4	25.0	23.0
20 - Professional	6.5	6.0	9.2	10.9
30 - Associate Profession	8.5	10.2	10.0	16.0
40 - Clerical	2.9	15.5	6.7	25.0
50 - Craft and Related	36.4	13.5	19.8	3.4
60 - Personal	1.4	14.4	6.5	8.2
70 - Sales	5.3	9.6	4.3	4.2
80 - Plant Operators	9.2	6.7	13.5	5.8
90 - Other	5.1	9.8	4.9	2.5
N	844	1789	3415	1622

Source: Own calculations from NCDS5 1991 data supplied by ESRC Data Archive.

Table 5.3
Employment Status by Gender and Children at age 33- NCDS5 1991

	Age of Youngest Child				
	<5	5-9	10+	All	None
	%	%	%	%	%
Women					
Economically Active	52	74	78	63	93
Paid Employment	51	72	75	61	89
Full-Time	16	24	42	21	81
Part-Time	35	48	33	40	8
Unemployed	1	2	3	2	4
Economically Inactive	48	27	22	37	7
N=	2299	1564	459	4322	1373
Men					
Economically Active	97	95	92	97	96
Paid Employment	93	90	83	92	88
Full-Time	92	89	81	91	87
Part-Time	1	1	2	1	1
Unemployed	4	5	9	5	8
Economically Inactive	2	4	7	3	4
N=	302	967	190	3459	2129

*Not all columns add up to 100% due to rounding
Source: Ward, C. *et al* (1993) 'Participation in the Labour Market' in Ferri, E. (1993) Life at 33: The Fifth Follow-Up of the National Child Development Study, National Children's Bureau, page 65.

Organisation and Place of Work

Table 5.5 provides characteristics on the type of organisation the respondent works for, the number of workers within that organisation and the main location of work.

Regardless of gender, the vast majority of respondents worked for a private firm. Interestingly, nearly ten per cent more male full-time workers worked for a private firm than male non-standard workers. Similar numbers of women full-time workers and women non-standard workers reported working for private firms.

A difference of almost ten per cent between male full-time and male non-standard workers is also observed in the second largest organisation type. Nineteen per cent of male non-standard workers worked for local authorities compared to ten per cent of male full-time workers. The figures for women were largely equal with around 20 per cent working for local authorities. However, what this may suggest is that the growth in male non-standard employment is being driven by the public sector.

Differences can also be observed in the relative size of the organisations the research samples worked for. Eighty six per cent of male non-standard workers reported that they worked for an organisation that had between one and ten workers compared to only 30 per cent of female non-standard workers and 12 per cent of male full-time workers. This is not a surprising result given the nature of the relative samples. The male non-standard group has a large percentage of self-employed workers compared to the women non-standard category where more part-time workers can be observed.

Full-time workers can be seen to be working, more for larger organisations rather than smaller ones. Around 50 per cent of male full-time workers suggest that they work for an organisation with more that 100 workers.

In terms of work location, except for male non-standard workers, the majority of the men examined worked from their employers premises.

Pay

The NCDS5 data set contained a large amount of data relating to the pay of the respondents. There were separate variable for gross and net pay, the period for which the pay covered and there were also separate variables relating to the pay of the self-employed. To make sense of this data a derived variable was generated based on the respondents net pay per week. The reason for this is that, in many ways, it represents the real or actual weekly earning power of the individual. Based on this variable a number of points can be made about the pay of the research groups. Table 5.7 provides pay distribution based on a weekly pay scale ranging from nothing to more than £1000 per week. Table 5.7 also provides data on the mean weekly pay for the research groups.

This data reveals some interesting differences and provides evidence of a pay divisions between full time and non-standard workers, between full-time male workers and full-time female workers and also a divisions between male and female non-standard workers. For example, around 60 per cent of women non-standard workers earned £100 or less per week compared to nearly 70 per cent of male non-standard workers who earned between £101 and £500 pounds per week.

Table 5.4
Example of Current Job Titles by Standard Occupational Classification for Male Workers - NCDS5 1991

10 - Managers

clerk to governors - school governors, sub contractor - agent contracting, site manager, managing director of estate agents, partner in firm of estate agents, agent, data communications consultant, osteopath, chartered accountant (sole proprietor), principle managing director manager, operations controller, manager in a catering outlet at heathrow airport, partner - chef manager, warehouse manager.

20 – Professional

director of marketing, director exploration geophysicist, consultant geologist, structural engineer s/e partner, self employed communications engineer, electronics engineer, computer consultant, ceramic tiling, general practitioner, lecturer, teacher handicapped people (m/h), music teacher, barrister, solicitor, chartered accountant, social worker.

30 – Associate Profession

self employed construction, vehicle technician, structural engineer technician, resurfacing technician, draughtsman, conservator of paintings, quantity surveyor, analyst/programmer, decorators merchants, ships captain, nurse, chiropodist, dispensing optician, psychotherapist, financial consultant.

40 - Clerical

civil servant, accountant, information assistant (Heathrow) clerk.

50 – Craft and Related

warehouseman, secretary, brick layer, monumental mason, sheet steel erector, plasterer, builder, self employed scaffolder, fire place builder, wall floor tiler, foreman carpenter, mastic asphalt construction, painter and decorator, French polisher, locksmith and engineer.

60 - Personal

security officer, day care officer, playground installer, barber, freelance lighting gaffer in films etc, golf professional, owner of shop.

70 - Sales

partner importer/wholesale, sales agent, photographer - own business, insurance associate, plant hire and ground work salesman/director, shop assistant part time, milkman, ice cream delivery roundsman, manager market stall.

80 – Plant Operators

bakery operative, leader of craft work, fishing, engineer, tool room machinist, assembly worker, mechanical inspector, pottery retailer, auto breaker scrap dealer, mate - on trawler, commercial diesel recovery driver, construction plant operator, building erector, taylor timber products owner, h.g.v. driver.

Table 5.4 continued

90 - Other   farm labourer, forestry timber contractor, factory worker, hod
                                  carrier, construction worker, labourer, ground worker to the
                                  construction industry, diver, furniture remover, postman, courier,
                                  kitchen assistant, restaurant assistant, cleaner.

Source: Own calculations from NCDS5 1991 data supplied by ESRC Data
Archive.

Table 5.5
Organisational Characteristics for Non-Standard Workers and all Full-Time Workers by Gender - NCDS5 1991

	Percentage of Men and Women			
	Men	Women	All F/T Men	All F/T Women
Organisation Type				
Private Firm	59.5	55.9	69.1	53.2
National Industry	6.3	3.6	8.7	6.1
LA / LEA	19.0	18.8	10.0	18.7
Health	2.5	12.0	2.6	9.6
Central Gov.	6.6	3.6	6.0	6.9
Charity	1.3	3.1	0.8	2.2
Other	3.8	3.0	2.7	3.3
Number of Workers				
1 - 10	86.0	30.0	12.0	13.7
11 - 25	5.2	19.6	12.6	16.1
26 - 99	4.1	18.8	24.5	24.0
100 - 499	1.8	15.4	26.9	22.0
500+	1.3	13.0	23.2	23.2
can't say	1.6	3.1	0.7	1.0
Ever Work ?				
Employers Premises	31.0	51.5	44.4	96.1
Driving Around	2.1	11.9	8.3	-
At Home	46.5	11.1	0.7	-
Other	14.0	12.8	9.5	-
Missing	6.4	13.7	36.0	-
N=	982	2919	4109	1843

Source: Own calculations from NCDS5 1991 data supplied by ESRC Data
Archive.

Table 5.6
Work Characteristics for Self Employed Workers by Gender - NCDS5
1991

Organisation Type	Men%	Women%
Own Firm	59.8	60.2
Work for Others	30.6	31.0
Both	6.8	5.7
Other	1.9	3.1
Value of Business		
Nothing	39.7	42.3
up to 10,000	13.4	12.8
10,001 - 50,000	12.7	12.0
50,001 - 100,000	6.3	6.5
100,001 - 250,000	6.9	6.0
250,001 - 500,000	3.8	4.0
500,000 +	4.5	3.9
Other	10.7	11.4

Source: Own calculations from NCDS5 1991 data supplied by ESRC Data Archive.

Overall the highest paid workers were full-time male workers, who earned an average of £311.20 per week. The lowest were female non-standard workers who had a weekly income of £69.50. However if one compares non-standard work with full-time work, regardless of gender, those who work full-time earn substantially more than their non-standard counterparts, nearly twice or three times as much.

Table 5.7
Weekly Pay for Non-Standard and Full-Time Workers by Gender -
NCDS5 1991 (percentage)

	Men	Women	F/T Men	F/T Women
Nothing	2.3	1.8	0.1	0.9
up to £50	6.4	29.3	6.1	0.5
£51 - 100	12.2	31.6	0.1	10.0
£101 - 200	29.4	16.7	1.2	52.3
£201 - 300	22.0	8.8	36.7	26.7
£301 - 500	18.2	6.6	35.3	5.8
£501 - 1000	6.5	2.8	16.0	0.4
£1000+	2.0	1.4	2.2	0.9
Mean Week Pay	£129.91	£69.93	£311.20	£209.83
N=	982	2919	4109	1843

Source: Own calculations from NCDS5 1991 data supplied by ESRC Data Archive.

The hours that the research samples worked per week are presented in Table 5.8, along with information on the variability of working hours and the extent on un-social working hours.

Male full-time workers appear to work the longest mean hours per week (45), with women non-standard workers working the shortest mean weekly hours (25). Male non-standard workers and female full-time workers both seemed to work around 40 hours per week. Indeed 44 per cent of male non-standard workers and 73 per cent of female full-time workers worked between 31 and 40 hours per week. For the vast majority of workers in the research groups these hours were fixed with only around 30 per cent in each experiencing variability in work hours.

Table 5.8
Hours Worked by Non-Standard Workers and all Full-Time Workers by Gender - NCDS5 1991 (percentage)

Hours Per Week	Men	Women	F/T Men	F/T Women
1 to 16	5.0	34.7	0.2	0.3
17 - 30	6.4	32.4	0.9	6.4
31 - 40	44.0	21.3	50.3	73.9
41 - 50	26.0	6.2	31.4	13.1
50+	16.6	5.5	16.2	5.4
Mean hours	39.2	25..2	45.1	39.2
Hours Fixed ?	66.1	70.0	66.2	66.0
Hours Vary ?	32.9	30.0	33.8	33.0
Do You Ever Work ?				
6pm til 10pm ?	4.7*	36.1	60.7	46.3
10pm til 4am ?	3.4*	15.4	26.9	15.4
4am til 7am ?	1.8*	10.3	32.5	12.6
On Saturday ?	4.1*	36.6	52.7	34.4
On Sunday ?	1.9*	21.0	34.5	23.1
N	982	2919	4109	1843

* Numbers are low due to missing Self Employment data.
Source: Own calculations from NCDS5 1991 data supplied by ESRC Data Archive.

The NCDS5 interviewer tried to ascertain the extent to which the respondents worked un-social hours. However in terms of this research, this data is incomplete as it was not collected for the self employed groups and this is therefore limited. However, from the data it is possible to see that 60 per cent of male full-time workers work between the hours of 6 and 10pm and that over 50 per cent work on Saturdays.

Partner's Employment Characteristics

NCDS5 also collected information on the employment characteristics of the respondents partner. The current status of partners is presented in Table 5.9. For the partners of non-standard workers there is a certain amount of stereotypical role occupation. For example, of those men who worked in non-standard roles, 24.1 per cent had partners who worked full-time, and 35.3 per cent had partners whose role was to look after the home and family. For those women with non-standard roles, 73.5 per cent had partners who worked full-time, whilst only 0.2 per cent of the partners were reported to be at home.

Table 5.9
Status at 33 of all Partners and Social Class of Father by Gender - NCDS5 1991 (percentage)

	Men	Women	F/TMen	F/TWomen
Status				
Full-Time Employee	24.1	73.5	32.2	79.7
Part-Time Employee	25.5	1.1	30.2	1.4
Full-Time Self-Employed	6.9	20.2	1.8	12.5
Part-Time Self-Employed	4.6	0.4	2.0	0.4
Home and Family	35.3	0.2	31.1	0.5
Other	3.2	2.8	2.6	5.6
Fathers Social Class				
I	5.5	4.2	5.2	5.2
II	16.3	13.1	13.8	15.6
III Non-Manual	9.2	9.2	11.0	11.2
III Manual	46.7	51.7	51.2	50.0
IV	12.0	13.4	11.4	11.5
V	8.3	8.4	6.5	6.5
N=	796	1816	3346	1298

Source: Own calculations from NCDS5 1991 data supplied by ESRC Data Archive.

These patterns are not too dissimilar for the samples of men and women who were working full-time. For full-time men, 32.2 per cent had partners who worked full-time, and 31.1 per cent had partners who looked after the family and home. For full-time women, 79.7 per cent had partners who worked full-time and only had 0.5 per cent of partners who stayed at home to look after the family.

The work patterns here seem to be breaking down along traditional gender lines to a certain extent. For both males who work in non-standard forms, and men who work full-time, there is a high percentage who have partners at home providing unpaid domestic labour. Whilst for both categories of women the same is not true.

Previous Job Characteristics of Male Workers

The longitudinal nature of NCDS5 means that certain statements can be made about the respondents previous employment and Tables 5.10 summarises this information. Of those males currently working in a non-standard form, 95.1 per cent report that they were an employee in their first job. Over four and a half per cent report that they were self-employed, compared to only 0.8 of male full-time workers and female non-standard workers.

The first job for men regardless of their current status at 33 was more likely to be full-time than anything else. Interestingly the likelihood of these men being employed on a full-time basis increased with their second job. Over ninety-nine per cent of current male non-standard workers, and 99.5 per cent of current male full-time workers worked full-time in their second job (this was from 98.2 and 98.4 per cent respectively).

For women, 2.6 per cent of current non-standard workers, and 3.5 per cent of current full-time workers worked part-time. This increased to 6.6 per cent and 5.2 per cent respectively by their second job, with full-time participation levels also falling for both sets of women.

There are some differences evident in the length of the respondents first job. Only 26.8 per cent of current male non-standard workers left their first job between 1 and 10 months. All other groups were more likely to leave in this period.

During their first job male non-standard workers were more likely than any other group to work for a private company.

In an examination of data from the previous NCDS sweeps one can determine the extent to which cohort members had worked part-time in their previous jobs. Interestingly, 12.2 per cent of male non-standard workers in NCDS5, reported that they had worked part-time in previous sweeps. The figure for full-time working males was 8.5 per cent. The previous participation of women in part-time work was much higher than that of men, with 85.3 per cent of women who currently worked in a non-standard way, reporting previous part-time working. The figure for female full-time workers was 30.7 per cent. There is a massive difference between these two groups of women of around 55 per cent. This suggests that women who are currently working part-time are nearly three times as likely to have worked part-time before than their full-time counterparts. It may also suggest evidence of 'repeatedly part-time working' for this group of women (e.g. always going for part-time work/jobs rather than just as a one off occurrence in between full-time jobs).

Table 5.10
First Job Characteristics of Non-Standard and Full-Time Workers by Gender - NCDS4 1981 (percentage)

	Men	Women	F/T Men	F/T Women
Employment Status				
An Employee	95.1	98.4	98.9	98.1
Temp	0.2	0.8	0.3	1.3
Self-Employed	4.7	0.8	0.8	0.6
Full-Time	98.2	96.4	98.4	96.4
Part-Time	1.8	2.6	1.6	3.5
Employer				
Private Company	84.2	72.3	74.7	66.6
Other	14.6	26.3	24.5	32.2
Don't Know	1.1	1.3	0.9	1.2
Length of Time for First Job in Months				
1-10	26.8	30.0	35.2	36.9
11-20	11.2	15.9	10.5	15.8
21-30	8.6	11.9	6.7	11.7
31-40	8.0	8.1	6.6	6.3
41-50	8.4	5.6	6.5	5.8
51-60	6.8	5.1	5.8	4.3
61-70	3.8	3.7	4.0	2.4
71-80	2.7	2.7	3.2	1.9
81-90	2.4	2.6	2.4	1.2
91-120	4.2	5.1	4.5	2.5
121-150	3.4	2.9	3.2	1.9
151-180	2.9	0.9	2.3	1.0
180+	0.9	0.1	0.9	0.4
Missing	9.0	5.2	6.2	5.9
N=	836	1789	3415	1591

Source: Own calculations from NCDS5 1991 data supplied by ESRC Data Archive.

In 1981 at the fourth sweep of NCDS, 82.6 per cent of those men currently in a non-standard employment form were working full-time. This had fallen to 73.5 per cent by 1991, with more men moving into self-employment at the age of 33.

NCDS4 also provides information on the Social Class of the father or male head of household, for all the current cohort members. This provides some interesting comparisons in that for all groups, male and female non-standard workers, and male and female full-time workers, the largest class grouping of their fathers was III Manual.

This, especially in the case of male-non-standard workers may suggest some evidence of inter-generational class mobility. For example, in NCDS5, 26 per cent of male non-standard workers were in class II, compared to only 16.3 per cent of their fathers.

Predicting Men's Current Labour Market Status: Logistic Regression

> Life and work history data are important...They are a recognition of the importance of the overlap in the chronology between individuals' lives and social and institutional structures as well as between related individuals. Both sets of these relationships are important for in trying to unravel social life...
>
> (Dex 1991: 2)

Work history information is usually investigated to examine for a relationship between the previous socio-economic circumstances of an individual and their later socio-economic status (Baker and Elias 1991). The National Child Development Study has developed quite a pedigree for work history analysis (Payne 1984; Elias and Blanchflower 1989), mainly due to the highly developed event history questions contained within the research instruments.

> investigation of this proposition required that two essential prerequisites should be fulfilled; the information on individuals' occupations and earnings must relate to a substantial part of their working lives and must be nationally representative. Only two sources of information fulfilled these conditions, the national birth cohort studies of 1946 and 1958.
>
> (Elias and Blanchflower 1987: 9)

Payne and Payne (1985), for example, used NCDS data to examine the effect of general labour market conditions on the level of occupational entry. Alternatively, Elias and Blanchflower (1987) used NCDS data to examine the relationship between social class, education, the decision to leave school and post-school work-histories and labour market attainment.

In this research a logistic regression model uses previous employment experiences to ascertain whether any of these characteristics can be used to 'predict' current employment status. This moves the discussion on from one that simply outlines the general work experiences of each of the male research groups on to a more sophisticated level of analysis, integrating the current concerns with the issues suggested by Hakim (1996) and the general changing nature of male employment (as outlined in chapter three).

Logistic regression models have proved highly successful in other gender related research (see Felstead, 1995, 1996) and unlike other linear regression, a logistic model allows predictions to made about whether a particular event will occur or not. In logistic regression it is possible to directly estimate the probability of an event occurring. The logistic model for one independent variable can be expressed as follows:

$$Prob(event) = \frac{eX}{1 + eX}$$

This equation is true for the probability of an event occurring, where x is the independent and where e is the base of the natural logarithms. Alternatively, if one wants to predict an event not occurring, one would divide the probability of an event by the probability of no event occurring. The model can be specified as

$$Prob(no\ event) = -1\ Prob(event)$$

The assumption that underpins these models is that an event will either occur or it will not. As such, in terms of the model presented in this analysis, the dependant variable of full-time work (FT-EMP) is assigned the value of 'zero' where the respondent is not working full-time. The value of 'one' is assigned where the respondent is currently working full-time. This is a 'dummy variable'. Some of the explanatory variables are also dichotomous or are strings of dummy variables representing variables that contain more information that are 'either or', such as Standard Occupational Classification or Social Class.

Table 5.11
Classification Table for not Working Full Time by Employment and Individual Characteristics - NCDS5 1991

	Predicted		
Observed	0	1	Percent Correct
0	840	2	99.76%
1	1	3459	99.97%
		Overall	99.93%
	Number of Cases in Equation		4302

Source: Own calculations from NCDS5 1991 data supplied by ESRC Data Archive.

Table 5.11 is a classification table for not working full time by employment and individual characteristics. This table is a useful starting point in the analysis of the logistic regression equation. From this table we can see that 840 of those men who are *not* currently working full-time were correctly predicted as not currently working full-time. Likewise, 3459 of those men who are currently working were correctly predicted to be doing so. Of those men who are not currently working full-time 99.76 per cent had been correctly predicted. Of those who are working full-time, 99.97 per cent were predicted to be doing so. Out of the total number of men used in this equation, 99.93 per cent were correctly predicted. As such this table suggests that the regression model used in this part of the analysis 'fits' very well, based on the comparison of predicted and observed outcomes with only a total of three men being misclassified.

Table 5.12 shows the 'parameter estimates for the logistic regression model and predicted probabilities of men not working full time'. The Table contains a wealth of information useful in predicting whether or not certain characteristics (or independent variables) increase the likelihood of an event (men not currently working full-time) occurring. For example, the R statistic can be used to examine partial correlation. R ranges from -1 to +1, with a positive value indicating that as the variable increases, so does the likelihood of an event occurring. Likewise if R is a negative value this suggests the opposite, or that as a variable increases the likelihood of an event decreases. Alternatively the regression coefficients can be used. In Table 5.14 the coefficient (B) for EVFULL (the respondent has previously worked full-time) is -1.4137. All other things being equal, this suggests that the log odds of a man not working full-time decreases by -1.41 if they worked full-time before. Putting this more simply, if an individual has previously worked full-time they are more likely to be working full-time rather than in a non-standard form of employment.

From Table 5.12 a number of main findings can be highlighted. The first main result to report is that the vast majority of the variables used in this model are not significant. The model suggests that previous employment characteristics such as length of job (LGUTIME), total time in employment (JOBTIME), experience of training (TRAIN74 and TRAIN81) or standard occupational classification, appear to have no significant impact on whether or not the individual male works full-time or not. However, four of the variables do seem to have a significant impact on the dependant variable and therefore may be useful in predicting men's employment status.

The first variable that displays a significant effect on whether a male works full-time or not is whether or not the man has previously worked in a temporary position. Table 5.12 reports that the coefficient (B) for EVTEMP is 5.1850. This suggests that if a male has previously worked in a temporary position their likelihood of not working full-time is decreased. Putting this more simply, these men are then more likely to work in a non-standard job.

The second variable that demonstrated significant impact on the dependant variable was the number of jobs held by the respondent (NJOB). The logistics regression model suggests that this variable has a positive impact on men not working full time. For example, in Table 5.12 the coefficient (B) for NJOB is 7.2617. This suggests that, with all other thing being equal, that the log odds of a man not working full-time increases by 7.26 the greater number of jobs that they have had. This implies that male non-standard workers are more likely to have a higher mean number of jobs than their full-time counterparts. An analysis of the responses associated with this model, presented in Table 5.13 supports this finding reporting the mean number of jobs for male full-time workers as being 2.07 compared to a mean of 2.90 for male non-standard workers.

The third variable which displays significant effect is the number of spells of unemployment experienced by the respondent (NUEMP). In Table 5.12 the coefficient (B) for NUNEMP is 2.1312. Like NJOB, this response suggests that, with all other thing being equal, that the log odds of a man not working full-time increases by 2.1312 the greater number of jobs that they have had. Again, the implication here is that male non-standard workers are more likely to have experienced more periods of unemployment than male full-time workers.

Having a NVQ or equivalent qualification above level three also seems to exert a positive effect on men not working full-time. The coefficient (B) for NVQ1 presented in Table 5.12 is 1.6198. This response suggests that, with all other thing being equal, that the log odds of a man not working full-time increases by 1.61 if they have qualification above the NVQ level three.

Table 5.12
Parameter Estimates for the Logistic Regression Model and Predicted Probabilities of Men not Working Full Time - NCDS5 1991

	B	Wald	R	Predicted Probability
EVFULL	-1.4137	0.1641	.0000	0.80
EVSEEMP	0.9395	0.0697	.0000	0.71
EVTEMP	*5.1850*	*3.6268*	*1960*	*0.96**
FCLASS1	7.1028	0.0013	.0000	0.99
FCLASS2	-1.0895	0.3845	.0000	0.25
FCLASS3	-2.1423	1.3753	.0000	0.10
FED	-0.6618	0.1609	.0000	0.34
FSJTIME1	-0.2984	0.0000	.0000	0.43
FSJTIME2	-0.0632	0.0000	.0000	0.48
FSJTIME3	3.7127	0.0000	.0000	0.97
FSJTIME4	0.0263	0.0001	.0000	0.50
FTJOB1	-3.7281	0.9068	.0000	0.02
FTJOB2	-0.9662	0.2113	.0000	0.27
FTJOB3	3.3076	0.0000	.0000	0.00
FTJOB4	0.2029	0.0077	.0000	0.55
FTJOB5	0.3313	0.0123	.0000	0.58
FTJOB6	-2.7973	0.0459	.0000	0.05
FTJOB7	-0.4882	0.0003	.0000	0.62
FTJOB8	-5.3815	0.0421	.0000	0.00
FTJOB9	5.6759	1.3719	.0000	0.99
FTJOB10	4.3261	0.0001	.0000	0.98
FTJOB11	-13.4344	0.0005	.0000	0.00
FTJOB12	5.6759	0.0001	.0000	0.99
JOBTIME1	-23.5361	0.0005	.0000	0.00
JOBTIME2	-9.4460	0.0000	.0000	0.00
JOBTIME3	-14.0069	0.0001	.0000	0.00
JOBTIME4	-5.4986	1.4153	.0000	0.99
JOBTIME5	-4.8775	1.1656	.0000	0.00
LGJTIME1	23.7142	0.0025	.0000	6.86
LGJTIME2	16.2178	0.0248	.0000	0.00
LGJTIME3	9.9516	0.3882	.0000	1.00
LGJTIME4	5.7429	1.4522	.0000	0.99
LGUTIME1	-0.0029	0.0000	.0000	0.50
LGUTIME2	-0.4259	0.0164	.0000	0.39
LGUTIME3	1.3393	0.1165	.0000	0.79
LGUTIME4	-2.3813	0.8313	.0000	0.08
NJOB	*7.2617*	*26.2347*	*.0075*	*0.99**
NUNEMP	*2.1312*	*3.5943*	*0194*	*0.89**
NVQ1	*1.6198*	*3.8528*	*0209*	*0.83**

110

Table 5.12 continued

PROFSOC1	2.9920	0.4786	.0000	0.95
PROFSOC2	-1.4437	0.2183	.0000	0.19
PROFSOC3	3.2479	0.5167	.0000	0.96
PROFSOC4	-1.0894	0.0915	.0000	0.25
PROFSOC5	-1.3268	0.0422	.0000	0.21
PROFSOC6	3.0846	0.0130	.0000	0.95
SERSOC1	2.4648	1.2944	.0000	0.92
SERSOC2	0.3758	0.0369	.0000	0.60
SERSOC3	-0.6585	0.0174	.0000	0.34
SERSOC4	4.7087	0.6113	.0000	0.99
SERSOC5	2.3039	0.0010	.0000	0.90
SERSOC6	-2.6010	0.0011	.0000	0.06
TRAIN74	0.4748	7.6320	.0364	0.61
TRAIN81	1.2829	0.7754	.0000	0.78
WIFEJ	1.3689	1.1569	.0000	0.80

* significance at the 0.05 level
Source: Own calculations from NCDS5 1991 data supplied by ESRC Data
Archive.

Concluding Remarks

This chapter provides a descriptive overview of the characteristics of male
workers within the fifth sweep of the National Child Development Study
and builds up a picture of the nature of male non-standard working. The
chapter also goes on to attempt to predict male non-standard working. The
chapter had two broad aims. First, the chapter aimed to outline the
characteristics and employment conditions of male workers in NCDS5, with
particular emphasis being placed on the characteristics of male full-time and
male non-standard workers and their labour market participation. The
second main aim of this chapter was to introduce a multivariate model to
explore whether male non-standard workers specifically, and all male
workers generally have some particular pattern in their previous
employment which could be used to predict current employment. Within
these broad aims, a number of specific research questions were raised. They
were :

i) Do men who work in non-standard forms have different employment
experiences than those men who work in full time employment ?
ii) Do those men who work in non-standard-forms have different
employment experiences to those of women ?

111

iii) Is it possible to predict men's current occupational status from other sociodemographic variables from earlier in their lives and careers ?

The main findings confirm that there are important similarities and differences between men who worked in non-standard forms and male and female full-time workers and female non-standard workers. Further to this, certain labour market experiences can determine future labour market status. The main findings can be identified as.

- Social class III 'skilled manual' accounted for 40.3 per cent of male non standard workers and for 46.6 per cent males who work full-time. For women who work in non-standard forms there was more of an even spread amongst class groupings II to IV, whereas women who work full-time seemed to be concentrated in classes III Skilled Non Manual and III Skilled Manual.

- Men in the non-standard working group are represented more in SOC 5. There is more of an even distribution for male full-time workers, however. Women non-standard workers are split more or less evenly between SOC 1 -Managers SOC 4 - Clerical SOC 6 - Personal Services .

- More male full-time workers worked for private firms than male non-standard workers. Similar numbers of women full-time workers and women non-standard workers reported working for private firms. Twenty per cent of male non-standard workers worked for local authorities compared to ten per cent of male full-time workers.

- Eighty six per cent of male non-standard workers reported that they worked for an organisation that had between one and ten workers compared to only 30 per cent of female non-standard workers and 12 per cent of male full-time workers. Around 50 per cent of male full-time workers suggest that the work for an organisation with more that 100 workers.

- Overall the highest paid workers were full-time male workers, the lowest were female non-standard workers. Those who work full-time earn substantially more than their non-standard counterparts, nearly twice or three times as much regardless of gender. However, regardless of status, women examined as part of this research were the lowest paid group.

- Male full-time workers appear to work the longest mean hours per week, with women non-standard workers working the shortest mean hours.

Male non-standard workers and female full-time workers both seemed to work around 40 hours per week.

• The results demonstrated that previous temporary working, the number of jobs held, the number of unemployment spells, and finally holding an NVQ 3 or equivalent qualification, all seemed to reduce the chances of a man working full-time and increased the likelihood of working in a non-standard job.

The importance of documenting male labour market experiences needs to be reiterated in light of this chapters findings as it is only by highlighting such experiences will men's work be understood. This data suggests that men indeed do experience the labour market very differently depending on whether or not they work full-time or as a non-standard worker. The results also show that men, whether full-time or non-standard workers, do have labour market experiences that are different to women in equivalent positions.

In terms of the final research question the data provided evidence that certain labour market characteristics are important as they can determine the current labour market status of men. Such a finding does have implications for the 'traditional' assumption that they will work full-time and throughout their lives. For some men, for example, those who experience temporary work or experience more than one spell of unemployment men, the social 'ideal' of full-male employment may become socially and economically impossible.

Yet alongside these findings, it is obvious that this data does little to counter the fact that women have largely limited labour market experiences when compared to men nor does it move away from the fact that issues such as women's pay is a cause for concern.

The next chapter moves the debate on to explore men's attitudes to work.

6 Men, Work and Gender Role Attitudes

Introduction

> Research directed to what men say about their work and family roles has generated less interest than what men do in the family. Studies examining attitudes toward the changing roles of women and men have focused almost exclusively on women's roles or included only women as respondents.
>
> (Willinger 1993: 108-109)

The previous chapter introduced the 'actuality' of the experiences of work for the NCDS5 male worker samples. In this chapter, the analysis turns to examine men's attitudes towards work and their gender role and addresses the point that Willinger (1993) makes. The use of attitudinal statements is beneficial for any sociological enquiry, and particularly for the study of gender and masculinity. If they do not give definitive predictors of gender behaviour, they can provide some insight into the gender role views held by the respondent and how these views may have changed over time.

Men, Work and Gender Role Attitudes

Attitudinal research is often described as the cornerstone of social psychology (Fiske and Taylor 1984), with many attitudinal indicators having been developed throughout this century. Most attitudinal measures are based on verbal responses that are usually standardised, and their measurement assumes that first the statement will mean the same to all, and secondly that it can be quantified[1].

Despite some disagreement about the precise definition of attitudes[2], social psychologists agree that attitudes and external action or behaviour have a reciprocal relationship. As Scott *et al* (1996) and others note (see La Piere 1934; Allport 1935; Rokeach 1968; Wicker 1969; Myers 1988), the extent of this relationship is subject to conjecture.

> Attitudes are important indicators of people's latent tendencies to respond to the opportunities and constraints that are posed by the structural conditions of life.

Clearly attitudes and behaviour are linked, although it is almost never possible to determine to what extent one might be the cause of the other.

(Scott et al 1996: 475)

The use of attitude research as Scott *et al* (1996) define (as indicators of the ability to respond to structural constraints) also has some pedigree in sociological research (see Goldthorpe *et al* 1968; Brown 1974; Agassi 1979; LaRocco 1983). For example, Blauner (1964), examined the behaviour and attitudes of a sample of manual workers, relating the attitudes generated by differing production technology to alienation. Goldthorpe *et al* (1968), questioned the work of Blauner and explored the 'similarity between the attitudes of affluent workers' regardless of technology. In terms of gender-role attitudes, more contemporary accounts of attitudes can be found in sociological literature (see Dex, 1988; Christian 1994; Simpson 1994; Blee *et al* 1995; Hills 1995; Scott *et al* 1996). Blee *et al* (1995) suggests that for women and girls, a substantial body of literature has documented the formation of their gender role attitudes, and the transmission of those attitudes (Blee *et al* 1995; p21; Willinger 1993). Yet less research has been conducted into the attitudes that men have towards their male gender-roles, or how such gender-role attitudes vary between different groups of men and how these attitudes change over time (Blee *et al* 1995; Willinger 1993) .

The neglect of studies of men's attitudes is linked to the nature of some of the research, and the idea that women want gender-role change and men do not (Willinger 1993). For example, family research suggests that, historically, gender roles have been mediated by the meaning of work and family, with men's attitudes reflecting their involvement in economic functions, and women's reflecting roles based on emotional support. Men are happy with this as they benefit from such relationships. Yet, in arguing about change, a response to such representations of women's attitudes to family and work, Dex (1988) suggests that :

There are many stereotypes and platitudes thought and voiced about women's attitudes, especially about their attitudes towards employment

(Dex 1988: 1)

The point that Dex (1988) makes is certainly correct, but also limited. The same assertion can be made of men's attitudes towards their employment (and the attitudes that women have towards men and men's employment). Men's (as well as women's) attitudes towards men and work are also largely mediated by 'stereotypes and platitudes'. For example, a respondent in Murcott (1983) suggests that :

you must think of your husband...it's a long day at work for him at work' usually, ...even if they have got a canteen at work, their cooking is not the same as coming home to your wife's cooking...I think every working man should have a cooked meal when he comes in from work.

(Murcott 1983: 81)

Such a view contains hidden attitudes about the nature of male work. Men's work is hard, strenuous labour that needs to be supplemented or supported with home-cooking. Far worse than this, it implies that this is how it should be - men should work hard and return home to the comforts provided by the female partner. Yet such an attitude ignores many issues, for example, the variance in the nature of men's work, the fact that this may only describe white, heterosexual men (Blee *et al* 1995), or that men (and women) may now be adopting more egalitarian gender role attitudes. What it also suggests is that to get round the stereotypes and platitudes more research needs to be done in mapping and exploring men's attitudes towards their own gender role.

To explore the themes suggested here, and to outline men's attitudes generally, one Hypothesis could be that the more men are supportive of a traditional masculine view, the less likely they are to support equality and extended women's roles. Before this is explored, initial work is required to examine the extent to which men do identify with their traditionally defined role and whether or not this is mediated by other characteristics. As such this chapter examines men's attitudes in three ways. First, it provides an outline of what men's attitudes are. Second, it explores if men's attitudes do vary between different groups of men or if men's attitudes are related to certain work characteristics. Finally, the chapter examines the extent to which male work based gender-role attitudes have changed between 1981 and 1991.

Data, Definitions and Methods

This chapter uses the attitude data contained within the NCDS survey. NCDS5 contained a number of self-completed attitude statements (55 in total) that cover a broad range of issues from the environment to sex equality (Wiggins *et al* 1993). All these statements appeared in the instrument *'What Do You Think?'* in the section *'Your Views'*. The statements were ranked and ranged from strongly agree to strongly disagree. Wiggins *et al* (1993) suggest the attitude statements in NCDS5 were based on a classic Likert scale ranking used in a study on family attitudes carried out by the Australian Institute of Family Studies. The questions

...included traditional versus liberal views, especially in relationships to separation and divorce; attitudes to marriage and children as an ideal, as opposed to single status; and attitudes to gender roles in marriage, especially equality of responsibilities between the sexes. This initial range of opinions was extended to tap other attitude domains through which modern citizenship is expressed.

(Wiggins and Bynner 1993:162)

Table 6.1
Factor Matrix for, Permissiveness about Work and Family; Support for Sex Equality; and Support for Work Ethic

Variable	Permissiveness	Sex Equality	Work Ethic
N509664			0.73241
N509559			0.70603
N509571			-0.63661
N509555		0.61407	
N509515		0.59340	
N509520		-0.57641	
N509573		-0.57321	
N509666		-0.56536	
N509561		0.53206	
N509713		0.47337	
N590526		0.31001	
N509513	0.64532		
N509517	0.42108		
N509525	-0.67541		
N509524	-0.18933		
N509522	-0.65093		
N509530	0.66154		

* For definition of these variables refer to Table 6.15.
Source: Own calculations from NCDS5 1991 data supplied by ESRC Data Archive based on Wiggins et al (1993).

To date analysis has been carried out by Wiggins and Bynner (1993) on the attitude data in NCDS5. They identified ten broad scales from 50 of the original attitude statements. These were, support for work ethic; support for authority; support for traditional marital values; permissiveness about work and family; opposition to family life; political cynicism; left-right beliefs; support for sex equality; environmentalism; and finally anti-racism (Wiggins and Bynner 1993: 164). Many of these themes are beyond the scope of this chapter. However the factor analysis that Wiggins and Bynner (1993) carried out can be usefully replicated here for three of their factor scales are central to this book. They are 'Permissiveness about Work and

Family', 'Support For Sex Equality At Work'; and 'Support for Work Ethic'. The individual attitude variables which contribute to these themes are outlined in the factor matrix above (Table 6.1).

These factors provide the measures of 'gender-role' attitudes. For example, factor one measures the 'masculine' gender-role, and explores the extent to which men in NCDS5 identify with work. Factor two provides us with a range of measures that indicate the extent to which men in NCDS are ready to accept equality in work. Factor three, permissiveness about work and family, examines the acceptance of non-family roles for women.

The attitude data generated by NCDS4 in 1981 is used later in the chapter for an exploration of men's work ethic attitude change in the intervening ten years between the NCDS sweeps.

Sociodemographic Data - A Cluster Analysis

One of the issues that has characterised research into gender roles and their attendant attitudes, is a neglect of the variations in expressed attitudes of men (Blee *et al* 1995). For example, attitudes to gender role may differ on the basis of ethnicity, social class or occupational group. There is good empirical evidence to support such a decision. For example, Willinger (1993) and Scott *et al* (1996) suggest that views on equality are affected by levels of education and income. Those with higher levels of education and income being more likely to retain traditional views about equality. Religious practice, marital status and employment status, were also shown to be influential (Willinger 1993: 126). By clustering men into groups based on personal characteristics, such variance in attitudes could be more fully explored. Men from the male worker samples were then broken then down in smaller groups via the technique of cluster analysis. Table 6.2 presents the clustering of the men in four cluster groups based their own individual characteristics identified in the other NCDS survey instruments. The following statements can be made about the characteristics of these four male cluster groups.

Group one contains 337 men of whom 64 per cent fell into the non-standard worker category (and presumably the majority of this group were self-employed). Only 19 per cent reported that they work for more than 20 hours per week. This group were more likely to vote conservative compared to the other groups and the least likely to belong to a trade union. Thirty two per cent had qualifications above NVQ level three. Forty six per cent of this group had partners that were not employed and 61 per cent had children under the age of fourteen. The mean social class grouping for this cluster was II and the mean standard occupational classification was one.

Table 6.2
**Response Percentage or Mean Breakdown in Scores for Each Cluster
on the Discriminating Variables**

Group	1	2	3	4
Full Time Employee	36	93	95	39
NS Worker	64	7	5	61
Works 20+ Hours pw	19	93	96	27
Mean Number of Jobs	2.59	2.11	2.10	2.63
Voted Conservative	63	56	47	59
Member of a Union	18	33	51	20
Partner Not Employed	46	47	45	50
Has Children Under 14	61	61	70	68
Mean SOC	1	2	6	5
Mean Social Class	II	II	IIIM	IIIM
Qualifications higher than NVQ level 3 ?	32	51	10	14
Paid Less Than £200 pw	86	32	58	64
N	337	1851	1992	911

Source: Own calculations from NCDS5 1991 data supplied by ESRC Data
Archive.

Group two contained 1851 men, ninety three per cent of who were full-time employees and worked more than 20 hours per week. Fifty six per cent of this group indicated that they voted conservative in the 1987 general election, and they were the second highest group in terms of unionisation. This cluster of men seemed to be the highest qualified, with fifty one per cent suggesting that they had qualifications above NVQ level three. Forty seven per cent had partners who worked full-time and 61 per cent had children under the age of fourteen. The mean standard occupational classification for this group was two.

Group three clustered together 1992 men, ninety five per cent of whom were full-time employees. Ninety six per cent indicated that they worked for more than twenty hours per week. This cluster of men were the least likely to vote conservative and the most likely to belong to a trade union. Only ten per cent had qualifications above NVQ level three. The mean social class grouping was IIIM and the mean standard occupational classification was six.

Group four clustered 911 men, 61 per cent of whom were not full-time employees. Only twenty seven percent suggested that they worked for more than twenty hours per week. The number of conservative voters was high in

119

this cluster and correspondingly the number of trade union members was low. This group had the lowest levels of qualifications, with only ten per cent indicating qualifications above NVQ level three. Mean standard occupational classification was five.

The cluster groups of men outlined above are used in the remainder of this chapter to structure the discussion and analysis. In the first instance the cluster groups are used in bivariate analysis to explore the relative levels of agreement or otherwise for the individual attitudinal scales contained in the three factors identified above. The percentages and mean scores are reported below. The cluster groups are then used in a regression analysis which explored the extent to which the three factors, permissiveness about work and family; support for sex equality at work; and support for work ethic, were linked to the personal and work- related characteristics of the male cluster groups. Finally, attitudinal data from NCDS4 is introduced to explore the extent to which the male cluster groups support of the work ethic had changed between 1981 and 1991.

Outlining Men's Attitudes to Work[3]

In one of the few studies of men's attitudes, Willinger (1993) makes use of three theoretical perspectives in understanding men's attitudes. They are 'cultural lag' which suggests that men's attitudes will become less traditional, with men supporting women's changed roles as they discover the advantages of such change. Second, 'sex segregation' approaches which suggest men will continue to deny the legitimacy of women's employment and reject equality as they benefit from the status quo. Finally the approach of 'political domination' suggests that whilst men may recognise the legitimacy of equality, men will resist it. Yet whilst many of these approaches has some appeal in studying men's attitudes, they ignore the fact that men themselves are socialised into a male gender role linked to occupations and work. As such changes in men's attitudes towards more egalitarian views, or the display of a commitment to equality may be mediated by the extent to which men themselves identify with the work based nature of their 'role'.

These notions can be explored using the cluster groups identified above and the attitudinal factors identified by Wiggins and Bynner being replicated in this research. Also basic cross- tabulation will give some indication of support for particular attitudes. Tables 6.3 to 6.5 present the data for each of the four cluster groups (and all women for comparison), on each of the attitudinal scales included in each of the above factors. Tables 6.12 to 6.14 provide the mean scores for each cluster group on all the attitudinal variables used in this analysis. Table 6.3 presents the data for 'Support for Work Ethic' attitude scales.

Table 6.3
Percentages on Work Ethic Attitude Scales by Cluster Group Membership- NCDS5 1991

	Cluster Groups				
	1	2	3	4	All Women*
'having any job is better than being unemployed'					
agree	49.7	50.1	57.0	54.4	37.6
'Once you've got a job it's important to hang on to it even if you don't really like it'					
agree	31.7	38.9	50.5	39.7	35.6
'if I didn't like a job I'd pack it in, even if there was no other job to go to'					
disagree	62.0	73.7	75.0	62.9	62.3
N	**337**	**1851**	**1992**	**911**	**4762**

* All Women who identified themselves as working.
Source: Own calculations from NCDS5 1991. Categories based on Wiggins, R.D and Bynner, J (1993) 'Social Attitudes' in Ferri, E. (1993) 'Life at 33' NCB.

This table shows that Cluster Group three exhibits the greatest support for a traditional male work ethic. Fifty seven per cent agreed that any job is better than being unemployed. 50.5 per cent agreed that it is important to hang on to a job even if they did not like it. Finally 75 per cent suggested that they would not 'pack a job in' if they did not like it, if they did not have another job to go to. This group, as discussed above, has certain characteristics which may offer some explanation to these views. First, they are the most likely of the four cluster groups to be a full-time employee. Second, they have the lowest mean number of jobs. Third, around 70 per cent have children under the age of fourteen. Finally, 45 per cent have partners who are not employed, and as a group they are the least qualified.

This can be compared with Cluster Group one, which is the groups that displays least support for traditional work ethic attitudes, 49, 31 and 62 per cent respectively. This group of men were more likely to be male non-standard workers, have a relatively high mean number of jobs, work fewer hours and are marginally better qualified.

Table 6.4
Percentage Scores Support for Sex Equality Attitude Scales by Cluster Group Membership- NCDS5 1991

| | Cluster Groups | | | | |
	1	2	3	4	All Women*

note lack of discrim. in agree values

'women should have the same chances as men to get some training or have a career'

	1	2	3	4	All Women*
agree	98.0	98.3	90.5	96.4	98.7

'men and women should all have the chance to do the same kind of work'

agree	91.1	87.6	77.7	83.7	91.7

'there should be more women bosses in important jobs in business and industry'

agree	52.5	57.0	49.2	49.4	73.1

'men and women should do the same jobs around the house'

disagree	30.2	26.2	24.1	25.1	19.5

'when both partners work full-time the man should take an equal share of the domestic chores'

disagree	6.5	2.9	4.0	5.0	3.3

'I would not want a women to be my boss'

agree	16.0	10.5	12.6	15.7	7.9

'if a child is ill and both parents are working it should usually be the mother who takes time off to look after the child'

agree	40.1	27.7	38.2	38.9	38.8

'it is less important for a woman to go out to work than it is for a man'

agree	30.1	21.8	25.8	28.8	18.8
N	337	1851	1992	911	4762

* All Women who identified themselves as working.
Source: Own calculations from NCDS5 1991 data supplied by ESRC Data Archive, categories based on Wiggins, R.D and Bynner, J (1993) 'Social Attitudes' in Ferri, E. (1993) 'Life at 33' NCB.

122

Table 6.4 presents the actual percentage responses of the male cluster groups for the attitude scales related to the factor 'Support for Sex Equality at Work'. During the lifetime of the NCDS5 sample, government legislation was introduced to try and reinforce sex equality for pay and in work. Such legislation would have been in force when this sample of 33 year olds entered the work force for the first time in the mid to late 1970s. Based on the full sample, Wiggins and Bynner (1993) demonstrate that the ethos of sex equality has been instilled in this group. Do the Cluster Groups, representing certain sub-samples of men, support the notions of sex equality?

Interestingly, following on from the suggestion that support for male work ethic by men may be important in determining support for equality, we can see in this table those who had the strongest work ethic support (Cluster Group three) displayed the lowest levels of support for sex equality of the four cluster groups. Conversely, those in Cluster Group one, who displayed the lowest levels of support for a traditional work ethic, were more likely to display the most positive attitudes towards sex equality at work. For example, 98 per cent of Cluster Group one think that women should have the same career and training chances as men compared to only 90.5 per cent of men in Cluster Group three. The figures for the statement that men and women should do the same kind of work were 91.1 per cent and 77.7 per cent respectively.

Table 6.5 presents the percentage responses of the male cluster groups on the attitude scales related to the factor 'Permissiveness about Work and Family'. Again, important differences can be seen. For example, 47.3 per cent of men in Cluster Group 3 suggests that a persons must have a job to feel a full member of society compared to only 38.7 per cent of the men in Cluster Group one. Around 48 per cent thought that a person could get satisfaction out of life without having a job, compared to 61.8, 65.5 and 55.8 per cent for Cluster Groups one, two and four respectively.

The analysis so far seems to confirm the view that one can only understand men's attitudes towards gender roles by first identifying men's level of commitment to that gender role.

Table 6.5

Percentages on Support for Permissiveness about Work and Family Scales by Cluster Group Membership- NCDS5 1991

	Cluster Groups				
	1	2	3	4	All Women*
'women who do not have a job are dull'					
disagree	91.0	91.2	91.0	91.3	91.4
'a marriage without children is not fully complete'					
disagree	61.5	66.4	62.0	62.1	70.1
'a person must have a job to feel a full member of society'					
agree	38.7	39.0	47.3	46.1	29.0
'being a housewife is just as fulfilling as working for pay'					
agree	32.9	34.8	34.5	37.7	42.1
'people can have a satisfying relationship without children'					
agree	88.2	86.7	83.7	84.1	86.6
'a person can get satisfaction out of life without having a job'					
agree	61.8	65.5	48.1	55.8	66.0
N	**337**	**1851**	**1992**	**911**	**4762**

* All Women who identified themselves as working.
Source: Own calculations from NCDS5 1991 data supplied by ESRC Data
Archive, categories based on Wiggins, R.D and Bynner, J (1993) 'Social Attitudes'
in Ferri, E. (1993) 'Life at 33' NCB.

Multivariate Analysis of Men's Attitudes and Sociodemographic Data

The chapter now turns to an exploration of the sociodemographic variables that may be associated with the male attitudinal factors identified above. Multivariate regression analysis was carried out using 'ordinary least squares' (OLS) estimation on the three attitudinal factors (Support for Work Ethic; Support For Sex Equality at Work; Permissiveness about Work and Family). The aim was to investigate which sociodemographic variables determined men's attitudes towards the three factors. The regressions were carried out on five groups of men, the whole male worker sample and the cluster groups one to four that were used and identified in the research above.

Various explanatory variables were included in the analysis such as employment status, social class, standard occupational classification, education and political views or levels of conservatism. The results of the OLS regressions are presented in tables 6.6 to 6.8.

Table 6.6
Determinants of Permissiveness about Work and Family (Factor 3)
Coefficients for Cluster Groups 1-4 and Whole Sample

Variable	All	1	2	3	4
Paid Less Than £200 pw	0.019	-0.081	-0.010	0.044	0.024
Number of Jobs	-0.016	-0.062	0.007	-0.011	-0.087
Qualifications higher than NVQ level 3	0.056‡	-0.038	-0.064	0.089†	0.169*
Partner Not Employed	0.047	0.025‡	-0.017	0.047	0.011
Children under 14	-0.210*	-0.222	-0.156†	-0.206*	-0.279*
Voted Conservative	0.062	0.023	0.078	-0.010	0.098
SOC	-0.031†	-0.037	0.030	-0.014	-0.056
Number of					
Unemployment Spells	-0.069	0.210‡	-0.008	-0.026	-0.021
Member of a Union	-0.025‡	-0.222	-0.007	-0.039	-0.024
Works Full-Time	0.023	0.133	0.039	0.023	0.055
Social Class	-0.025	-0.130	-0.081	-0.039	-0.036
Works 20+ Hours pw	-0.003	0.088	-0.064	-0.007	0.028
R-Sq	3.0	10.4	1.6	2.1	5.0
N	5091	337	1851	1992	911

*p<0.001 †p<0.01 ‡p<0.05
Source: Own calculations from NCDS5 1991 data supplied by ESRC Data Archive.

Table 6.6 presents the data exploring the sociodemographic determinants of 'Permissiveness about Work and Family'. If one examines the whole male research sample to begin with one can ascertain that a number of variables are important in determining this attitude. The results suggest having a qualification above NVQ level 3, having children under 14, Standard Occupational Classification and being a Member of a Union all affect 'Permissiveness about Work and Family'. Having a qualification above NVQ level three seemed to increase permissiveness, whereas all the other variables were negatively associated. However, the impact of these variables must be put into perspective as they only explain 3 per cent of the variance in the dependent variable.

The largest amount of variance in the dependent variable explained by the sociodemographic variables occurred in the analysis for Cluster one. Here the sociodemographic variables explained 10.4 per cent of variance. However for this group, it was employment status of the man's partner or number of unemployment experiences that affected permissiveness. This is further explained by this groups characteristics (outlined in full above). This group were less likely to work for more than twenty hours per week. They were the least likely to belong to a trade union. Over half had partners that were employed and they had the most mean number of jobs.

Table 6.7
Determinants of Sex Equality Attitudes (Factor 2) Coefficients for
Cluster Groups 1-4 and Whole Sample

Variable	All	1	2	3	4
Paid Less Than £200 pw	0.018	0.011	0.077†	0.046	0.003
Number of Jobs	-0.045	-0.034	-0.077‡	-0.021	-0.010
Qualifications higher than NVQ level 3 ?	0.043	0.086	0.194*	-0.005	-0.058
Partner Not Employed	-0.096†	-0.358‡	-0.090	-0.096	-0.007
Children under 14	0.143*	0.215	0.344	0.164†	0.159
Voted Conservative	-0.199*	-0.218	-0.293*	-0.062	-0.184‡
SOC	0.009	-0.213‡	0.007	0.015	0.023
Number of Unemployment Spells	-0.044	-0.067	0.011	-0.101‡	-0.022
Member of a Union	0.892‡	-0.057	0.132‡	0.030	0.123‡
Works Full-Time	-0.045	0.020	-0.316	0.254	-0.072
Social Class	0.077†	0.250	0.029	0.017	0.219
Works 20+ Hours pw	-0.285*	-0.297	0.187	-0.314	-0.329‡
R-Sq	4.0	19.3	9.0	2.0	9.0
N	5091	337	1851	1992	911

*p<0.001 †p<0.01 ‡p<0.05
Source: Own calculations from NCDS5 1991 data supplied by ESRC Data Archive.

Table 6.7 displays the data for the exploration of the determinants of 'Sex Equality Attitudes'. The R-Sq for the whole male sample suggests that the sociodemographic variables used in the analysis explained around 4 per cent of the variance in the dependant variable. The explanatory power of the model rose to 19.3 for Cluster one, was at around 9.0 per cent for Cluster groups two and four. Its lowest explanatory power for was Cluster group three.

For the whole sample, the important variables were employment status of partner, having children under 14, voting Conservative, being unionised, social class and working hours. Having a partner who was not employed, voting Conservative and working for more than twenty hours per week decreased support for sex equality. Being unionised and having children under 14 increased support for sex equality. Voting Conservative was also linked to decreasing support for sex equality in Cluster groups two and four.

Table 6.8
Determinants of Support for Work Ethic (Factor 1) Coefficients for Cluster Groups 1-4 and Whole Sample

Variable	All	1	2	3	4
Paid Less Than £200 pw	0.007	0.043	0.071‡	0.005	-0.006
Number of Jobs	-0.014	-0.067	-0.013	-0.033	0.017
Qualifications higher than NVQ level 3 ?	-0.016	-0.029	-0.013†	0.015	0.069
Partner Not Employed	-0.039	-0.024	-0.005	-0.109‡	-0.028
Children under 14	-0.126†	-0.050	-0.170†	-0.098	-0.002
Voted Conservative	0.324*	0.435†	0.429*	0.239*	0.139
SOC	-0.010	0.097	0.063‡	-0.034	-0.008
Number of Unemployment Spells	0.164*	0.284‡	0.182*	0.107†	0.281*
Member of a Union	-0.055	-0.174	-0.051	-0.039	-0.081
Works Full-Time	-0.156	-0.156	-0.167	-0.178	-0.170
Social Class	-0.069‡	-0.028	-0.044	-0.015	-0.261‡
Works 20+ Hours pw	-0.049	0.064	0.294	0.032	0.084
R-Sq	5.1	11.0	10.5	5.0	6.0
N	5091	337	1851	1992	911

*p<0.001 †p<0.01 ‡p<0.05
Source: Own calculations from NCDS5 1991 data supplied by ESRC Data Archive.

Table 6.8 presents the data for the factor Support for Work Ethic. Again the predictive powers of the regression equation presented here is limited. At best, for Cluster groups one and two, the equation explains 11 per cent of the variance in the dependent variable. The predictive power is reduced to explaining around 5 per cent of variance for the male sample as a whole and Cluster groups three and four.

The sociodemographic variables that appear to be important in determining Support for Work Ethic are having children under the age of 14, voting for the Conservative party, having experienced unemployment and social class. Voting Conservative and experiencing unemployment seemed to improve an individual males support for the work ethic. However, variables such as having children and social class reduced the individuals commitment to the work ethic.

Men, Work And Gender Role Attitude Change 1981 - 1991

...men's attitudes appear to be influenced as much by the social and historical period in which we now live as by personal experiences or objective characteristics.

(Willinger 1993: 127)

One of the most widely accepted important attributes of the National Child Development Study is its longitudinal nature (Ferri 1993; Fogelman 1976; Butler and Bonham 1968). The survey spanning 33 years, as has been already noted, collects data on every aspect of the respondents lives and this includes their attitudes and aspirations over time.

According to Scott *et al* (1996), one possible explanation for change is characteristics of the period, for example, the state of the economy or employment. This view has been supported elsewhere, with other research suggesting that such intra-cohort change being more likely to be due to changes in circumstances than other explanations such as cohort-replacement. Attitudes may change overtime due to a number of factors such as changing lifestyles, experience, age and other life events. (see Mason and Yu-Hsia, Lu 1988; Alwin 1991; Davis and Robinson 1991; Willinger 1993). Although attitudes can be seen to change and the factors for such a change be identified, actually measuring change may be problematical. A full account of these debates are provided by Dex (1988) and will not be explored here suffice to say change in this research will be measured based on the following definition.

The most common definition of change, is that different frequencies of individuals occur at two points in time with a particular characteristic.

(Dex 1988: 19)

Such views can be explored to some extent within the framework of the NCDS cohorts. The fourth sweep of NCDS took place in 1981, when the respondents were aged 23. As these individuals had now been working for some time, it was pertinent to ascertain their individual work related attitudes, and in NCDS4 the attitude scales closely address the extent to which individuals value their work. These attitude scales can then be matched up with the respondents in the current sweep and compared.

The changes in agreement or support with matched attitudinal statements are presented in Tables 6.9 to 6.11. The analysis uses two time points, NCDS4 (1981) and NCDS5 (1991) when the respondents were 23 and 33 years of age respectively. In this analysis the change in support for the attitude statements is measured for the male worker samples as a whole and for the four male cluster groups identified above. The figures for each group can be read from the rows in the tables. the change in support is presented in the two last columns, net-change and the column marked Δ^*.

The net-change column simply represents the change in support for the attitudinal statement as represented in the raw data. However, before any useful analysis can be offered, it is important to note there is a significant difference in the response rates for the attitudinal questions for each cluster group over the ten year period. One can only speculate as to the reasons for this, with the main explanation probably being linked to the difficulty of matching variables to individuals between cohorts in longitudinal analysis. In the current research more men seemingly answered the questions in 1991 than in 1981. Whilst this may limit the true value of the data, for the purposes of this research the results should not be rejected out of hand. For example, the raw data does give some indication of the direction of change for changing attitudes and may therefore suggest trends. Secondly, there are well established techniques for weighting data to give a more precise analysis of data from differing sample sizes (SPSS, 1990). The weighted data is presented in the tables in italics. The column marked Δ^* presents the change in attitude scores for the weighted data which accounts for the differences in sample size. For simplicity, the discussion will refer to the weighted data.

Table 6.9 presents the analysis of the data for the work ethic statement 'Can Get Satisfaction out of Life Without Having a Job'. The data for this attitude statement shows some variation between the cluster groups and over the ten year period between sweeps. The data suggests that over the ten year period the trend has been one of a general decline in support for this statement. This suggests that as the men in this research have aged, their own life satisfaction has become linked further with work. The analysis suggests that there has been a mean decline in support of around 21 per cent since 1981.

There are also interesting differences between the sub-samples of men represented by the clusters. For example, in 1981 nearly 90 per cent of

Cluster Group one thought that life satisfaction was possible without having a job. Yet by 1991 support for this viewpoint by Cluster Group one had fallen by 28 per cent.

The extent of this decline may be explained by the characteristics that these respondents display in Table 8.2. For example, this attitude suggests a greater identification with work, and indeed this group had the second highest mean number of jobs, 46 per cent had partners who were not employed. This can be compared to Cluster Group two who experienced the smallest decline in support for this attitude statement. This group were more likely to be full-time employees, unionised and well paid.

Table 6.9
Changes in Agreement with 'Can Get Satisfaction Out of Life Without Having a Job' 1981- 1991, all Sample and Cluster Groups 1-4

Group	1981	1991	Net Change +/-	Δ*
All	87.2 78.7 (843)	56.8 58.6 (4785)	-30.4	-20.7
Cluster 1	88.1 89.6 (185)	61.8 61.6 (293)	-26.3	-28.0
Cluster 2	86.8 79.1 (106)	65.5 69.3 (1781)	-21.2	-9.8
Cluster 3	88.2 79.0 (69)	48.1 54.9 (1855)	-40.1	-24.1
Cluster 4	86.7 78.0 (483)	55.8 55.8 (856)	-30.9	-22.2
			mean change	-20.92

* 'N' in Brackets; Figures in italics represent weighted scores. Δ* Change for weighted samples.
Source: Own calculations from NCDS4 1981 and NCDS5 1991 data supplied by ESRC Data Archive.

Table 6.10 presents analysis of the attitudinal data for the statement 'Must Have a Job to feel a Full Member of Society'. The data suggests that the general trend for the cluster groups has been an overall increase in the support for this view. The mean change in support was an increase of 26 per cent.

The largest increase in support for this view comes from Cluster group four who witnessed an increase of 37 per cent. This group have experienced the greatest number of jobs and 50 per cent have partners who are not employed.

Table 6.10
Changes in Agreement with 'Must Have a Job to Feel a Full Member of Society' 1981- 1991, all Sample and Cluster Groups 1-4

Group	1981		1991		Net Change +/-	Δ*
All	29.1 (843)	*13.0*	43.4 (4785)	*45.5*	+14.3	+32.5
Cluster 1	30.3 (185)	*21.5*	38.7 (293)	*24.2*	+8.4	+2.7
Cluster 2	28.3 (106)	*9.3*	38.9 (1781)	*42.6*	+10.6	+33.3
Cluster 3	42.0 (69)	*15.7*	47.3 (1855)	*40.3*	+5.3	+24.6
Cluster 4	26.9 (483)	*12.5*	46.1 (856)	*50.0*	+19.2	+37.5
					mean change	+26.12

* 'N' in Brackets; Figures in italics represent weighted scores. Δ* Change for weighted samples.
Source: Own calculations from NCDS4 1981 and NCDS5 1991 data supplied by ESRC Data Archive

Table 6.11 presents the data for the statement 'Any Job is Better than No Job'. Support for this statement has generally increased over the ten year period by 11.2 per cent based on the weighted scores. However, for cluster group four, this statement has seen a decrease in support of -6.8 per cent suggesting that for this group at least, fewer men believed that any job was better than no job.

Concluding Remarks

This chapter aimed to do three things. First to map the attitudes that four different groups of male worker samples held towards their work, and work-related issues. Second, it examined the possibility of linking these attitudes to the particular labour market and individual characteristics displayed by male workers. Finally, this chapter explores the notion of men's attitude change between the period 1981 and 1991. Despite having identifiable problems, the attitudinal data can provide us with a useful picture of the men's work related attitudes.

In terms of mapping men's attitudes, this chapter has confirmed the view that attitudes do vary between different groups of men, and as such one cannot discuss men's attitudes in the way that perhaps Dex does - that is by not accounting for difference and the issues which affect them. Men's attitudes are also largely mediated by 'stereotypes and platitudes'.

Table 6.11
Changes in Agreement with 'Any Job is Better than No Job' 1981-1991, all Sample and Cluster Groups 1-4

Group	1981		1991		Net Change +/-	Δ*
All	67.9 (843)	50.0	53.4 (4781)	61.2	-14.5	+11.2
Cluster 1	62.2 (185)	43.6	49.7 (293)	44.6	-12.5	+1.0
Cluster 2	65.1 (106)	46.8	50.1 (1781)	55.8	-15.0	+9.0
Cluster 3	71.0 (69)	52.8	56.7 (1855)	56.8	-14.3	+4.0
Cluster 4	70.2 (483)	52.9	54.4 (853)	46.1	-15.8	-6.8
					mean change	+6.4

'N' in Brackets; Figures in italics represent weighted scores. Δ Change for weighted samples.
Source: Own calculations from NCDS4 1981 and NCDS5 1991 data supplied by ESRC Data Archive.

The data also seems to suggest that men's attitudes towards their work, their support for sex equality and their permissiveness about family and work are linked to various work related or sociodemographic variables. For example, the results of the cluster and factor analysis, used in the multivariate model suggest that support for sex equality and support for a traditional work ethic for some men are mediated by their political affiliations. Permissiveness about work and family for others is mediated by whether or not they have children within their household.

The final part of the analysis also suggests that men's attitudes are not stable or always consistent over time and that change will occur. The data suggested that men's support for the work ethic as indicated by the attitude statements does actually increase over time and becomes stronger.

These findings suggest that men's attitudes cannot be taken as 'given' and that, like women's attitudes (see Dex), they are affected by a multiplicity of variables. The final important point to make here is that men's attitudes also vary between groups of men and as such they cannot be treated as a homogeneous group.

Notes

1   The most common measurements are (i) Likert Scale (1932) - this comprises of a statement against which the respondent has to indicate whether they strongly agree, agree, undecided, disagree, strongly disagree; (ii) The Bogardus Social Distance Scale (1925) - is a measure of racial attitudes that comprises a series of social statements representing degrees of distance between and racial groups that the subject would not tolerate; (iii) The Semantic Differential, Osgood, Suci and Tannebaum (1957) - is a set of pairs of each of which there is a seven point scale ranging from positive too negative.

2   Secord and Beckman (1964) suggest that most definitions comprise of three elements (i) the cognitive or what the person believes about an object; (ii) the affective or what the person feels about an object; (iii) the behavioural how the actually responds to the attitude.

3   Some of the figures here represent own calculations on NCDS5 data, based on categories and factor analysis suggested in Wiggins, D., and Bynner, J., (1993) 'Social Attitudes' in Ferri, E., (1993) 'Life at 33' NCB. For a general view of the attitudinal responses of all the NCDS5 survey, this please refer to this chapter.

Table 6.12
Mean Scores on Work Ethic Attitude Scales by Cluster Group Membership- NCDS5 1991

	1	2	3	4	All Women*
having any job is better than being unemployed'					
	1.84	1.80	1.72	1.77	2.83
'Once you've got a job it's important to hang on to it even if you don't really like it'					
	2.15	2.04	1.82	2.02	3.06
'if I didn't like a job I'd pack it in, even if there was no other job to go to'					
	2.42	2.62	2.63	2.40	3.49
N	337	1851	1992	911	4762

* All Women who identified themselves as working.
Source: Own calculations from NCDS5 1991 data supplied by ESRC Data Archive, categories based on Wiggins, R. et al (1993) 'Social Attitudes' in Ferri, E. (1993) .

Table 6.13

Mean Scores on Support for Permissiveness about Work and Family Scales by Cluster Group Membership- NCDS5 1991

	1	2	3	4	All Women
'women who do not have a job are dull'					
	4.33	4.34	4.25	4.23	4.24
'a marriage without children is not fully complete'					
	3.47	3.63	3.51	3.56	3.71
'a person must have a job to feel a full member of society'					
	3.11	3.15	2.87	2.92	3.33
'being a housewife is just as fulfilling as working for pay'					
	2.91	2.86	2.90	2.84	2.89
'people can have a satisfying relationship without children'					
	2.00	1.97	2.06	2.05	2.00
'a person can get satisfaction out of life without having a job'					
	2.54	2.43	2.83	2.65	2.00
N	337	1851	1992	911	4762

Source: Own calculations from NCDS5 1991 data supplied by ESRC Data Archive, categories based on Wiggins, R.D *et al* (1993) 'Social Attitudes' in Ferri, E. (1993) .

Table 6.14
Mean Scores on Support for Sex Equality Attitude Scales by Cluster Group Membership- NCDS5 1991

	1	2	3	4	All Women
'women should have the same chances as men to get some training or have a career'					
	1.03	1.03	1.05	1.05	1.45
'men and women should all have the chance to do the same kind of work'					
	1.15	1.20	1.26	1.26	1.80
'there should be more women bosses in important jobs in business and industry'					
	1.64	1.59	1.66	1.67	2.26
'men and women should do the same jobs around the house'					
	1.69	1.63	1.58	1.62	2.15
'when both partners work full-time the man should take an equal share of the domestic chores'					
	1.19	1.10	1.12	1.15	1.68
'I would not want a women to be my boss'					
	2.53	2.65	2.56	2.52	3.95
'if a child is ill and both parents are working it should usually be the mother who takes time off to look after the child'					
	2.06	2.27	2.08	2.04	3.15
'it is less important for a woman to go out to work than it is for a man'					
	2.24	2.42	2.32	2.27	3.64
N	**337**	**1851**	**1992**	**911**	**4762**

Sources: Own calculations from NCDS5 1991 data supplied by ESRC Data Archive, categories based on Wiggins, R.D *et al* (1993) 'Social Attitudes' in Ferri, E. (1993).

135

Table 6.15
Attitude Variables Used in Analysis

Variable	Definition
N509664	Once you have got a job it is important to hang on to it even if you don't really like it
N509559	Having almost any job is better than being unemployed
N509571	If I didn't like a job I'd pack it in, even if there was no other job to go to
N509555	Men and women should do the same jobs around the house
N509515	There should be more women bosses in important jobs in industry
N509520	If a child is ill and both parents are working it should usually be the mother who takes time off to look after the child
N509573	I would not want a women to be my boss
N509666	It is less important for a woman to go out to work that it is for a man
N509561	When both partners work full-time, the man should take an equal share of the housework
N509713	Men and women should all have the same chance to do the same kind of work
N590526	Women should have the same chance as men to get some training or have a career
N509513	A person must have a job to feel a full member of society
N509517	Women who do not have a job are dull
N509525	A person can get satisfaction out of life without a job
N509524	Being a housewife is just as fulfilling as working for pay
N509522	Person can have a satisfying relationship without children
N509530	A marriage without children is not complete

Source: Own calculations from NCDS5 1991 data supplied by ESRC Data
Archive.

7 Men and Work Related Training

Introduction

> No capitalist skill formation system...can do without employers, and a high-skill system needs high-skill-using employers to predominate...An in-depth knowledge of modern technology can be acquired only through participation in the workplace...The recognition of the workplace as an important source of learning is now appearing in the work of psychologists.
>
> (Ashton and Green 1996: 101)

The two previous empirical chapters have considered men's participation in the labour market generally, men's attitudes to their work. This chapter considers another increasingly important aspect of men's working lives, namely the access to and participation in work related education and training. This chapter begins with a brief introduction to the debates and issues. The discussion will then proceed to examine the issues both in existing literature and in the education and training data available for the male research samples.

> For some time now, the reform and expansion of training and education in Britain has been placed high on the political agenda. This imperative derives from the recognition that training and education levels are relatively low overall in the British Workforce.
>
> (Green 1994: 242)

The value placed on education and training experiences in most capitalist economies is high, and goes without question (Brown 1991; Green 1994; Ashton and Green 1996), and its links to the workplace and future employment experiences are well established within academic literature (Ashton *et al* 1986, 1991, 1996; Brown 1991; Bynner and Fogelman 1993; Felstead 1994, 1995). Various aspects of the impact of education and training experiences on employment have been explored elsewhere, such as transition to work from school (see Ashton *et al* 1986; Bynner 1991); on unemployment (see Brown 1991); on employee development (Maguire *et al* 1994; Devlin *et al* 1995); on career paths (Devine 1994); and on the attainment of professional qualifications (Crompton and Sanderson 1986; Crompton *et al* 1990; Goodwin and Sung 1994; Ashton and Goodwin 1996). Education and training experiences have also been explored in terms of more personal characteristics such as ethnicity and age, and along with these, it is suggested that education and training experiences are also affected by an individuals gender. Felstead (1995) suggests that the impact of gender on education and training experiences in the past has taken the following form, the access or participation in education or training; the occupational segregation of work related training opportunities; the type of academic subjects studied by men and women. However, he goes on to argue that the distribution of vocational qualifications (and training) by gender has been less frequently considered.

However, a gender analysis of education and training, in line with all other areas of gender enquiry, tends to take the relative education and training attained by women as the focal point, and uses men as the 'yardstick' against which to measure women's participation (see Wickham 1986; Clarke 1991; McGiveney 1994; Istance and Rees 1994; Rees 1994; Felstead 1994; Gibbins 1994; Green 1994; Felstead Goodwin and Green 1994; Ashton and Green 1996).

For example, Felstead (1994), focuses upon the gender implications of exposing government funded training delivery and take-up to market forces. Yet in reality, the paper focuses on women's overall participation rate in government-funded training (Felstead 1994: 3). In later research Felstead (1995) suggests that men and women have an unequal chance of getting their vocational skills certified and that there is evidence to suggest that women are relatively poor attainers of vocational qualifications. Even though Felstead (1994, 1995) draws these conclusions, there is very little consideration, if any, of men's education and training experiences *per se*. There is no consideration of whether it is the case that *all* men that have better chances for training or getting their vocational skills certified or just certain groups of men. For example, do all men receive the same training or does it differ depending on occupation, social class, family responsibilities, parents educational experiences or/and whether the individual male currently works full-time or in non-standard work ? Regardless of the factors used in the analysis, research needs to consider the work-related training experiences of men *per se*.

Men, and Work Related Training: Issues for Research

Education and training participation and attainment have been explored within the National Child Development Study. Indeed, Bynner and

Fogelman (1993), to some extent have already examined the educational and training experiences of the whole NCDS5 cohort. They provide an exploration of the changes that have occurred in the educational and training experiences of men and women between 1981 and 1991. In general they report that at 23, 30 per cent of the whole NCDS sample had undertaken no education or training since leaving school (39 per cent women and 21 per cent men) and that 28 per cent had no qualifications at all above CSE grades 2-5.

Beyond NCDS5, certain other issues can be drawn from existing research of the gender effect on training to serve as a model for the analysis here. For example, Felstead (1994) in an analysis of the 'training market' using QLFS, Gibbins (1994) using an analysis of the LFS, and Green (1994) using GHS, and Ashton and Green (1996) assert that gender differences are revealed in the following ways: Men are more likely to get job-related training; Men are more likely to get their training paid for; Men are advantaged in the acquisition of skills; and finally, Men in unskilled manual occupations have relatively long training hours.

Yet such statements, for the purposes of this research, can act as little more than a guide in researching men's participation in work related training. The rationale for this is that these 'definitive statements' are generated about men in research which compares women's with men's participation and does not consider a comparison of training differences between different groups of men. For example, it may well be the case that men are more likely to participate in work-related training than women, however does this statement apply to all men or just certain groups of men. The research presented here aims to explore these points. As such a number of refined research questions can be asked :

i) Which men are more likely to participate in work-related training ? Does such participation differ depending on factors such as tenure, job type or organisation ?;

ii) Are men who are working in non-standard ways less likely to get job related training than those men who are full-time employees ?;

iii) Do all men participate in similar or different types of work-related training ?

iv) Do certain employment characteristics determine whether or not men will participate in work related training ?

Such research questions can be fully explored within the context of the male worker samples in NCDS5, as this survey contains a wealth of data relating to training generally and work related training specifically.

Male Differences in Work Related Training

The general theme of men being more likely to get work-related training can be explored initially by examining participation data from the Labour Force Survey.

Table 7.1 outlines the 'Participation in Job Related Training as a Percentage of All employees by Gender' for the ten years between 1984 and 1994. This table provides some basic information on men's participation in work-related training compared to that of women for the ten year period. The trends which this table suggest implies that there has been an increase in work-related training for all employees, with training increasing from 8.3 per cent in 1984 to 13.4 per cent in 1992. However if one examines this trend by gender, one can see that the increase in work related training has been greater for women employees than it has for male employees. For example, in 1984, 8.5 per cent of male employees and 7.9 per cent of women employees participated in work related training. However between 1987 and 1988 women's participation in work related training began to increase and outstrip that of male employees.

Table 7.1
Participation in Work Related Training as a Percentage of all Employees by Gender[#] - LFS 1984 to 1994

Spring	All Persons	Men	Women
1984	8.3	8.5	7.9
1985	9.4	9.0	8.7
1986	9.8	9.3	9.3
1987	9.8	9.9	9.7
1988	12.3	12.2	12.4
1989	13.4	13.2	13.7
1990	14.4	14.1	14.7
1991	13.8	13.5	14.1
1992	13.4	13.2	13.7
1993*	-	12.8	14.6
1994*	-	13.2	15.6

* Figures are for Great Britain, [#]Men aged 16-64 and Women aged 16-59
Source: Labour Force Survey Historical Supplement (1993), Government Statistical Office, No.9 page 12. and Employment Gazette (1994) 'Women and Training', November, pages 391-402.

Between 1987 and 1988 men's participation increased by 2.3 per cent, for women the increase was 2.7 per cent. This trend continued throughout the 1980s and into the 1990s. In 1994 men's participation had increased to 13.2 per cent with women's participation at 15.6, a gender difference of 2.4 percent. If one considers the period as a whole the percentage increase in work related training for women was 7.7 per cent, compared to an increase of an 4.7 per cent for male employees. These trend can be summarised as, up until 1987 and 1988 a greater percentage of all male employees received work-related training compared to women employees. However after this period this situation is reversed with a greater percentage of women employees receiving work related training compared to men.

Table 7.2
Men and Work Related Training by Employment - NCDS5 1991

NCDS5 Question   All Men

Any Work Related Training Courses Since 1981
                                    YES   56.8   NO 43.2

Were Any Work Related Training Courses Since 1981
of more than 3 days duration ?
                                    YES   80.6   NO 19.4

Number of Work Related Training Courses Since 1981
                                    1   28.7
                                    2-5   45.8
                                    6-10   15.4
                                    10+   10.1

Source: Own calculations from NCDS5 1991 data supplied by ESRC Data Archive.

Characteristics of Men's Work Related Training

Tables 7.2 to 7.4 provide general information on men's participation in work-related training based on the male worker samples from NCDS5.

Table 7.2 provides some basic information on men's participation in work-related training for the male worker samples in NCDS5. From this table one can see that 56.8 per cent of the 5593 male workers participated in work-related training between the survey dates of 1981 and 1991. This is much higher than the LFS data on employees participation.

Over 80 per cent of these men participated in work-related training that lasted for three or more days and that vast majority had been on between one and five such work related training courses. Table 7.3 explores the characteristics of this work related training in slightly more detail and Table 7.12 provides a selection course titles for the most recent work-related training.

Using the data presented in Table 7.3 one can see that the overriding reason for participating in work-related training was that the work related training was needed for the respondents current job. This figure is largely to be expected, however more than 9 percent of the respondents participated in the training as they wanted a better job. If one looks at the figures for male non-standard workers this figure increases to nearly 15 per cent.

The vast majority of respondents participated in full-time training (83.2 per cent), on the premises of the employer (41.3 per cent) and did not have to pay for the training themselves (93.0 per cent). All the respondents were asked if they used the skills which they has gained from the work related training course, and the majority suggested that they had. However around one quarter of all men asked suggested that they used the skills hardly ever or indeed never.

Which Men Participate in Work Related Training ?

Literature of training seems to suggests that those who participate in training, generally display certain characteristics or are drawn from certain occupational or work groups (see Green 1991; Drew *et al* 1992; Istance and Rees 1994; Felstead 1995; Gibbins 1994; Green 1994; Ashton and Green 1996). For example, (Green 1994) suggests that those with higher educational qualifications are more likely to receive training. Gibbins (1994) also suggests, in an analysis of labour force data, that the incidence of training was higher for those individuals educated to A level standard. Felstead (1995) also provides an analysis of employment characteristics and vocational qualifications, suggesting that those in certain occupational groups are more likely than those in other occupational groups to hold vocational qualifications above level three. Also analysing employment characteristics, Gibbins (1994) suggests that the incidence of training reduces with the length of time spent with a single employer.

Table 7.3
Work Related Training Issues by Employment* - NCDS5 1991

	All Men	NS Men	F/TMen
Main Reasons for Participation in Work Related Training			
Needed for Job	74.2	70.3	75.1
Wanted Better Job	9.2	14.7	8.6
Another Reason	16.2	15.1	16.3
Can't Say	0.4	0.0	0.4
Was The Work Related Training Full or Part-Time ?			
Full-Time	83.2	73.2	84.3
Part-Time	16.3	26.4	15.2
Can't Say	0.5	0.4	0.5
Where did the Work Related Training Take Place ?			
Technical College	3.4	3.2	5.2
College of Education	1.0	1.0	1.3
Further Education	1.9	1.7	3.9
Tertiary College	0.0	-	-
Inst. of HE	0.3	0.3	0.4
Polytechnic	1.1	1.1	0.9
University	2.6	2.6	2.6
Adult ed Centre	1.1	1.0	2.2
Government Skill Centre	2.1	1.6	6.5
Private College	12.1	12.1	12.1
Employers Premises	41.3	43.3	24.6
Other	32.7	31.9	40.5
Can't Say	0.3	0.2	-
Did you have to Pay for the Work Related Training Course ?			
Yes	7.0	4.6	28.8
No	93.0	95.4	71.2
Was The Work Related Training Meant To Lead To a Qualification ?			
Yes	21.7	32.0	20.6
No	77.8	68.0	78.9
Can't Say	0.4	0.0	0.5
Have You Used The Skills Gained From The Work Related Training Course ?			
Most or all the time	36.9	36.6	37.0
Some of the time	37.3	33.1	38.3
Hardly Ever	13.5	15.5	13.1
Never	12.2	14.8	11.7

* Figures may not add up to 100% due to rounding.
Source: Own calculations from NCDS5 1991 data supplied by ESRC Data Archive.

Using data from NCDS5, it is possible to ascertain whether or not it is particular groups of men who gain access to and participate in training. The discussion here will mainly centre on all men and their employment related characteristics. Certain useful personal characteristics used elsewhere (for example in Felstead) are not available in NCDS5[1]. The data which was available was cross tabulated with the positive responses to the NCDS5 question 'Since 1981 Have you Participated in any Work Related Training?'. Tables 7.4 and 7.5 present the results of this analysis for three groups of men; All Men; Male Full-Time Employees; and Male Non-standard Workers.

Men's participation in work-related training differs by standard occupational classification, and the results presented here do not significantly differ in nature from figures reported elsewhere (see Felstead 1995). For example, participation of men in 'Craft and Related' occupations was at 39.3 per cent, whereas for those in 'Professional' occupation participation was at 74.8 per cent. High percentages of men who worked in female dominated occupations also participated in training, for example, 70.5 per cent of those men working in 'Clerical and Secretarial' occupations participated in work-related training.

Social class also seems to be important in determining participation in work-related training. It is possible to see that those men in lower class groupings are the men least likely to get training. For example, 73.3 per cent of those in the 'professional' grouping participated in work related training compared to only nearly 22 per cent in the 'unskilled' grouping. Further to this, there seems to be a very clear dividing line between those who participate in work related training and those who do not based on the manual versus non-manual split. Around 70 per cent of each of the top three groupings participate in training compared to 40 per cent or below for the lower three class groupings.

Employment type, working hours and job tenure had some impact on men's participation in work related training. Those men who were full-time employees seemed more likely to participate in training than non-standard workers. Likewise, the more hours the particular man worked increased the likelihood of participation. Job tenure has been explored elsewhere (Felstead) and like other research, job tenure in NCDS5 seemed to affect participation in work-related training. Those individual men most likely to participate were those employed between six and twelve months. Those at either extreme, employed six months or less, or five years and over, were the least likely men to participate in work-related training.

Table 7.4

**Men and Work Related Training by Employment Characteristics -
NCDS5 1991**

	All	FT Men	NS Men
By Occupation			
Managers and Administrators(1)	60.1	76.5	38.5
Professional (2)	74.8	77.3	62.2
Associate Professional & Technical (3)	68.6	72.3	50.6
Clerical & Secretarial (4)	70.5	70.4	71.4
Craft Related (5)	39.3	47.6	20.4
Personal and Protective Services (6)	72.4	75.1	21.4
Sales (7)	60.4	65.7	42.3
Plant & Machine Operatives (8)	39.1	40.4	31.1
Other (9)	33.3	34.2	30.0
By Social Class			
Professional	73.3	75.3	65.2
Intermediate	70.6	76.1	40.8
Skilled (Non-Manual)	72.4	75.6	53.9
Skilled (Manual)	40.6	47.1	22.1
Partly Skilled	41.2	43.2	39.7
Unskilled	21.8	20.5	24.3
By Employment Type			
Full-Time Employee	62.2	-	-
Non-Standard Worker	34.4	-	-
By Working Hours			
Works 20+ hours per week	62.8	63.0	52.7
Works Less than 20 hours	26.7	42.9	21.7
By Job Tenure			
Less Than 6 months	55.9	57.3	51.1
6-12 months	62.6	64.8	53.1
More than 1 year but less than 3	57.8	61.5	39.2
3-5 years	58.1	62.7	37.3
5 or more years	56.1	62.8	29.1
By Establishment Type			
Private Firm	58.5	58.9	38.3
Nationalised Industry/Company	68.9	69.1	60.0
LA/LEA	71.9	73.0	46.7
Health Authority	60.0	61.4	-
Central Government	80.9	80.8	83.8
Charity or Trust	78.6	77.9	-
Other	68.6	70.7	-
By Size of Establishment			
1-10 people	46.9	47.6	36.0
11-25 people	58.3	59.0	22.0
26-99 people	62.7	62.9	50.0
100-499 people	65.3	65.7	40.0
500 or more	69.7	69.8	61.5

Source: Own calculations from NCDS5 1991 data supplied by ESRC Data Archive.

Type of establishment and other establishment variables also seem to be important in determining men's participation in work-related training. For example, the results seem to suggest that men are more likely to participate in work related training if they do not work for a private firm. Men working for 'Central Government', 'Charities' and 'Local Authorities/Local Education Local Authorities' seem to be those most likely to participate in work-related training. The size of the establishment is a further determining factor. For example, the data presented in Table 7.4 suggests that participation in work related training increases as does the size of the establishment.

Table 7.5
Men's Participation in Work Related Training by Other Characteristics - NCDS5 1991

Weekly Pay	All	FT Men	NS Men
£1-£50	30.6	40.0	29.8
£51-£100	32.3	32.1	32.4
£101-£200	48.7	51.7	30.2
£201-£300	66.4	71.7	27.8
£301-£500	70.0	79.0	40.5
£501-£1000	73.2	85.7	60.3
£1000+	68.7	72.5	56.3
Number of Previous Jobs			
1 Job	68.7	68.7	-
2-5 Jobs	62.3	62.3	34.0
6- or more	46.8	60.5	50.0
Number of Unemployment Periods			
1 Period	53.5	58.2	35.2
2-5 Periods	46.9	49.7	36.0
6 or more	26.3	31.3	-
NVQ Level of Highest Qualification			
No Qualifications	29.5	33.0	16.9
NVQ1	48.2	52.6	27.3
NVQ2	47.2	54.4	24.7
NVQ3	60.8	68.5	31.1
NVQ4	77.0	80.4	57.7
NVQ5	77.4	80.5	59.8

Source: Own calculations from NCDS5 1991 data supplied by ESRC Data Archive.

146

Table 7.5 presents men's participation in work related training by other characteristics, including education level, pay, number of jobs and number of employment spells. These variables also reveal some interesting possible determinants of men's participation in work- related training. Indeed, as suggested elsewhere (Green 1994) educational qualifications seem to impact quite significantly on participation in training. The qualification data here has been translated into NVQ levels for ease of analysis. This data certainly suggests that those with higher qualifications or their NVQ equivalent participate more in work-related training. Conversely, those without qualifications are the least likely to participate. From this descriptive analysis, the discussion has shown that various employment related characteristics may impact on men's participation in work-related training.

Factors Affecting Men's Participation in Training: A Multivariate Analysis

The analysis above provides a descriptive account of the educational and training experiences of each of the male research groups. However, to understand or reflect further on the data a logistical regression model is used as this technique has proved highly successful in other gender and training research (see Felstead, 1995, 1996). The features that underpin this technique are outlined in Chapter five and need little further reflection here. Suffice to say that unlike the linear regression models that are used elsewhere in this research, logistic regression allows predictions to made about whether or not a particular event will occur. For example, the tables above suggest that certain characteristics seem to relate to whether men participate in work-related training. Men who are categorised as Professional seem more likely to get training than those who are deemed 'Unskilled'. Likewise male full-time employees seem twice as likely to get work-related training compared to those men who are not.

To test these issue more thoroughly, these variables can be built into a logistic regression equation which will allow us to explore whether or not factors such as being professional or working full-time are predictors of participation in work-related training. In terms of the model presented in this analysis, the dependant variable of work-related training (ANYTRAIN) is assigned the value of 'zero' where the respondent has not experienced any work related training. The value of 'one' is assigned where the respondent has experienced work related training. Some of the explanatory variables are strings so dummy variables representing these variables, such as Standard Occupational Classification or Social Class, (for definition of all variables used see Table 7.8) needed to be developed. Table 7.6 is a classification table for work related training by employment and individual characteristics.

This table is a useful starting point in the analysis of the logistic regression equation. From this table we can see that 1387 of those men who did not experience work-related training were correctly predicted to have not experienced work related training. Likewise, 2123 of those men who had experienced work related training were correctly predicted to have done so. Of those men who had not experienced work related training, 62.9 per cent and 73.5 per cent had been correctly predicted. Out of the total number of men used in this equation, 68.9 per cent were correctly predicted

Table 7.7 shows the 'parameter estimates for the logistic regression model and predicted probabilities of men having work related training'. This table contains a wealth of information useful in predicting whether or not certain characteristics (or independent variables) increase the likelihood of an event (work-related training) occurring.

For example, the R statistic can be used to examine partial correlation. R ranges from -1 to +1, with a positive value indicating that as the variable increases, so does the likelihood of an event occurring. Likewise if R is a negative value this suggest the opposite, or that as a variable increases the likelihood of an event decreases. Alternatively the regression coefficients can be used. For example, in Table 7.7 the coefficient (B) for FULLT (the respondent works full-time) is 0.5745. All other thing being equal, this suggests that the log odds of a man experiencing work-related training increases by 0.57 if they work full-time. Norusis (1990) suggests that it is, however, easier to think of 'odds' rather than 'log odds'. In this example the odds are increased by a factor of 1.776, as shown in the *EXP (B)* column in Table 7.7.

However, returning to the problem of this chapter, the aim here is to use logistic regression to predict men's participation in work-related training based on the values of the various employment related characteristics used in the equation. Following Felstead's (1996) method and rationale, when all the dummy variables have a value of zero, we have a 'base case'. In this research, this is an individual with the following characteristics: a male non-standard worker (not a full-time employee) who is doing skilled manual work in a craft related occupation, not working for a private company that has between one and ten other employees. It would be this individuals sixth job after six or more periods of unemployment. The base case works between one and twenty hours per week for a weekly wage of £300 or less. This individual is qualified below NVQ level 3 standard. The probability of this event happening is 0.1149.

Table 7.6
Classification Table for Work Related Training by Employment and Individual Characteristics - NCDS5 1991

	Predicted		
Observed	0	1	Percent Correct
0	**1387**	815	62.99%
1	766	**2123**	73.49%
		Overall	**68.95%**
	Number of Cases in Equation		**5091**

Table 7.7
Parameter Estimates for the Logistic Regression Model and Predicted Probabilities of Men Having Work Related Training - NCDS5 1991

Variable	B	Wald	R	Exp(B)	Probability	Odds
CLASS1	1.1228	19.7951	.0505	3.073	0.5255†	1.1
CLASS2	1.1163	25.8825	.0586	3.053	0.5239†	1.1
CLASS3	1.0808	87.9013	.1111	2.946	0.5150†	1.0
CLASS4	-.1782	2.9661	-.0118	0.836	0.0998	0.1
CLASS5	-.8356	11.1277	-.0362	0.433	0.1355†	0.15
FULLT	.5745	13.4212	.0405	1.776	0.3902†	0.63
HED	.7478	75.0092	.1024	2.112	0.2034†	0.25
LENGTH1	.1076	0.2754	.0000	1.113	0.2863	0.40
LENGTH2	-.1357	1.0176	.0000	0.873	0.2393	0.38
LENGTH3	-.1073	0.5628	.0000	0.898	0.2421	0.39
LENGTH4	-.1699	1.9159	.0000	0.843	0.2333	0.30
PRIV	-.3219	19.0750	-.0495	0.724	0.3321	0.49
PROFSOC1	-.2459	1.2800	.0000	0.782	0.2198	0.28
SERSOC1	-.0569	0.4245	.0000	0.944	0.2539	0.30
JOB1	.2982	5.8131	.0234	1.347	0.3268	0.48
JOB2	.0216	0.0699	.0000	1.021	0.2691	0.36
NJOB1	-.1971	8.5808	-.0307	0.821	0.2283	0.29
NJOB2	-.3819	9.2613	-.0323	0.682	0.2578*	0.34
ORG2	-.1746	2.5053	-.0085	0.839	0.2578*	0.34
ORG3	-.0367	0.1852	.0000	0.963	0.2578	0.34
KIDS	.0882	1.7740	.0000	1.092	0.2824	0.39
TIMED	.7782	29.6896	.0631	2.177	0.4397†	0.78
Base Case	-1.020	46.5073	-	-	0.1149	0.12

* significance at the 0.01 level † significance at the 0.001 level.
Source: Own calculations from NCDS5 1991 data supplied by ESRC Data Archive

The regression equation allows us to explore the effect of each of the independent variable on men's participation in work-related training. Such an exploration suggests that men's participation is increased by changing one of the base characteristics. For example, if the man was a full-time employee rather than a non-standard worker, if the man was in either the Professional, Managerial, or Skilled Non-Manual class grouping rather than the Skilled Manual grouping. The probability of this man participating are also increased if he had obtained qualifications above the NVQ level 3 rather than below it.

Similarly the probability of this man participating in work related training is reduced if he belongs to an unskilled class grouping. The probability of training would also have been reduced if he had less unemployment or worked for an organisation with eleven to twenty five employees.

Concluding Remarks

This chapter acknowledges the increasing importance of education and training experiences, and that such experience has become a key factor of working life. However, it has also been noted that when commentators address the gender divisions that exist in participation and attainment, they tend to focus on women primarily, and on men as a yardstick against which to measure. In many respects this may not actually say anything about the education and training experiences of men *per se*.

To address these issues this chapter sets out to explore men's work-related training in relation to four main research questions; Which men are more likely to participate in work-related training? Are men who are working in non-standard ways less likely to get job-related training than those men who are full-time employees?; Do all men participate in similar or different types of work-related training?; and finally, do certain employment characteristics determine whether or not men will participate in work-related training?

In answering these questions on men's work-related training it is possible to draw certain conclusions. First that the overarching consensus in academic literature that men participate more than women in work related training needs clarification. Indeed it should be suggested that it is only certain groups of men who participate more than women and other men, and that variation in participation occurs amongst men. In this research it has been shown that men's participation in work-related training differs depending on factors such as Education, Standard Occupational Classification and/or certain other establishment variables.

Second, that certain labour market and other characteristics are actually significant in determining men's participation in work-related training. The logistic regression model demonstrated that men's likely participation in work-related training increases if they work full-time, are educated above NVQ level three and are of a relatively high social class grouping. Men's participation is reduced if they belong to class groupings four or five, have a large number of jobs and work for an organisation with few employees.

Third and finally, given what has just been suggested it is not simply enough to talk about gender based differences *per se*. Whilst it goes without question that certain groups of men do participate more in training than women, certain other male (and female) groups need to be targeted if training is to be equitable. For example, lower class males and men with lower levels of education. If the distribution of education and training for a high skills economy is to be addressed fully then a gender based dichotomy is only partially the answer.

Note

1   For example Felstead uses 'AGE', however all the NCDS5 respondents are 31. Also ethnicity is used elsewhere, but because of low responses in NCDS5 this variable is very difficult to operationalise here.

Table 7.8
Analysis of Work Related Training Prediction Model- NCDS5 1991

Variable	Definition	Coefficient	t-statistic
Class1	Professional	1.1228	4.44
Class2	Managerial	1.1163	5.08
Class3	Skilled nm	1.0808	9.37
Class4	Partly skilled	-0.1782	-1.72
Class5	Unskilled	-0.8356	-3.33
Fullt	Works full-time	0.5742	3.66
Hed	Qual above nvq3	0.7478	8.66
Length1	In work 6to12 months	0.1076	0.52
Length2	In work 1 to 3 years	-0.1357	-1.00
Length3	In work 3 to five years	-0.1073	-0.74
Length4	In work or more years	-0.1699	-1.38
Priv	Works inPrivate company	-0.3219	-0.43
Profsoc1	Professional manager soc	-0.2459	-1.13
Sersoc1	In service soc	-0.0569	-0.65
Job1	Only one job	0.2982	4.41
Job2	Two to five jobs	0.0216	0.26
Njob1	Only one unemployment spell	-0.1971	-2.92
Njob2	1-5 unemployment spells	-0.3819	-3.04

Table 7.8 Continued

Org2	11 to 25 employees	-0.1746	-1.58
Org3	26 to 99 employees	-0.0367	-0.42
Kids	Children under 14	0.0882	1.33
Timed	Works 20+ hours per week	0.7782	5.44

Number of Cases in equation   5091   -2 log Likelihood   6,964.6346 * Given the degrees of freedom the value of *t* must be equal to or greater than 1.960 to be significant at the 0.05 level.
Source: Own calculations from NCDS5 1991 data supplied by ESRC Data Archive.

Table 7.9
Qualifications and Related NVQ Levels - NCDS5 1991

Level	*Description of Equivalents*
LEVEL 1	RSA 1; CSE Grades 2-5; Other Business/Technical qualifications
LEVEL 2	JIB Technicians Cert; CGLI Operative; Insignia Award and Other Qualifications; RSA 2 and 3; Scottish Standard O Grade; O Level, CSE 1, GCSE.
LEVEL 3	TEC, BEC, BTEC National Certificate or Diploma; JIB ONC/OND; CGLI Pt II, Scottish Cert of 6th Form Studies, GCE and Scottish Highers, A level
LEVEL 4	Training College Certificate; Unvalidated Diploma or Certificate, Nursing Qual; Professional Qual; BTEC HND; JIB HNC/HND; CGLI Full Technical.
LEVEL 5	First Degree; Postgraduate Diploma, Higher Degree.

Source: Bynner, J. and Fogelman K. (1993) 'Making the Grade: Education and Training Experiences' in Ferri, E (1993) 'Life at 33' NCB.

Table 7.10
Qualifications- NCDS5 1991

Qualification	Percentage Of Men and Women[*]			
	Men	Women	F/TMen	F/T Women
CSE 2-5	20.0	24.1	17.2	16.1
CSE1/GCE/GCSE A-C	12.1	15.0	1.0	13.9
A Levels	3.5	2.3	3.7	2.8
Scottish O	0.3	1.5	0.6	1.4
Scottish Standard	0.0	0.0	0.1	0.1
Scottish Higher	0.3	0.5	0.5	1.0
C&G/RSA	25.7	21.2	18.6	4.3
ONC/HNC	11.9	6.6	16.0	5.8
Professional	4.4	7.6	6.1	11.0
Degree	9.4	8.8	14.1	16.8
Other	11.5	11.5	13.4	14.4
N	982	2919	4109	1843

*Percentages may not total 100% due to rounding.
Source: Own calculations from NCDS5 1991 data supplied by ESRC Data Archive.

8 Men, Households and Private Work

Introduction

In this chapter men's household participation is considered. The introduction carries on with an outline of the debates. The theoretical framework developed by Coverman (1985) is introduced and discussed in terms of being an appropriate model to aid our understanding of men's household participation. The Coverman Hypothesis is then explored empirically.

> His wife says he does 'just little things', which turns out to mean clearing the table after the main meal and making a pot of tea at intervals during the day…He does no cleaning, shopping, washing or washing up.
>
> (Oakley 1974: 140)

The relative roles that men and women play in the home has attracted considerable attention (both empirical and theoretical) during the last thirty years or so (for example see, Miller and Swanson 1958; Blood and Wolfe, 1960; Gavron 1966; Oakley, 1974; Sharpe 1976; Gove and Hughes, 1980; Coverman 1985; Weiss 1990; Blair 1992; Cohen 1993; Simons, 1995; Johansson *et al* 1996; Benjamin 1996; Nielsen *et al*, 1997). This is largely a consequence of the second wave feminists in the early seventies. Other theorists go further back, and locate the discussion of the household division of labour in the writings of classical theorists such as Marx and Durkheim, and in turn onto others such as Parsons' instrumental roles and the functionalist tradition (see Cohen, 1987, 1988, 1993; Pleck 1976, 1985).

Within the 'empirical' accounts of housework, it is possible to identify four differing approaches. First, time budget research, or the amount of actual time individual household members spend in household work. (Walker and Woods 1976; Messiner 1975). Second, survey items on distribution of tasks, or who do what tasks (Pahl *et al* 1985; Ross 1987). Third, survey items on responsibility, who has responsibility for aspects of the household (Brannen and Moss 1991). Finally, resource allocation research, who controls household resources (Pahl, 1989, 1993).

Regardless of its theoretical or empirical pedigree, such research usually shows a scene where men undertake little, if any, domestic labour. Indeed, despite the different strands of the research, all suggest that very little has changed in terms of men's involvement (Glazer 1980; Berk 1985; Seymour 1992; South *et al* 1994). This is regardless of whether the partners of these men are employed or not (Walker and Woods 1976; Geerken and Gove 1983). This has lead to the suggestion that the marriage relationship was (and still is) fundamentally exploitative of wives and women (Oakley 1974; Blair 1992), as Blair writes

Virtually every study investigating the division of household labour has come to two basic conclusions: women perform approximately twice as much labour as men: and women perform qualitatively different types of chores than men.

(Blair et al 1992: 570)

Yet, while these findings may be true, very little work exists that explores the different levels of participation in household labour for certain 'groups' of men. Indeed very little is really known about men's experiences of the family, or how men balance home and work. Much of the work that has gone before, contains a gender bias in that it mainly focuses on women and the impact that men's limited housework participation has on such women. Men's roles within the home are ignored or at best, marginalised to accounts of 'how little housework men do', or have been of little empirical interest (Willinger, 1993; Dench, 1996). Where men are considered in such research they are often treated as a homogeneous group and considered using data collected primarily for studies of women and mothers (Blood and Wolfe, 1960; Miller and Swanson 1958; Oakley 1972).

This is not to suggest that women's participation in the home should go unquestioned. Indeed, it goes without refutation that women do carry much of the burden of domestic work and those women in paid public labour experience the conflict of duality. However, by only concentrating on women there is a systematic neglect of the home and work conflicts for men (Doucet 1991; Hearn 1987; Goodwin 1993). As Duncombe and Marsden (1992) suggest

...if we are fully to gauge the extent and thoroughness of change in men's behaviour, we must recognise the way that men's role performance is bound up with conceptions of masculinity...

(Duncombe and Marsden 1992: 20)

Traditionally, sociological analysis has provided a pessimistic view of the possibility for a change in the domestic division of labour and the conclusion is no different here. Men have increased their participation, but not sufficiently to offset women's participation in the labour market (Berk 1985; Pleck 1985; Brannen and Moss 1991; Seymour, 1992). For many the basic essence of masculinity is closely linked with public work, with men's power stemming from a breadwinner status (Berdo *et al* 1987; Hochschild and Machang 1989). However, it is important to note that although the breadwinner versus homemaker model remains culturally dominant in the UK and in much of the West, some allege that a new form of 'fatherhood' and male household participation is emerging and that certain men may participate more in household work (Bronstien *et al* 1988; Pleck 1985, 1987; Benjamin *et al* 1996). Such assertions have fuelled an explosion of research on fathering in the United States (see Bronstien and Cowen 1988; La Rossa 1988; Lewis and O'Brien 1987). In the new 'fatherhood' role, emphasis is placed on egalitarianism within the family, and it encourages expressiveness and a more caring role (Dennehy and Mortimer 1993; p88). Indeed, Segal (1990) argues that men have a wide range of 'masculinities' available as alternatives to the traditional oppressive masculinity. Studies also show that men can benefit greatly from more involvement in family life (Pleck 1976; Gove and Hughes 1980; Brod 1987; Weiss 1990).

All this research seems to herald the emergence of the 'new father'. However, alongside this there is some pessimism about the nature of such change (Daniels and Weingarten, 1982; Lewis 1986; Pleck 1985), whilst others doubt this change totally (La Rossa 1988).

> There has been a significant trend in the past decade for men to recognise the legitimacy of both women's employment and men's family work However, men remain reluctant to accept the kind of restructuring that would enable men and women to participate equally in both work and family roles.
>
> (Willinger 1993: 120)

To recap, what we do know is that men undertake less housework relative to women; that this has not changed due to men's (and societies) linkage of masculinity to work and economic provision; and that studies of housework have perhaps not explored men's household participation explicitly and that where men are considered, they are usually treated as a homogeneous group within such analysis.

It is now important that the 'actuality' of men's participation in household tasks is understood. To do this, two themes will guide the empirical research in the remainder of this chapter. First, there has been a wealth of data produced on who does what in the household, or the gender division of labour. The central tenet of some of the debate seems to centre on the fact that, despite an increase in women's, and a decrease in men's, labour market participation, men still do less work within the household than women. What has not been fully explored is the extent to which differing 'male roles' may lead to a re-negotiation of household tasks. Second, research must ask why (or why not) this is the case. As Duncombe and Marsden (1992) point out, sociological discussions have tended to focus on changes in the instrumental performance of household tasks. This is also a view that treats the household too economically (Duncombe and Marsden 1992; 82). The problem with this research is that if focuses on 'actual' participation rather than the factors that influence this participation. It is one thing to document the relative in-activity of men in the household, it is another to identify and examine the factors that influence men's household participation.

> In order to understand better the structure of gender role behaviour, we must investigate the factors influencing husband's participation (or lack of it) in domestic activities.
>
> (Coverman 1985: 81)

Rather than just documenting who does what, the focus will be trying to explain what influences who does what in the household division of labour. This will be done using Coverman's (1985) Hypothesis. This can be summarised as, first, the more resources (i.e. education, earnings and status in occupational position) a husband has, both in absolute terms and relative to his wife, the less domestic labour the man does. Second the more traditional the husband's sex role attitudes, the less domestic labour he does. Finally, the more time available the more likely the husband is to do housework.

These issues will be explored via an examination of the relative household division of labour for a group of men who work full-time and in a non-standard way, and compare this to women who work in either full-time occupations or in non-standard forms.

Understanding Men's Household Participation

Coverman identifies three broad sets of factors which may influence the household participation of men. These are resources, sex role attitudes, and available time, and all have had some coverage in academic debates.

Resources

The relative access to and control of resources have attracted considerable commentary within the household work debate. This work has two bases. The first suggests that the division of labour in the household is based largely on differential power relations within the home. The individual who holds 'most power' can minimise their participation in household work and that 'power' in the household stems from socio-economic status in society (Perrucci *et al* 1978; Blood and Woolf 1960). The second is based on micro-economic assumptions about the rational division of labour within the home. For example, those with most earning power in paid work devote their time to the market (Farkes 1976; Greeken and Gove 1983). However these analyses do not take the analysis further than a consideration of power issues or they make very simplistic assumptions about rational decision making. They do not explore the potential impact that resources can have in determining household participation.

The impact of resources such as education, earnings, status and occupational position have been explored individually elsewhere. For example, education has been used as a predictor of participation in household work. Research also suggests that men's education will affect the extent to which men become involved in child care and housework. For example, Bonney *et al* (1994) taking data from the Sino-Japanese Survey of Working Women's lives, argued that the husbands of graduates were more likely to be involved in domestic work. Farkas (1976) goes further linking ideology with education and suggests that more educated men are less likely to hold traditional sex-role ideas and are more likely to see housework as a burden to their wives.

Occupation has also been used as an indicator of household participation. Glover (1994) suggests that women's home/employment relationships vary between and within white collar occupations and teaching. Greeken and Grove (1983) suggest a more curvilinear relationship with middle income men having higher levels of household participation.

Sex-Role Ideology

The second influencing factor that Coverman suggests is traditional sex-role ideology arguing that there is some evidence to suggest that men who adhere to traditional sex-role ideology perform fewer household chores than those with non-traditional ideas. The development of such traditional sex-role ideology is usually assumed to be consequence of early, intensive socialisation by parents, teachers and society about 'appropriate behaviour' and the notion that sex-role ideology and socialisation effects sex-role behaviour is now a well established theme (Coverman, 1985 ; Lennon *et al* 1994; DeMarris *et al* 1996).

The impact of role ideology on housework participation has also been developed further. For example, Fassinger (1993) argues that the problem with men's participation is how domestic work itself is perceived by men. Using interviews Fassinger argues that some tasks were invisible to men as when they were married their wives did them. DeMarris *et al* (1996) builds on this theme and also suggest that household participation is linked to gender role identification. They suggest that the less an individual ascribes to traditional role ideology, the more likely they are to perceive housework as being a burden to their partners.

Time Demands

The final theme in Coverman's thesis is the time demands on men and that one explanation of men's poor household participation is that they do not have available time (Coverman, 1985; Perrucci *et al* 1978; Presser 1994).

> ...women worked roughly 15 hours longer each week than men. Over a year they worked an extra month...Over a dozen years, it was an extra year of twenty four hour days.

> (Hochschild 1989: 4)

However, as Pleck (1985) notes, men face structural barriers, such as inflexible and demanding work schedules that made it difficult to meet family obligations. The lack of attention to the impact of men's paid work time on their household labour time may reflect the fact that there is *less* variability in men's paid labour than women's (Shelton and Johnson 1993). Indeed existing research finds that men's time spent in paid work is negatively associated with household work (Rexroat and Shehan 1987), whilst others find no association (Kingston and Nock, 1985). Coverman (1985) also found that variables relating to time were the *most* powerful predictors of husbands hours of housework.

> ...even if a man works part-time, he probably will not spend much time in domestic work if there is little demand placed on him to do so (for his spouse, other family members, or hired individuals can do the work)...

> (Coverman 1985: 84)

Again, research exists that has tried to explore the available time Hypothesis and men. For example, Pleck (1985), argues that there has been some change in the husbands time spent on household labour. His research shows husbands of employed wives spend 1.8 more hours per week in housework and 2.7 more hours on child care compared to husbands of full-time homemakers. However, South *et al* (1994), drawing data for the National Survey of Families, in the USA, found that in all family situations women spent more time than men doing housework. The 'gender gap' in participation was widest amongst married couples, with men who were

159

divorced or separated doing substantially more housework than men in other household forms. One other finding from the research related to the impact of children on the division of domestic labour.

Goldscheider and Waite (1991) demonstrated that husbands do more housework in response to the relative number of hours worked by their wives. Berk and Berk (1979) found that husbands in dual-earner households participated in more housework in the evenings than any other times of the day. Being at home while wives are at paid work may reduce the pressures on husbands to be involved as wives are not there to tell them.

Husbands also perform less household labour when spouses have different employment schedules. Presser (1994) hypothesised that the presence of men at home whilst their partners were at work increases participation of husbands, and decreases women's participation, in household tasks. Presser found that the more hours the husband is not employed, the more likely he is to do housework that is traditionally done by females. One can also suggest that the extent of a husband's participation will depend on whether he or his partner work non-standard hours.

In exploring male full-time workers and male part-time workers, one other possible hypothesis exists. Namely, that men who work in non-standard forms have different home lives than those men who comply with the traditional roles. This group of men actually spend more time in the household, and as a consequence, are more likely to participate in domestic labour. This assertion falls loosely in with the assumption that men's participation in domestic labour will increase as men's actual labour market participation decreases, and women's increases.

Data, Definitions and Issues

Coverman's model provides an adequate framework around which to build an analysis of men's household participation using the National Child Development Study Sweep 5 (NCDS5). Coverman's analysis uses the explanatory variables of resources, sex role attitudes, and available time and these are operationalised using NCDS5 as follows.

Resources

In Coverman's analysis the resources variables cover education, earnings, occupation and status, all of which are covered in NCDS5 to a greater or lesser extent. For example, the NCDS data set contains a wealth of information about the educational experiences of the cohort members and the qualifications that they obtained. To make these meaningful for this aspect of the research, the National Vocational Qualification (NVQ) coding system devised by Bynner and Fogelman (1993) is replicated. The value of this coding is that it ranks vocational as well as traditional academic qualifications into comparable levels. The data on highest qualifications can also be sub-divided and re-defined into advanced (NVQ 4 and 5) and basic education (NVQs 1-3). These variables then provide the basis to explore the effect of qualification, particularly the effect of highest qualifications, on household participation. However, unlike Coverman (1985), the data here can only be used to provide an absolute measure of the level of education achieved by the male sample, as educational data for the respondents partners was not collected. Thus a relative education variable cannot be derived.

Earnings are also extensively covered in the data. Respondents and their partners provided information as to their total earnings for their respective jobs, including overtime, bonuses and any commission, both before and after tax. Here, the after tax variable is used as this represents take home pay, and has some implications for the influence of pay in that this represents 'real' earning power. The data was then divided by the length of time for which the respondent indicated that the amount specified was for a week, fortnight and so on. From this data a relative income variable can also be operationalised by calculating whether the respondent earns less than, the same as, or more than their partner. The hypothesis being that those men who earn similar amounts or more than their partners will participate less.

For occupation and status NCDS5 contains absolute measures of occupation in terms of a three digit code based on the Standard Occupational Classification, for current job, for both the man and his partner. However, three digits provide too much information for the purposes of this chapter, so the codes were aggregated up to their two digit equivalent.

Sex-Role Ideology

The research instrument 'What Do You Think' in the NCDS survey provides a rich and valuable source of data on family life. These attitudinal statements are used as a measure of traditional (or otherwise) sex-role ideology. An overall 'Traditional Views' variable was constructed from these attitude statements. Where males did not exhibit traditional views they were given a score of 0, where they did they scored 1.

The data set also included the a number of issues on which the respondent had to indicate whether or not they disagreed with their partner. On household issues, these included issues included 'Handling family finances' and 'Sharing household tasks'. These were then combined to produce a derived variable 'Disagrees about Household Matters'. If there was more disagreement one could assume that the household would adopt a different domestic labour pattern to where there was no disagreement about household tasks.

Available Time

The actual time spent on household tasks, or the amount of time individuals have available for tasks was not measured in NCDS5. However it is possible to derive a proxy variable for this by using the 'hours worked each week' variable. The assumption here would be that the fewer labour market hours worked by the respondent the more likely they would be to participate in household tasks.

Other Explanatory Variables

Coverman's analysis in this instance is supplemented with a number of other variables readily available in NCDS that may have some explanatory effect on men's household participation. The extra variables are fathers social class, political views, autonomy at work, partners employment status and the presence of children under the age of 14. The further explanatory power that these variables may offer adds further depth to the discussion. For example, NCDS5 contains two measures of power and autonomy within the particular occupation and job which took the form of attitudinal statements, 'I am able to vary the pace at which I work' and 'I can only take breaks at certain times'. Although these are quite crude measures, they were combined and assigned a value of either 0 or 1. The higher the value the more control the respondent reports they have over their work. Control over work may or may not be transferred into the household.

Household Participation

Coverman (1985), used a measure of the time spent engaged in housework or child care as the dependant variable. One problem with the NCDS5 data set was that no such comparable data existed, and it was not possible to derive a suitable alternative for the purposes of this discussion. However, NCDS5 contained a series of statements which asked who did what household chore *most of the time*. The chores were, 'Preparing and Cooking the Main Meal'; 'Doing the Shopping'; 'Cleaning the Home'; 'Laundry and Ironing'; 'Household Repairs, DIY and Decorating'; 'Looking after Household Money and Paying Bills'; 'Looking after Children when they are Ill'; 'Teaching Children Good Behaviour'; 'Generally Being with and Looking after Children'. These statements were examined and explored in relation to the explanatory variables.

162

This chapter uses two main methods to analyse the data. First to begin the analysis it seems pertinent to provide a brief descriptive overview of some of the data, thus allowing us to examine any basic relationships that may exist between the explanatory variables and the housework dependent variables. Such bivariate analysis is really a base line analysis. Second, to isolate the effect of particular explanatory variables on household participation a multivariate model is required as this allows the estimation of the probability of male worker with particular characteristics participating in household tasks. In both instances the participation of male non-standard workers and male full-time workers will be the focus of enquiry.

Results

Participation in Household Tasks

The data for this part of the discussion is contained within tables 8.3 to 8.6. Within this research, a baseline picture of men's household participation can be provided and as Ferri (1993) suggests, there is a remarkable degree of correspondence in their reports of who was responsible for domestic labour 'most of the time' and gender. The routine household chores fall to women, with men only taking the lead in DIY. From the current analysis it can be seen that 7.7 per cent of male non-standard workers and 6.8 per cent of male full-time workers report that they take responsibility for cooking the main meal. Seventy eight per cent and 72.5 per cent respectively suggest that their partner does it.

For women, either non-standard or full-time workers, around 60 per cent take responsibility for cooking the main meal. Interestingly 25.5 per cent of women non-standard workers report that their partner does it, compared to only 12.2 per cent of women working full-time. This is interesting in that men seem to be willing to help a women when she is working in a non-standard way more so that if she was working full-time.

Eight per cent of male non-standard workers and 7.0 per cent of male full-time workers do the shopping most of the time, with 64.7 per cent and 54.6 per cent respectively leaving it to their partners.

Fifty two per cent of female non-standard workers and 49.1 per cent of female full-time workers take responsibility for the shopping. As with cooking, women in non-standard jobs can expect more help from their partners than can their full-time counterparts. Five per cent of male non-standard workers, compared to 65 per cent of their female counterparts did the ironing. However the data suggests that male non-standard workers, and male full-time workers have low levels of participation in household

163

cleaning compared to their partners. The reverse was true for women regardless of their status.

Household repairs represents a change in the gender allocation of tasks. Men, whether non-standard workers, or full-time workers take the lead in DIY (68.9 and 70.9 per cent respectively). The partners of male non-standard workers are nearly twice as likely to be involved in household repairs that the partners of male full-time workers.

The pattern of household money management is less clear cut. However, on a whole women do tend to take responsibility for it most of the time (42.6 per cent female non-standard workers, and 44 per cent female full-time workers). The partners of male non-standard workers and full-time workers also seem to take responsibility for this matter. However, in all instances, around 30 per cent of men in the sample do take some responsibility for money management. They are therefore more likely to be involved in this than any other household task.

Such descriptive data suggests that 'actual' participation in household tasks demonstrates it is still the responsibility of women and that this differs very little from previous research (see Glazer 1980; Berk 1985; Seymour 1992; South *et al* 1994) . However, this can be compared with the fact that 58.3 per cent of male non-standard workers and 65.7 per cent of male full-time workers agreed with the statement that men and women should do the same jobs around the house. Although there is obvious support from men for an equality in the household sexual division of labour, it does not materialise in practice in relation to women, but may imply some variations between men.

Factors Influencing Household Participation - Regression Results

The second part of the analysis involves the development of a multivariate model. In this instance the advantage of a multivariate model over a bivariate model is that it allows focus to shift away from the actual percentage figures of who does what, to one where it is possible to estimate the probability of certain male workers with particular characteristics participating in household tasks (Felstead 1995). Two multivariate regression analyses using ordinary least squares (OLS) estimations were conducted using the responsibility for housework and a number of socio-demographic variables. The aim was to explore what factors determine i) the actual number of household tasks a male participates in and ii) to explore what factors determine low male household participation where the partner takes main household responsibility. The regressions were carried out for three groups. First, the whole male worker sample, second male full-time workers and finally the sample of 982 male non-standard workers.

164

Table 8.1 presents the regression co-efficients for the variables used in the regression model exploring the determinants of male household participation based on number of household tasks undertaken. This model should allow the exploration of which socio-demographic variables are likely to affect the number of household tasks participated in by men.

Table 8.1
Regression Co-efficients for Variables in Analysis of Determinants of Male Household Participation: Number of Household Tasks Done- NCDS5 1991

Variable	All Men	Full-Time	Non-Standard Worker
Employment Characteristics			
Income	-0.023**	-0.006*	-0.045
SOC	-0.010**	-0.130*	0.010*
1-20 Hours Work	0.674*	-0.303*	0.797*
21+ Hours Work	0.101	-0.026	0.330
Non-Standard Worker	0.168*	-	-
Autonomy at Work	0.024	-0.440	-0.823
Ideology			
Traditional Views	0.050	-0.210*	-0.087**
Disagreement about			
Household Task	0.828*	-0.284	-0.379
Politically Conservative	-0.024	-0.126*	-0.034*
Fathers Social Class	-0.018	-0.006*	-0.067*
Personal Characteristics			
Basic Education	0.024	-0.811*	-0.011*
Advanced Education	0.028	0.039*	0.192
Partner Employed	0.046	-0.124	0.114*
Partner Week Pay	0.046*	0.021	0.045
Partner SOC	-0.002	-0.002*	-0.023
Child Under 14	0.177*	-0.056	-0.124**
R-sq=	19.0%	8.0%	24.0%
N=	5091	4109	982

*p=.01   **p=.05; Based on the analysis of Coverman (1985) 'Explaining Husbands' Participation in Household Tasks' The Sociological Quarterly, Vol.26, No. 1 pages 81-97.
Source: Own calculations from NCDS5 1991 data supplied by ESRC Data Archive.

A number of variables included in the model were significant, but when the model is examined in totality the variables explain very little of the

165

variation in the actual number of household tasks undertaken by men. The model for the total male worker sample only explains 19 per cent of the variation experienced in the male research samples. The explanatory power of this regression model is reduced still further for the other male worker samples. However, despite the fact that the model is not that good in determining which men do most household tasks, there are number of dependant variables which exert some influence.

The results of the multivariate regression suggests that variables such as income, standard occupational classification and having at least one child under the age of fourteen have a significant effect on the number of household tasks participated in by men. Each of the significant explanatory variables will be explored in turn.

For the whole male sample, income appeared to have a negative effect on the number of household tasks participated in. Likewise standard occupational classification (SOC) also had a negative effect for the whole sample and male full-time workers. The exception to this was that for male non-standard workers, household participation increased significantly along with SOC.

In the regression model two variables were used to explore the impact of men's labour market working time. The first variable indicated that the men worked between one and twenty hours per week in the labour market. For the whole male worker sample and for those male non-standard workers, working 20 or fewer hours in the labour market had a significantly positive impact on the number of household tasks undertaken. This suggests that the fewer labour market hours a man does, the more likely he is to participate in household tasks and take responsibility for them. This is also supported by the non-standard worker variable which suggests being a non-standard worker increases the likelihood of housework participation.

A number of male full-time workers also indicated that they worked for twenty or less hours per week and this seemed to have a negative effect on the number of household tasks they undertook. The variable for men working more that 21 hours per week appeared to exhibit no significant effect for any group.

In exploring the impact of ideological factors on the number of household tasks undertaken, one can see that three out of the four variables appeared to have a significantly negative effect. If the male full-time workers and the male non-standard workers held traditional views about housework, were politically conservative and had a father who was working class, it was likely that the household participation of these men would be reduced. Interestingly, however, the more the whole male sample disagreed with their partners about housework, the more these men did.

The remaining set of explanatory variables, labelled personal characteristics, also appeared to have some impact on the number of household tasks participated in. For example, for both male full-time workers and male non-standard workers, only having a basic education (equivalent to NVQ level 1-3), had a negative impact on the number of household task participated in. Conversely, for male full-time workers, having a higher education had a positive impact on participation.

Table 8.2
Regression Co-efficients for Variables in Determining Low Male Household Participation Where Partner Takes Main Household Responsibility- NCDS5 1991

Variable	All Men	Full-Time	Non-Standard Worker
Employment Characteristics			
Income	0.113*	0.008*	-0.031*
SOC	-0.027**	-0.013	0.017
1-20 Hours Work	0.895**	-0.161*	-0.070
21+ Hours Work	-0.452*	-0.356**	-0.109*
Non-Standard Worker	-0.018	-	-
Autonomy at Work	0.053	-0.207	-0.255**
Ideology			
Traditional Views	0.709	0.034	0.051*
Disagreement about			
Household Tasks	0.279*	-0.119	-0.160
Politically Conservative	-0.107	-0.037	-0.173*
Fathers Social Class	0.073	-0.003*	-0.461*
Personal Characteristics			
Basic Education	0.050**	-0.644*	0.149*
Advanced Education	-0.246**	0.060	0.263
Partner Employed	-0.130	-0.081	0.126*
Partner Week Pay	-0.136*	0.013	-0.007*
Partner SOC	0.037*	-0.004*	-0.008*
Child Under 14	1.643*	0.023*	-0.201
R-sq=	53.2%	20.6%	26.0%
N=	5091	4109	982

*p=.01   **p=.05; Based on the analysis of Coverman (1985) 'Explaining Husbands' Participation in Household Tasks' The Sociological Quarterly, Vol.26, No. 1 pp 81-97.
Source: Own calculations from NCDS5 1991 data supplied by ESRC Data Archive.

The impact of the partner's working life were also explored. For male non-standard workers, having an employed partner increased their household participation, and for the whole sample partner's pay had a similar effect. For male full-time workers, a partner's SOC had a negative impact.

Having at least one child under the age of 14 increased the number of tasks participated in for the whole male sample, but significantly reduced it for the male non-standard worker group.

Table 8.2 presents the regression co-efficients for the variables in determining low male household participation where the partner takes main household responsibility. Here a number of variables can be seen to have a significant impact in determining low participation. For example, variables such as disagreement about household tasks, and the presence of a child under the age of 14 seems to exert an influence on the men's partners having to shoulder the burden of domestic work. Other variables in this regression model also support this, such as only having a basic education, partners income, men working more than 21 hours per week in the labour market, income and partner's occupation. When taken together for the whole male sample, these variables explain 53 per cent of the variation in the low levels of male housework participation.

Concluding Remarks

This discussion started by suggesting that, whilst it is agreed that women still take the biggest responsibility for household work, men's participation has not been fully explored. Where it has been examined men are usually treated as a homogeneous group, with their experiences not being explored *per se*. The argument was that men's participation in housework need to be explored in order to examine the possible home and work conflicts experienced by men. It was also suggested that men should not be treated as homogeneous as certain men may experience this conflict in different ways. To explore this, the data from the National child Development Study could be used to provide a descriptive account of men's participation and to develop a regression model. The regression model was based on Coverman's (1985) hypothesis.

The descriptive analysis confirms earlier discussions that, despite an increase in men's participation, women seem still largely responsible for household work (Oakley 1989; Hochschild 1989; Morris 1990 1993, Brannen and Moss 1991, Doucet 1991). The exception to this, as one would expect was household repairs. The data presented in Table 8.3 also goes some way in supporting the view that women's employment does lead to men's 'improved' participation in household tasks, as suggested by other research (see Hoffman and Nye 1974; Huber and Spitze, 1983; Ross 1987; Brannen and Moss, 1991). However in this instance men tend to be involved more in those tasks that are pleasurable and many see it as an option rather than a definite commitment such as cooking.

The descriptive analysis also suggests that, in line with Ferri's (1993) analysis of the same data, men in this research expressed largely supportive views about equality in the household. However, highlighted here (unlike Ferri) is the fact that such support does vary between particular groups of men and that not all men support these views to the same degree. This is also supported in the exploration of Coverman's hypothesis.

Coverman's hypothesis had three main facets all of which find some support in the data presented here. First, that the more resources (such as education, earnings and status in occupational position) a male has the less domestic labour he does. For example, the results suggests that those male full-time workers and that male non-standard workers with an advanced education did fewer household tasks. The results for men's earnings and standard occupational classification also correspond with Coverman's Hypothesis and the higher the income or SOC, the fewer households tasks men participate in.

Coverman's second hypothesis is that the more traditional the man's sex role attitudes, the less domestic labour he does. This aspect of Coverman's hypothesis also attracts a great deal of support from the data presented here, and those men who had traditional views about housework and are perhaps politically conservative are less likely to participate in household tasks.

Finally, Coverman suggests that the more time available the more likely the male will do housework. This is also supported with the data presented here. The data shows a clear relationship between lower levels of market work and participation in household tasks. Further to this, an addition to this aspect of Coverman's position was that male non-standard workers would be more likely to participate in housework as they would have more available time. The data suggests that this may in fact be the case.

Such results lead to three broad conclusions. First, authors such as Pleck (1985) assert that due to the importance of the occupational role for men, a reduction of a man's workload would not increase men's participation. Contrary to this, the data here suggests that different groups of men with different working arrangement do have different participation rates. The results presented here do not really question the fact that women's participation is still overarching. However what the results begin to question is treatment of men as a homogeneous group and that variation in participation is evidenced between different male working groups.

Second, that in explaining men's differing rates of participation in domestic labour Coverman's hypothesis may actual be a useful predictor. It may seem obvious to state that a man's household participation may be determined by his available time, yet this often appears to attract very little commentary.

Third, along with authors such as Willinger (1993) one could argue that change is taking place both in men's attitudes towards household equality. However, the structure and culture of men's work roles and women's family roles have yet to undergo the changes necessary for complete gender equality to occur (Willinger). One step towards this may be the increasing flexibility in men's work, freeing time for men to participate in household work. A further step, must also be an acknowledgement amongst researchers and commentators, that not all men react in the same way to household participation. Research which suggests men do so, must be limited.

Table 8.3
All Research Samples, in Your Family, who Does Each of These Things Most of the Time ? - NCDS5 1991

		Men	Women	All F/T Men	All F/T Women
Cooking:	I do	7	60	6	59
	Partner	78	25	72	12
Shopping:	I do	8	52	7	92
	Partner	64	22	54	8
Cleaning:	I do	4	59	2	56
	Partner	76	22	71	4
Laundry:	I do	5	65	2	71
	Partner	85	25	83	3.4
Repairs:	I do	69	24	70	5
	Partner	6	48	2	62
Managing Money	I do	33	42	34	44
	Partner	38	29	36	22
Care Sick Child	I do	3	47	0.5	28
	Partner	53	16	49	1.9
Gen. Child Care	I do	3	34	1	16
	Partner	42	12	36	2
Teaching child:	I do	3	12	3	7
behaviour	Partner	10	4	8	2
N		744	2449	3151	1242

Source: Own calculations from NCDS5 1991 data supplied by ESRC Data Archive.

Table 8.4
Attitudes to Allocation of Household Tasks- NCDS5 1991

	Percentage of Response*					
	Strongly Agree	Agree	Uncertain	Disagree	Strongly Disagree	N
'Men And Women Should Do The Same Jobs Around The House'						
Men	9.7	48.6	11.3	27.7	2.7	905
Women	17.6	50.5	8.7	22.1	1.1	2780
F/TMen	13.3	52.4	10.1	23.0	1.3	3891
F/T Women	28.3	52.0	6.0	13.3	0.6	1782
'When Both Partners Work Full-Time, The Man Should Take An Equal Share Of Domestic Chores'						
Men	22.1	65.7	6.4	5.1	0.8	982
Women	37.0	56.1	3.4	3.0	0.4	2784
F/TMen	30.5	61.9	4.3	3.1	0.3	3878
F/T Women	47.9	47.6	1.3	3.1	0.1	1785
'Being A Housewife Is Just As Fulfilling As Working For Pay'						
Men	6.8	33.0	36.9	20.0	3.3	888
Women	9.0	36.9	21.2	27.5	5.3	2755
F/TMen	5.9	28.1	40.4	22.3	3.3	3818
F/T Women	6.9	29.3	28.4	28.9	6.5	1772
'If A Child Is Ill And Both Parents Are Working It Should Usually Be The Mother Who Takes Time Off To Look After The Child'						
Men	8.4	35.8	17.4	30.9	7.5	982
Women	7.8	37.6	11.9	35.3	7.4	2779
F/TMen	4.2	28.0	16.8	40.6	10.5	3891
F/T Women	3.9	24.7	9.6	47.0	14.8	1780
'It Is Less Important For A Woman To Go Out To Work Than It Is For A Man'						
Men	4.8	28.2	15.2	43.5	8.4	904
Women	2.8	23.6	11.5	49.7	12.3	2774
F/TMen	2.1	21.2	15.8	50.2	10.7	3865
F/T Women	1.6	9.8	7.9	55.5	25.5	1778

* Percentages may not total 100% due to Missing Cases Source: Own calculations from NCDS5 1991 data supplied by ESRC Data Archive.

Table 8.5
Percentage of How Much Partners Agree or Disagree About Sharing Household Tasks- NCDS5 1991

	Always Agree	Often Agree	Both	Often Disagree	Always Disagree	N
Men	18.3	35.8	31.1	10.9	1.8	758
Women	21.7	31.9	31.4	10.5	2.6	2459
F/TMen	23.7	35.8	30.0	8.4	1.5	3179
F/T Women	31.9	31.3	24.3	8.9	2.3	1278

Source: Own calculations from NCDS5 1991 data supplied by ESRC Data Archive.

Table 8.6
Current Status of Partner by Status of Sample - NCDS5 1991

	Percentage Of Men and Women			
	Men	Women	All F/T Men	All F/TWomen
Full-Time Employee	24.1	59.0	32.2	79.7
Part-Time Employee	25.6	8.4	30.2	1.4
Full-Time Self-Employed	6.9	16.4	1.8	12.5
Part-Time Self-Employed	4.6	1.7	2.0	0.4
Unemployed	1.1	2.4	0.7	3.3
Other	37.5	12.2	33.0	14.5
N	796	2544	3346	1298

Source: Own calculations from NCDS5 1991 data supplied by ESRC Data Archive.

9   Psychological Health and Men's Work

Introduction

The final empirical chapter explores the possible impact of men's work on their mental ill-health experiences. The chapter begins with an introduction to the issues and the identification of four existing research hypotheses. These hypotheses are explored both in terms of the data and the literature. A multivariate model and a cluster analysis technique are used to explore any possible links between men's work and mental ill-health.

> You don't suffer real physical hardship on two quid a week, and if you did it wouldn't matter. It is in the brain and the soul that lack of money damages. Mental deadness, spiritual squalor - they seem to descend upon you inescapably when your income drops...
>
> (George Orwell 1936)

Orwell's contributions to social science were based mainly on his own experiences of unemployment, hardship and poverty. Although, one cannot agree with the statement in its entirety, one can find an identifiable theme in current academic literature.

> in addition to the material hardship there is al loss of self-esteem through ceasing to be a breadwinner and through becoming the recipient of unemployment benefit. Financial strain is likely to be greater when there are dependant children to feed, clothe and educate and financial problems are a major source of emotional distress.
>
> (Warr 1984 in Gross 1992: 711)

The linkage of psychological ill health to employment characteristics is now well established, and a number of differing research themes can be identified. For example, the psychological difficulties caused by loss of employment (Burchell 1990; Willot and Griffin 1996); the fear of losing one's job (Kasel and Cobb 1982); job insecurity (James 1984; Knox 1985; Jacobson 1987; Burchell 1990); gender differences and mental health experiences (Wladron 1995); coping with job-related stress (Norman *et al* 1995); low income and depravation (Frese 1985); psychological difficulties and older workers (Mitchell *et al* 1989); role overload (Glass *et al* 1994); psychological difficulties and working conditions (Lowe *et al* 1989); psychological difficulties, unemployment and suicide (Wasserman 1984; Canetto 1995); unemployment and identity (Willot *et al* 1996); lack of control over one's working life (Greehalagh and Rosenblatt, 1984); and finally the impact of such anxieties on employment (Pinder 1995; Yelin *et al* 1996). The importance of such work is noted.

> Over the past century, the health of the population as a whole has improved. However, inequalities in longevity and health between different social groups within the population still exist on a substantial scale and are subject of widespread concern and debate. Relationships between work and health are likely to be complex and reciprocal, and also embedded in broader processes of social stratification and the gender division of labour.
>
> (Joshi and Macran 1991:451)

However, given the importance of such work, only a few authors seem to suggest that men can now be identified as a vulnerable group in terms of mental ill health and even suicide (Robins 1977; Beskow 1979; Wasserman 1984; Kposowa 1995; Canetto 1995) and that work may be the cause (Burchell 1990). However, using the previous discussion, it may be possible to further identify this linkage between work and men's mental ill-health and suggest an explanation for such a link. For example, throughout this book it is has been argued that there has been a change in the nature of work and, therefore there has been a change in masculinity for some men. Yet socially, perceptions of masculinity have not changed and are still linked to work. Indeed, notions of masculinity are closely linked with work, the ability to work and the provision of income (see Social Attitudes 1997). Traditional notions of masculinity suggest that men will work full-time and permanently throughout their lives. However, during the last decade there has been a shift towards 'flexibility' and a low pay and low skilled economy making it more difficult for men to find full-time permanent jobs.

Within the changing nature of work, one could argue, there is a possible explanation of work related psychological ill health for men. The yardstick against which masculinity in Britain is traditionally measured - work - has changed, but perceptions of masculinity have not. Men are still expected to work full-time throughout their lives although the possibilities of doing so have greatly diminished. For men's self-identity this fact alone could have a catastrophic impact. Such a view is supported by Simon (1995) who suggests that men still perceive that the ability to provide economically is an essential part of the male role. Eighty per cent of the men in Simon's (1995) study supported the view that negative consequences would result for a man's self-image if they could not provide economically. Simon argues that when men experience such role conflict they are more likely to suffer from mental ill-health. It is also important to note that this issue is not only confined to the industrialised nations of the West, as Lai (1995) acknowledges :

The urban Chinese are show to be able to exhibit psychological distress...Work and family stressors are related to psychological well-being among the Chinese. Due to the centrality of work roles for the Chinese, work stressors have stronger consequences...To conclude, as China is undergoing rapid social and economic transformations, changes might also be expected in work and family roles for men...Future research needs to focus on how these changes in the work and family spheres affect the status of Chinese mental health.

(Lai 1995: 30-31)

Returning to the present study, the effects of mental-illness, emotional and behavioural problems, and social maladjustment have also been a historic concern of the National Child Development Study. In the report of the first follow up, NCDS1 in 1965, when the respondents were 7 years of age, a whole section is devoted to behaviour and adjustment. At this age 136 out of the 14,528 sample had attended a child guidance centre. Interestingly, twice as many boys as girls attended the session (Davie 1972).

The aim of this chapter is to link this historic concern with the current labour market experiences of men in NCDS5, and explore men's mental health in relation to work and work-related issues. In order to structure such a project, existing research can be used to develop four main hypotheses for exploration with the male research groups.

Hypothesis One - Men who work in non-standard forms have more problems with mental health, than their full-time counterparts as a mere consequence of their employment status. For example, Burchell (1990) reveals that employees, where their labour market position is disadvantaged, also have as poor psychological health as the unemployed. Burchell suggests that existing analyses are limited as they only account for the psychological ill health caused by unemployment and not job insecurity (for example see Fryer and Payne 1983) .

Analysis...reveals that those employees in the most disadvantaged labour market segment...have psychological health as poor as the unemployed. Furthermore, for unemployed males, re-employment is only accompanied by an improvement in psychological health if the new job is felt to be secure. It is concluded that insecurity can be more of a threat to psychological health if the new job is felt to be secure.

(Burchell 1990: 2)

175

If the suggestion of Burchell is correct, the general shift towards flexibility and insecure employment will have drastic consequences for the psychological health of many workers. It is possible to take the model developed by Burchell and apply it specifically to a comparison of full-time male workers and male non-standard workers.

It is possible to develop a two by two contingency table, taking Burchell's model further and applies it to a comparison of male full-time and male non-standard working. The assumption here is that both male full-time working and male non-standard working will have one of two effects (beneficial or harmful) on psychological health and that individual males will appear in two of the four categories. As such, the possibilities are 'full-time work and good psychological health'; 'full-time work and poor psychological health'; 'non-standard work and good psychological health'; and finally 'non-standard work and poor psychological health'. One can the compare the cells to examine if there is any general pattern of men with a particular working pattern experiencing more or less harmful psychological ill health.

Hypothesis Two - If a male has experienced previous spells of unemployment, this may increase job insecurity and therefore increase the risk of psychological ill health.

> research has consistently pointed to the particularly negative impact of unemployment on the affective well-being of middle-aged men, especially those with families in need of financial support.
>
> (Warr 1987: 226)

The linkage of unemployment and psychological ill-health has featured very strongly in the literature. For example, Raphel (1984) distinguishes between sudden, unanticipated loss of work and retirement. She suggests that the loss of work is very similar to other forms of loss. The initial response is shock and disbelief. If similar work is available, this feeling will be transitory. Despite this Raphel (1984) suggests that some sense of loss will remain, and where no alternative job can be found the feeling of loss will be intense. However, one aspect that is largely ignored is the long-term affects that spells of unemployment may have in the long-term vis-à-vis the work and mental health of the individual. Does experiencing unemployment make an individual more susceptible to psychological problems in subsequent jobs?

Hypothesis Three - The third hypothesis worthy of exploration is the suggestion that lower levels of control and skill use, lead to increased mental ill-health problems. As Warr (1987) suggests restrictions on skill use may be of two kinds. First are those which prevent people from using skills which they already possess...second are restrictions on the acquisition of new skills, requiring people to remain at low levels of skilled performance.

(Warr 1987: 4)

In Warr's (1987) research nine environmental features linking work, unemployment and mental health are identified. Of interest here are the first two, 'Opportunity for Control' and 'Opportunity for Skill Use'.

The first determinant of mental health is assumed to lie in the opportunities provided by the environment for a person to control activities and events.

(Warr 1987: 3)

According to Warr mental health is enhanced in situations where an individual has control over events, and reduced in situations to the contrary. There are two factors to control that Warr identifies, (i) the ability to decide and act in one's chosen way; (ii) the ability to predict the consequences of action. Warr is not alone in suggesting such a relationship. Johansson *et al* (1996) in exploring the stresses experienced by informal caregivers, suggests that stress will increase and the less life control an individual has. Ross and Wu (1995) also suggest that an individual with a high level of education is more likely to have control over their life and will also experience greater life fulfilment.

The second element that Warr identifies is skill use. He suggests that it is expected that those workers with greater opportunity for skill use will tend to be mentally more healthy than those in jobs with limited skill use opportunities.

Hypothesis Four - The fourth and final hypothesis is that when differing work patterns are combined with traditional ideological notions of being the breadwinner there is likely to be an increased incidence of emotional problems. Several studies have explored this and highlighted how men's employment orientations lead to difficulties when they become unemployed, as it can lead to involuntary home centredness (Russell 1983 1987; McKee and Bell 1986; Wheelock 1990). Men (and women) think that their authority, or a fundamental aspect of their masculinity is affected by periods of unemployment (McKee and Bell 1986).

Given that men have a strong link to bread winning, it is difficult for men to adjust to their new roles as homemakers or fathers when society views these as being non-traditional. High paternal participation is unlikely to occur unless their is strong societal support for the role (Doucet 1991).

Data and Definitions

As noted above the literature identifies many factors which can affect the mental health of individuals. In this section the operationalisation of these factors will be identified within NCDS5.

Table 9.1   Emotional Problem Indicators

- Feeling low, depressed, sad ?
- Feeling generally anxious, jittery ?
- Feeling anxious or scared about objects or situations ?
- Feeling overexcited, overconfident ?
- Feeling compelled to repeat actions or thoughts ?
- Hearing or seeing things ?
- Problems with drink or drugs ?
- Other feelings of worry, tension, anxiety, depression or nerves.
- Do you feel tired most of the time ?
- Do you often feel miserable or depressed ?
- Do you often have bad headaches ?
- Do you often worry about things ?
- Do you usually have difficulty in falling or staying asleep ?
- Do you usually wake unnecessarily early in the morning ?
- Do you often get into a violent rage ?
- Do people often annoy or irritate you ?
- Do you suddenly become scared for no good reason ?
- Are you scared to be alone when friends not near you ?
- Are you easily upset or irritated ?
- Are you frightened of going out alone or meeting people ?
- Does every little thing get on your nerves and wear you out ?
- Have you ever had a nervous breakdown ?

Source: NCDS5.

The NCDS5 Cohort member interview contained quite a lengthy section relating to the health of the respondent between the last sweep in 1981 and the current research. Every aspect of health was addressed, ranging from general health questions such as the incidence of smoking, back trouble, asthma, exercise, accidents and assaults, hospital admissions and GP consultations. Aspects relating to mental health can be found in two areas. First a section on 'emotional problems' collected such data. The questions here ranged from numbers of emotional problem incidents since 1981, to numbers of admissions and data relating to consultation of GP and/or Specialist provided eight indicators of mental health.

Data on age when the problem started and the extent of the problem at the time of the research were also collected. The main questions in this section are outlined in Table 9.1

This section also asked if and how many times they had suffered such problems since 1981, how many hospital consultations they had and so on. From this it was possible to construct a variable 'Number of Malaise Events', One Malaise Event, Two to Four Events, Five+ Malaise Events.

Second, a section on 'supplementary health questions' contained fourteen indicators of mental ill-health or more general symptoms associated will emotional distress. These are outlined in Figure 9.1 This data provide a very detailed history of the individuals mental state during the ten years between the NCDS sweeps.

From this data it was possible to ascertain the nature of the problem, the average age when the particular emotional problems began and the extent to which these emotional problems still effect the lives of those individuals concerned.

As suggested elsewhere in this research it is possible to derive the other required variables from those variables which already exist within the data set (such as previous spells of unemployment). Importantly for hypothesis three, for example, NCDS5 contains two measures of power and control in the form of attitudinal statements, (I am able to vary the pace at which I work; I can only take breaks at certain times). These can be used as measures of control.

Linking Men, Work and Psychological Ill Health

Before the hypotheses are considered in any detail it is possible to offer some initial descriptive analysis. Basic frequencies are presented in tables 9.2 to 9.4 and these tables suggest that for male non-standard workers the most commonly reported emotional problems were: 'Feeling Low, Depressed or Sad' (6.4 per cent), 'Other Tension, Anxiety' (3.8 per cent) 'Felling Generally Anxious, Jittery' (2.1 per cent) 'Feeling Anxious or Scared about Objects or Situations' (1.7 per cent). All other emotional problems were reported by 1 per cent or less. The average age at which these four conditions commenced was 25.25 years. Of those who reported experience of emotional problems, 45 per cent suggested that these emotional difficulties were still a problem.

179

Table 9.2
Have Seen a GP or Specialist for the Following Conditions Since 1981
(% of Research Samples) - NCDS5 1991

	Percentage Of Men and Women			
	Men	Women	All F/T Men	All F/T Women
'Feeling Low, Depressed or Sad'				
Yes	6.4	14.8	6.2	16.7
Mean Start Age	26	26	26	27
Still A Problem ?	40.9%	42.0%	37.0%	47.4%
'Feeling Generally Anxious, Jittery'				
Yes	2.1	3.9	2.0	0.1
Mean Start Age	24	24	26	27
Still A Problem ?	52.2%	55.0%	35.0%	-
'Feeling Anxious or Scared about Objects or Situations'				
Yes	1.7	3.0	1.5	0.1
Mean Start Age	25	25	25	25
Still A Problem ?	36.8%	57.0%	37.0%	-
'Feeling Overconfident or Overexcited'				
Yes	0.2	0.3	0.3	0.4
Mean Start Age	16	18	30	25
Still A Problem ?	-	-	-	-
'Feeling Compelled to Repeat Actions or Thoughts				
Yes	0.5	0.7	0.4	0.4
Mean Start Age	27	24	27	27
Still A Problem ?	-	-	-	-
'Hearing or Seeing Things'				
Yes	0.2	0.6	0.7	0.5
Mean Start Age	24	21	26	26
Still A Problem ?	-	-	-	-
'Problems with Drink or Drugs'				
Yes	1.0	0.6	0.8	0.7
Mean Start Age	23	26	24	28
Still A Problem ?	81.8%	-	-	-
'Other Tension, Anxiety etc.'				
Yes	3.8	8.4	4.4	10.0
Mean Start Age	26	26	27	26
Still A Problem ?	53.8%	64.0%	46.2%	60.0%
N	982	2919	4109	1843

Source: Own calculations from NCDS5 1991 data supplied by ESRC Data Archive.

Table 9.3
Percentage of Positive Responses to General Malaise Questions by Current Status and Sex - NCDS5 1991

	Men	Percentage Of Men and Women Women	All F/T Men	All F/T Women
Do you feel tired most of the time ?				
	14.8	20.8	13.2	20.4
Do you often feel miserable or depressed ?				
	8.6	11.3	6.8	12.0
Do you often have bad headaches ?				
	7.1	16.0	8.0	19.6
Do you often worry about things ?				
	25.6	36.2	22.9	37.5
Do you usually have difficulty in falling or staying asleep ?				
	10.2	11.1	9.6	12.1
Do you usually wake unnecessarily early in the morning ?				
	15.6	14.5	15.6	16.6
Do you often get into a violent rage ?				
	2.4	4.7	2.8	3.8
Do people often annoy or irritate you ?				
	22.0	20.8	19.8	22.6
Do you suddenly become scared for no good reason ?				
	1.7	4.6	2.3	5.1
Are you scared to be alone when there are not friends near you ?				
	0.4	3.3	0.9	4.2
Are you easily upset or irritated ?				
	11.5	17.7	10.7	17.0
Are you frightened of going out alone or meeting people ?				
	1.8	5.1	2.0	5.7
Does every little thing get on your nerves and wear you out ?				
	1.1	2.8	1.4	2.1
Have you ever had a nervous breakdown ?				
	2.4	2.7	1.2	2.2
N	982	2919	4109	1843

Source: Own calculations from NCDS5 1991 data supplied by ESRC Data Archive.

Table 9.4
Percentage of Positive Responses to General Malaise Questions by Actual Current Status and Sex - NCDS5 1991

	Full-Time		All NS		Self-Employed		Part-Time	
	Men	Women	Men	Women	Men	Women	Men	Women
Do you feel tired most of the time ?								
	13.0	20.3	14.8	20.8	13.7	17.0	21.1	23.9
Do you often feel miserable or depressed ?								
	6.8	12.0	8.6	11.3	7.8	8.9	17.4	13.3
Do you often have bad headaches ?								
	8.0	19.6	7.1	16.0	6.5	10.1	12.8	20.7
Do you often worry about things ?								
	22.0	37.6	25.6	36.1	25.0	28.9	32.0	42.0
Do you usually have difficulty in falling or staying asleep ?								
	9.7	12.1	10.2	11.1	9.9	9.2	13.8	12.6
Do you usually wake unnecessarily early in the morning ?								
	15.7	16.6	15.6	14.5	14.8	13.4	20.2	15.3
Do you often get into a violent rage ?								
	2.8	3.7	2.4	4.7	2.2	3.7	5.5	5.5
Do people often annoy or irritate you ?								
	19.8	5.1	22.0	20.8	21.8	22.1	23.0	19.9
Do you suddenly become scared for no goo reason ?								
	2.3	5.1	1.7	4.6	1.3	3.3	5.5	5.6
Are you scared to be alone when there are not friends near you ?								
	0.4	4.2	0.9	3.3	0.2	1.7	1.8	4.6
Are you easily upset or irritated ?								
	10.7	17.0	11.5	17.7	10.5	13.5	20.2	21.0
Are you frightened of going out alone or meeting people ?								
	1.8	17.0	2.0	5.1	1.3	3.1	6.4	6.8
Does every little thing get on your nerves and wear you out ?								
	1.4	2.1	1.1	2.8	0.6	1.4	5.5	3.8
Have you ever had a nervous breakdown ?								
	2.3	2.2	1.2	2.7	2.3	2.4	3.7	3.0

Source: Own calculations from NCDS5 1991 data supplied by ESRC Data Archive.

Those men who worked full-time reported the same emotional problems as male non-standard workers. Around 6 per cent reported that they had experienced 'Feeling low, Depressed or Sad' to 1.5 per cent reporting anxiety about situations or objects. The average age at which emotional problems commenced for male non-standard workers was 26 years. Thirty eight per cent of those who reported emotional problems expressed that they were still affected by these conditions.

For women, regardless of their current status of either being a non-standard worker or a full-time worker the reporting of particular emotional problems was higher overall than that of men. More women (on average 15.7 per cent) suffered from 'Feeling Low, Depressed or Sad' and more women than men (on average 9.2 per cent) suffered from 'Other Tensions or Anxiety'. For all women the average age at which these emotional problems commenced was 26 years. For female non-standard workers it was 26 years. For 53 per cent of all women, the emotional problems that they had suffered from still had an impact upon their lives.

Tables 9.3 and 9.4 present data generated on emotional/psychological problems by the supplementary health questions in the cohort member interviews. The data here is presented as a percentage of positive responses in the first instance by gender and full-time or non-standard worker status. This data requires little commentary and the discussion now turns to examine the initial research hypotheses.

Exploring the Hypotheses

The first hypothesis suggested that men who work in non-standard forms have more problems with mental health, than their full-time counterparts as a mere consequence of their employment status. The data presented in Table 9.5 suggest that there were 2310 individual men within NCDS5 that fell into the 'Harmful' psychological health.

This means that around 45 per cent of the male work sample in NCDS5 had in the past experienced emotional problems or that they general suffered from at least one of the identified malaise questions. If one turns to examine the hypothesis specifically we can see that very little difference exists between the two employment status groups. Indeed, 45 per cent of male non standard workers (448) appear in the harmful psychological health with also 45 per cent of the male full-time workers (1862). This view is confirmed in calculation of a chi-square for this table. At the 0.05 two-tailed level with one degree of freedom, the value of 0.035 is smaller than the 3.84 value required. In other words the psychological health of the male workers sample does not differ significantly when broken down by current employment status.

Table 9.5
Labour Market Effects on the Psychological Health of Men in NCDS5 - Observed and Expected Frequencies

	Beneficial	Harmful	Total
Full-Time Working	2230	1862	4902
	(2226)	(1866)	
Non-Standard Working	528	448	976
	(531)	(445)	
Totals	2758	2310	

Source: Own calculations from NCDS5 1991 data supplied by ESRC Data Archive.

Hypothesis two suggested that previous unemployment may increase job insecurity and therefore increase the risk of psychological ill health. Table 9.6 provides a contingency table breaking down the data by a previous unemployment variable.

This table suggests that 42 per cent of the male worker sample had experienced unemployment, with the remaining 58 per cent indicating that they had been employed since leaving school. However, if we explore the 'harmful' cells in more detail we can see that 55 per cent of those who experienced emotional problems had not in fact experienced any previous unemployment at all.

Table 9.6
Unemployment Effects on the Psychological Health of Men in NCDS5 - Observed and Expected Frequencies

	Beneficial	Harmful	Total
No Unemployment	1657	1270	2972
	(1593)	(1334)	
Previous Unemployment	1101	1040	2141
	(1165)	(976)	
Totals	2758	2310	

Source: Own calculations from NCDS5 1991 data supplied by ESRC Data Archive.

Of the 42 per cent who had experienced unemployment, less than half reported experiencing harmful psychological health. However, the calculation of a chi-square for this table suggests that the two variables are not independent and the null hypothesis (that previous unemployment and psychological ill-health are not associated) can be rejected. At the 0.05 two-tailed level with one degree of freedom, the value of 13.2 is larger than the 3.84 value required to be statistically significant. In other words the psychological health of the male workers does differ significantly when broken down by previous experience of unemployment.

Hypothesis three posits the suggestion that lower levels of perceived control over life events and lower levels of skill use, lead to increased mental ill-health problems. The contingency table for this hypothesis is table 9.7. For ease of calculation two initial desecrate groups were formed. Those who perceived themselves to have little control over their life and did not use skills that they possessed. The second group contained those men who did use their skills and reported that they had control over their life. As one would expect the first group is relatively small and indeed this group only accounts for around 10 per cent of the male worker sample.

Table 9.7
Life Control and Skill Usage Effects on the Psychological Health of Men in NCDS5 - Observed and Expected Frequencies

	Beneficial	Harmful	Total
No Control or Skill Use	207	306	513
	(279)	(234)	
Control and Skill Use	2551	2004	4555
	(2478)	(2076)	
Totals	2758	2310	

Source: Own calculations from NCDS5 1991 data supplied by ESRC Data Archive.

If we turn to the hypothesis, an examination of the data shows that 86 per cent of those who experienced emotional problems reported that they had control over their life and used the skills that they had. This fact obviously brings into question the hypothesis. However this does not mean that the two variables are independent. This crosstabluation produced an observed significance level lower than 0.00001 (based on the combined data). The results seem to support the theory that those who have control over their life and use skills will experience emotional problems in a different way to those who perceive they have no control and do not use the skills that they have.

Hypothesis four suggested a relationship between differing work patterns combined with traditional ideological notions of being the breadwinner with increased incidence of emotional problems. For ease of analysis, this hypothesis was tested via two contingency tables 9.8a and 9.8b.

Table 9.8a suggests that a total of 427 men within the male worker sample held traditional sex-role attitudes, 328 being full-time workers and 99 being male non-standard workers. Forty five per cent of these men (191) indicated that they had experienced emotional problems. If broken down by employment status, 43 per cent of the male full-time workers with traditional attitudes experienced emotional problems, compared to 48 per cent of their non-standard worker counterparts.

Table 9.8a
Traditional Sex Role Ideology and Employment Status Effects on the Psychological Health of Men in NCDS5 - Observed and Expected Frequencies

	Beneficial	Harmful	Total
NS Men	52	47	99
	(55)	(44)	
Full-Time	184	144	328
	(181)	(148)	
Totals	236	191	

Source: Own calculations from NCDS5 1991 data supplied by ESRC Data Archive.

Table 9.8b casts doubt on this hypothesis. If this hypothesis were correct, relatively fewer men without traditional sex role attitudes should appear in the harmful psychological health category. However as with the previous table around 45 per cent of this group of men report experiencing emotional problems. One can conclude therefore that very little difference exists between the two employment status groups regardless of their sex-role ideology. Once again, this view is confirmed in calculation of a chi-square for this table. At the 0.05 two-tailed level with one degree of freedom, the values of 0.2613 and 0.00003 respectively are smaller than the 3.84 value required. In other words the psychological health of the male workers sample does not differ significantly when broken down by current employment status and sex-role ideology.

Table 9.8b
Non-Traditional Sex Role Ideology and Employment Status Effects on the Psychological Health of Men in NCDS5 - Observed and Expected Frequencies

	Beneficial	Harmful	Total
NS Men	476	401	877
	(477)	(400)	
Full-Time	2046	1718	3764
	(2045)	(1719)	
Totals	2522	1119	

Source: Own calculations from NCDS5 1991 data supplied by ESRC Data Archive.

Modelling Employment and Psychological Well-Being

The main problem with the four hypotheses posited here is that they all consider the influence of certain factors, such as employment status or previous experiences of unemployment, in isolation from each other. To make the exploration more meaningful two further procedures can be used. The first is regression analysis. This allows the assessment of certain explanatory variables on a dependant variable (in this instance the 'number of emotional problems'). This can be used to test a general hypothesis that the number of emotional problems a respondent experiences is due to (or influenced by) certain labour market characteristics.

The second procedure, following the work of Burchell, is a cluster analysis technique. Here men are divided up into more homogeneous sub-groups using the labour market data presented in the previous four hypotheses[1] .The groups, displaying particular social characteristics can be examined to ascertain whether they display certain mental health characteristics.

Regression Analysis

The results of the regression analysis are presented in Table 9.9. This table suggests that there is no support for the hypothesis that the number of emotional problems experienced is due to (or influenced by) certain labour market characteristics. Indeed this equation overall only explained 1.1 per cent of the variation in the number of emotional problems experienced. Only very weak support for this hypothesis comes from two variables used in the equation. The equation suggests that the more emotional problems are experienced the less life control an individual perceives they have, and secondly the more spells of unemployment that they have experienced.

Table 9.9
Determinants of Number of Emotional Problems for Men, Coefficients, Means and Standard Deviations

Variable	Coef	mean	s.d
N.Emotional Problems	-	1.3	0.80
Status	-0.02	1.19	0.39
Number of Jobs	0.01	2.25	0.84
Number of Unemployment Spells	0.04**	0.55	0.65
Ever Made Redundant ?	-0.02	1.08	0.94
Traditional Attitudes ?	0.02	1.91	0.27
No Skill Use ?	0.00	0.57	0.84
No Control Over Life ?	-0.25*	0.86	0.33
SOC	0.00	4.1	2.6
NVQ	0.00	2.0	1.7
Paid Less Than £200 pw	0.01	1.41	0.62

Note: *$p<.01$ **$p<.05$. Source: Own Calculations based on data from NCDS5

Cluster Analysis

The cluster analysis was carried out by linking experiences of psychological ill-health with certain labour market characteristics. Table 9.10 provides an outline of the cluster groups when broken down by the experience of emotional problems.

Table 9.11 gives the positive response percentage breakdown for each cluster on each of the discriminating variables. When these discriminating variables are linked to the data presented in Table 9.10 it is possible to see if certain groups with certain characteristics are more likely to experience emotional problems. Certain themes can be identified here.

Table 9.10
Percentage and Mean Response of Cluster Groups of 'Experienced Emotional Problems' for Men in NCDS5

Group	No	Yes	Mean Number of Problems	N
1	0	100	3.80	112
2	54	46	0.58	1050
3	57	43	0.51	1708
4	55	45	0.54	2133

Source: Own calculations from NCDS5 1991 data supplied by ESRC Data Archive.

Table 9.11
Response Percentage or Mean Breakdown in Scores for Each Cluster on the Discriminating Variables

Group	1	2	3	4
Full Time Worker	81	82	77	82
NS Worker	19	17	23	18
Mean Number of Jobs	2.35	2.29	2.21	2.20
Ever Unemployed ?	56	48	42	38
Mean Number of Unemployment Spells	0.79	0.62	0.52	0.56
Ever Made Redundant ?	14	13	11	8
Traditional Attitudes ?	10	7	6	7
No Skill Use ?	16	15	8	13
No Control Over Life ?	24	10	7	9
Mean SOC	3	8	5	2
Qualifications Lower than NVQ level 3 ?	43	20	29	55
Paid Less Than £200 pw	50	57	49	30
N	112	1050	1708	2133

Source: Own calculations from NCDS5 1991 data supplied by ESRC Data Archive.

First, group one, although very small, was the group which experienced the highest mean number of emotional problems. The characteristics of this group were that the men it contained mainly worked full-time, over 50 per cent of them have experienced unemployment in the past, with around 14 per cent reporting that they have been made redundant. Twenty four per cent report that they have no control over their life, with a further 16 per cent reporting that they have skills which they do not use. Forty three per cent of them have qualifications lower than NVQ level 3 and 50 per cent earn less than £200 per week. This group are more likely to be in SOC 3. This groups has the highest mean number of jobs and the highest mean number of unemployment spells.

Group two experienced the second highest mean number of emotional problems. This group was comprised of men who also worked full-time. Yet *al*ongside this, 48 per cent had experienced unemployment between leaving school and the survey date in 1991. Of the group 13 per cent reported being made redundant in the past with 10 per cent also reporting that they do not have control over their life. Only 20 per cent of this group has qualifications lower than NVQ level 3 and over 57 per cent of this group earn less than £200 per week. The average SOC category for this group was 8.

Group three had the lowest mean average of emotional problems. This is a group of men who mainly worked full-time. However 23 per cent of male non-standard workers also appeared in this group. Like group 2, they have experienced quite high levels of unemployment. Around 11 per cent report that they have been made redundant in the past, with 6 per cent also expressing traditional sex role attitudes. Of the group 8 per cent had skills they did not use, and 9 per cent had no control over their life. A high proportion have a qualification above NVQ level 3 and over 50 per cent are paid more than £200 per week.

The final group contains 82 per cent male full-time workers. Of this group 38 per cent have experienced unemployment between leaving school and the survey date in 1991. Eight per cent report being made redundant. They are more likely to have control over their life. Fifty five per cent have a qualification lower than NVQ level 3 and 70 per cent are paid more than £200 per week.

Concluding Remarks

This chapter aimed to explore men's mental health in relation to work and work related issues. This was aided by drawing on previous studies to conceptualise the links via four initial hypotheses as a framework. The hypotheses were explored to ascertain certain possible linkages between the psychological ill-health experienced by male workers and certain work related characteristics, such as the extent of non-standard working or previous experiences of unemployment. The initial hypotheses were 'Men who work in non-standard forms have more problems with mental health, than their full-time counterparts as a mere consequence of their employment status'; 'Previous unemployment may increase job insecurity and therefore increase the risk of psychological ill health'; 'Lower levels of control and skill use, lead to increased mental ill-health problems'; and finally, 'When differing work patterns are combined with traditional ideological notions of being the breadwinner there is likely to be an increased incidence of emotional problems'.

Using the male worker sample data from NCDS5, the results suggested that there was little support for three out of the four hypotheses when carrying out basic descriptive analysis. The only exception was in the exploration of hypothesis two which links previous unemployment to psychological ill health. The analysis of this data suggested that there is some association between the psychological health of the male workers and previous experience of unemployment.

Given the limited explanatory power of these descriptive models and to further enhance our understanding, two more analytical models were developed using the more comprehensive techniques of regression analysis and cluster analysis. The regression analysis offered little support for the hypothesis that the number of emotional problems experienced is due to certain labour market characteristics. However, weak support for this hypothesis came from two variables. The data suggested that more emotional problems are experienced the less life control an individual perceives they have. Secondly that the number of emotional problems experienced links to the individual males experiences of unemployment.

The cluster analysis grouped those men who exhibited very similar labour market characteristics. Four main groups were identified. Certain linkages were made in this analysis between the characteristics of the group and the number of emotional problems experienced. For example, group one, although the smallest group, experienced the highest mean number of emotional problems. This groups was characterised by the highest mean number of employment spells, the most traditional attitudes, limited skill usage and a lack of life control. Such characteristics can be compared to group four who had the lowest mean number of emotional problems. This group experienced the lowest mean number of employment spells, were less likely to report no skill usage and more likely to have perceived control over their life.

To conclude, when each aspect of this chapter is considered in isolation from other aspects of the analysis, it would be fair to conclude that it is difficult with this data to establish a clear link between labour market experiences and mental ill health. However when taken together the explanatory power of the techniques are enhanced as each seems to imply the same variables are important. Namely, that the experience of unemployment and lack of life control are important in determining men's experiences of mental ill-health. For example, the regression results and the results from the exploration of hypothesis two suggest that a man's experiences of mental ill-health are linked to the experiences of unemployment. This is also the finding of the cluster analysis.

The importance of unemployment experiences cannot be underestimated. Indeed, although the results presented here are limited, they are interesting and lend some support to the initial suggestion that there is a societal mis-match between men who do not work and the masculine ideal. As suggested above this mismatch is evidenced in the fact that there has been a change in the nature of work and men are often unable to work full-time and permanently throughout their lives. Yet, men *are* still expected to work full-time throughout their lives although the possibilities of doing have greatly diminished. These results suggest that unemployment may lead to emotional problems in that, as Simon (1995) suggests, they become unable to provide economically which is an essential part of the male role. As reported above, eighty per cent of the men in Simon's (1995) study supported the view that negative consequences would result for a man's self-image if they could not provide economically. The evidence presented here on unemployment may actually support Simon's view.

Note

1   Other variables were also introduced at this stage of the analysis to either increase the explanatory power of the regression equation or to ensure the homogeneity of the groups. Variables such as experience of emotional problems, how many emotional problems, weekly pay, highest qualification, standard occupational classification and ever made redundant from work were also used.

10 Conclusion: Moving Male Work Further ?

The extent to which data from any particular data set can generate general and widely applicable conclusion is open to question. However, this book has attempted to offer an original contribution to the sociology of gender generally, and the study of men and work via an analysis of the literature and the NCDS5 dataset. The importance of this contribution is that the research is based on the premise that empirically grounded (as well as theoretical) research on men should become an integral part of the gender-based enquiry. Further, that men should be studied in their own right, and that men do not have to be appended to, or studied by accident in, the study of women. Within this it was argued that (to date) an adequate analysis of men has been largely absent in empirical gender based sociology and that such a project could take place within a study of men and work. Given these broad objectives, four specific aims were developed. They were to:

(i)   establish that there is a real absence of an empirical understanding of men in British gender based sociological research;

(ii)   explore the link between men and work by examining and using existing accounts of gender theory and feminism;

(iii)   examine men's recent experiences of the British labour market; and finally;

(vi)   provide an empirical account of men's work via an analysis of existing data. To do so using established hypotheses and notions of full-time and non-standard work to illustrate the analysis.

The first four aims were explored, and largely established, in the first 'part' of the book in chapters one to three. The final aim was explored in chapters four to nine. Here the research was designed to provide an empirical account of men's work via an analysis of existing data. The book made use of data from the National Child Development Study. This data allowed the empirical exploration of men, work and work related issues, and whilst limited to a particular age group (33 year olds) and the fact that the

193

sample was largely white and heterosexual, a number of important themes were identified. The themes were identified and explored by using established hypotheses and notions of full-time and non-standard work to illustrate the discussion. Within this part of the book there was a methodological chapter and five main empirical chapters. The themes explored in these chapters were: 'Male Work in NCDS5; Men's Attitudes and Work Orientation; Men, Training and Skills; Men, Households and Private Work; and finally, Psychological Ill-Health and Men's Work.

This final concluding chapter reflects on these aims and considers what has been achieved in the discussion. This is done initially by reflecting again the themes contained in the research. Secondly, by using the findings to illustrate the themes and debates. Third, by setting the achievements and contributions of this book, alongside its limitations. Finally, a consideration of the implications that this book has for the future research agenda.

Men's Work and Male Lives: Main Themes and Findings

Within the broad aims and objectives outlined above it is evident that a number of themes permeate this research. For example, the initial chapters set to the context of the debate, and considered the need for a gender based sociological exploration of men (the theme of an *absence of men*). They explored those theories that link men and work (the theme of *the link between men and paid work*). Finally, they reviewed the nature of male employment in the UK for one group of 33 year old men (the theme of *men's working lives*). One can counter the problem of the former (*an absence of men*), and consider the link between men and work by offering an exploration of the latter (*men's working lives*). For example, in chapter three, and chapters six to nine, the issue of male invisibility was addressed by exploring issues relating to men's work.

An Absence of Men

In terms of the first theme, one can return to issues contained within the introduction and chapter one and cite Brod (1987) who argues that

> Men's studies argue that like women's studies corrects the exclusion of women from the traditional cannon caused by androcentric scholarship's elevation of a man as male to man as generic...While seemingly about men, traditional scholarship's treatment of generic man as the human norm in fact systematically excludes from consideration what is unique men qua men.
>
> (Brod 1987: 40)

Harry Brod's (1987) argument, that the 'unique attributes' of men are not explicitly studied in sociological research, was one of the underpinning motivators for this research. It seemed strange that since Brod wrote these words (ten years ago), very little empirical research has been carried out which exclusively considers men with the aim of exploring their 'uniqueness'. This perhaps suggests a great deal about the nature of sociological knowledge and 'who does what' in the sociological paradigm.

> We are...suspicious about the timing of the recent burst of activity around TNMS. The boom in conferences and books about men and masculinity would have been almost unthinkable ten or even five years ago...Why do they all appear now, when further and higher education are increasingly threatened both politically and financially (at least in the UK) and when areas like women's studies are becoming increasingly beleaguered? Is it a coincidence that TNMS is being constructed, in the present context, as a source of potential research, publishing deals and (even more) jobs for the already-well-paid boys holding prestigious positions ?

> (Cannan and Griffin 1990: 208)

Is the explicit study of gender, whether of men, women or both, an area reserved for women researchers with a particular political (as well as academic), agenda? Is there something less valuable in a man offering and empirical account of men's lives? Whatever the cause or origins of this debate, it seems self evident that many sociological researchers do not always recognise the need for an increase in the empirical considerations of male lives. The evidence for this has to be the limited numbers of scholars who are working on considerations of men's issues, and the lack of any real critical, empirically argued, literature on men and work or masculinity coming from men themselves. This must have something to do with 'institutionalised' and unquestioning support for 'feminised' academic and 'women oriented' gender research.

> It is possible to see such arguments as part of a 'backlash' by men against the impact of feminism: a determination to fight even the smallest gains which women have been able to achieve, in order to preserve male superiority. It is true that a there is now a small but vociferous men's movement ready to argue that men are now the oppressed sex. And it is also true that if it is a bad time to be a man, it is still, in almost every area of life, a worse time to be a woman. But what has to be understood...is how far and fast that privilege has been undermined...
> (MacInnes 1997: 6)

Authors such as Christian (1994) acknowledge the fact that since the 1970s women have achieved many advances in the study of gender. The feminist critique of social science has brought gender analysis into consideration. However, despite an obvious lack of concentration on women in the past, this well intentioned feminist critique, has led to a situation where men are increasingly 'hidden' in gender-based research. In chapter one this point was explored and, indeed, on examination of the literature, an analysis of men has been largely absent in empirical gender based sociology. The point was made that a sociological study of men is not only required, but essential if a fuller understanding of 'gender' is to be gained. Further, this was also an argument for a study of men in their own right. Other researchers, such as Carrigan *et al*, have acknowledged this point and have suggested that the empirical content of men's studies turns out to be slight and that good quality research on men is rare. What is required is an empirical analysis of men that provides an outline of their lives, how they actually are and not how they should be or how ideologically we would like them to be.

Having established that men have not been a main focus for empirical sociological enquiry, an obvious site for such an empirical enquiry (the site where men could be made visible) was a man's working life. This brings us to the second theme.

The Link Between Men and Work

The second of the main themes was that work is linked to men's lives and that this is the product of long-term social, historical, relational and cultural processes. It was argued that in the current time the work ethic for men is more fundamental that just an ideology of production based on gender. It was suggested that one of the keys to understanding this is the interrelationship between patriarchy (a set of social relations based on gender) and capital (a set of social relations based on production). The way that these historical, cultural, social and economic relationships develop over time affects the nature of masculinity (and femininity) over time, and the form of the masculinity that we have today is a consequence of this process. As a result the idea of the linkage between masculinity and work is expressed in the fact that traditionally, it is the man who is perceived to be the breadwinner, and the individual concerned with production outside of the home. The role of men, the nature of masculinities, was (and still is to some extent) defined by full-time, permanent employment.

Evidence to support the view that work is central to men's lives can be found in chapters six, eight and nine. For example, chapter six examined the attitudes that four different groups of male worker samples held towards their work, and work-related issues; it examined the possibility of linking these attitudes to the particular labour market and individual characteristics displayed by male workers.

It was confirmed in this chapter that attitudes do vary between different groups of men, and as a consequence it is problematic to discuss men's attitudes in the way that has been done so previously. For example, the data suggested that men's attitudes towards their work, their support for sex equality and their permissiveness about family and work were linked to various work related or socio-demographic variables. It was also found that men's attitudes are not always stable or consistent over time and that change does occur. However, the data also suggested that men's support for the work ethic and traditional working roles becomes stronger with time. That is to say, at the age of 33, when these men have responsibilities and families, the breadwinner role/work ethos takes on greater importance.

In chapter eight men's participation in housework was explored. The results of the descriptive analysis confirmed that women seem still largely responsible for household work and that the only exception to this was household repairs. There was some evidence to suggest that women's employment does lead to men's 'improved' participation in household tasks, but it was argued that men tend to be involved more in those tasks that are pleasurable and many see it as an option rather than a definite commitment, such as cooking.

From the regression analysis, the results suggested that men with only a basic education did fewer household tasks. Conversely, those full-time male workers with a higher education did more. Secondly, that men who had traditional views about housework, and are perhaps politically conservative, are less likely to participate in household tasks. Finally, the data showed a clear relationship between lower levels of work and participation in household tasks. Such data suggest that the household, and participation in household tasks is of secondary importance to work for men.

The importance of working for men can also be illustrated with the findings from Chapter 9. Using regression and cluster analysis in chapter nine it was found that the experience of unemployment and lack of life control are important in determining men's experiences of mental ill-health. So in the first instance, this suggests that a lack of employment has an impact on men's lives.

Men's Working Lives

The third main theme is men's working lives *per se* and the 'actuality' of the 'male working experience'. This book acknowledged the point that amongst the many changes that have occurred in the labour market over the past thirty years, one of the most drastic has been the increase of women's participation in paid employment and the decrease in male employment. However, women's experiences of labour market change have been explored fully at this juncture, and it was argued that most existing analyses are limited in that they only use men as a reference point against which to measure women's participation. Further, men's experiences of the labour market, and labour market issues have become lost in the broader 'gender and work based' research and that men's labour market experiences are not examined *per se*.

The data presented in chapter three suggested that the nature and content of male work had changed (and is continually changing) and that male employment has been characterised by a series of important historical shifts. Such historical shifts in work have led to fluctuations in the nature, type and amount of work available for men and that male full-time work has been declining despite such an association with traditional forms of masculinity. For example, the data showed that there has been a ten per cent decrease in the number of men working. There has been a decline from 80.5 per cent in 1971 to 72.6 per cent in 1995 and down to a projected 70.0 per cent by the year 2006. The data also pointed out that for men there has been a drastic decrease in working in industries such as mining, manufacturing and construction whilst working in areas such as distribution, hotels, catering and repairs, or financial and business services, have increased.

The changing nature of male work was evidence in the data that suggested that continuous full-time work had been declining despite such an association with men. For example, Table 3.5 suggested that in 1951, male full-time employment stood at 15,262,000 yet by 1995 this had fallen to 12,954,000. Conversely women's full-time employment had increased from 784 thousands to 6,302,000 in the same period. Given this trend, it may now be more appropriate to re-conceptualise the work that men do.

The data reported in chapter five suggested that there was a great variety of working experiences amongst the men studied. Chapter five also reiterated the importance of documenting male labour market experiences as it is only by highlighting such experiences that men's work will be understood. This data suggests that men indeed do experience the labour market very differently, depending on whether or not they work full-time or as non-standard workers. The results also show that men, whether full-time or non-standard workers, do have labour market experiences that are different to women in equivalent positions.

Chapter seven on the other hand demonstrated that there was a qualitative difference between the working experiences of men in differential rates of access to training. Indeed it was found that certain labour market and other characteristics are significant in determining men's participation in work-related training. The logistic regression model demonstrated that men's likely participation in work-related training increases if men work full-time, are educated above NVQ level three and are of a relatively high social class grouping. Men's participation is reduced if they belong to class groupings four or five, have a large number of jobs and work for an organisation with few employees. As a consequence it was suggested that, whilst it goes without question that certain groups of men do participate more in training than women, certain other male (and female) groups need to be targeted if training is to be equitable.

In conclusion, it seems evident that there is value in exploring the lives of men specifically and it should become a regular sociological pursuit. This book has established and provided an account of men's lives, both in general terms and in relation to the sample of 33 year old men from NCDS5. The data suggests that these men's lives appear to be far more complex, and less homogeneous than some would have us believe. For example, men do experience different working forms, they do experience differing levels of education and training, men do have varied attitudes towards work and home, and experience health differently. Indeed, the discussion demonstrates such male diversity now exists in working life that it is now difficult to consider men as a homogeneous group of full-time workers. Men need now to be conceptualised as men first and foremost and then as part-time workers, homeworkers, temporary workers, casual workers, self-employed workers, job-sharers or non-workers, as well as full-time workers. Despite the fact that such findings *may* only apply to this sample, such a finding has implications for the 'traditional' assumption that men will work full-time and throughout their lives. For some men, for example those who experience temporary work or experience more than one spell of unemployment, the social 'ideal' of full-male employment may become socially and economically impossible. Sociology must now explore and take account of this.

Men's Work and Males Lives: Limitations and Reflections

This research has to be viewed as a part of a larger and ongoing exploration into men and masculinity in Britain and elsewhere, and whilst it seems largely unique in arguing for an empirical approach, this research does contain limitations. It is very important that such limitations are acknowledged, not only so that future work can be adequately undertaken using this research as a framework, but also because the findings presented here should be set within the correct context.

The research makes use of a secondary analysis of data from mainly one source, the National Child Development Study 1991. Whilst this data is wide ranging and very comprehensive, this data was collected with very different aims and objectives than the present study. In places this may have limited the discussion. For example, as suggested above in the discussion of housework, the actual time spent by the male respondents on housework was not recorded.

One may also reflect on the fact that such secondary analysis is purely quantitative.

> One often seems to feel that only statistical analysis can provide the impersonal certainty expected of a sociological enquiry. Statements not based on measurements of quantifiable properties are frequently dismissed as 'impressionistic', as 'merely descriptive' or as 'subjective'. Other investigators before must have been troubled by the inadequacy of a conceptualisation which implied that any verbal statement which bears no direct reference to statistical data is necessarily unreliable, imprecise and scientifically suspect...
>
> (Elias and Scotson 1964: 8)

The addition of more qualitative data that reflects the depth of men's lives would have added greatly to the value of this project.

Age also limits the applicability of this data. All the men in this study were aged 33, and although it has been possible to use data from when they were younger, the full impact of a man's life course could not be explored. Indeed it seems logical to suggest that men at different stages in the life cycle may have very different concerns and as such future work should be undertaken to explore this possibility.

> ...sociological problems can hardly ever be adequately framed if they seem to be concerned with social phenomena exclusively at a given point and time - with structures which, to use the language of films, have the form of a 'still'.
>
> (Elias and Scotson 1964: 11-12)

Along with age a further limitation is that the impact of 'culture' is not considered. This research only focuses on men in the UK and does not explore men's lives elsewhere, where it is highly likely different themes and issues would appear. This on one level is justified as the original aim was to explore British men's lives, however if a more comprehensive understanding of men and masculinity is to be obtained this would could have been expanded to include empirical analyses from men in other countries and cultures. The value of such research would be unquestionable.

The use of other datasets may also have enhanced the scope and validity of the findings. For example, by further using the Labour Force Survey, further data would have been collected on the actual labour market experiences of a wider group of men. Alternatively data sets such as the General Household survey or the Family Expenditure Survey could have been used to shed new light on the household experiences of many in Britain.

Concluding Remarks: The Future of Male Work

Despite the limitations with the research and the data, the author remains committed to the fact that this research has been a worthwhile and essential task. As stated in the introduction, the contribution that this book has made to both gender and work debates are: first it has highlighted and acknowledged the absence of an adequate, empirically based study of men in British gender based sociology. Where men have been explored in the past, the focus has been largely theoretical or that men were treated as a homogeneous empirical grouping against which to compare women. The book suggested that this fact needed to be rectified if gender is to be fully understood. Second it has reflected upon the centrality of work to a group of 33 year old men's lives and uses a large scale quantitative dataset to explore issues relating to men's work experiences.

Such points need to be reiterated time and time again if men's studies is not to become a discrete topic within the British sociological enquiry. To avoid this researchers could return to the guiding principles outlined in chapter one which suggested that::

- It is important to consider male experiences of work from within the sociological paradigm making men more visible within gender sociology;

- There is a need to reflect critically on the impact on the forward moves made by feminism and the concept of patriarchy;

- There is a need to explore men's experiences empirically as well as theoretically. Further that work and employment provide one useful site for an empirically based sociological consideration of men. The reason for this is that men and work are inextricably linked and in most Western societies one defines the other;

- Finally, unlike in other 'gender' based research, men must not be treated as a homogeneous grouping.

It is also important that men's experiences of work and employment (and other areas such as work and sexuality) are (and continue to be) documented and brought back to the attention of the sociological research.

The reason for this is that work remains to be of central importance to men despite the fact that the nature of work has changed and continues to change. What sociologists need to do now is further document the nature of this change and the impact that it has on men. Yet this fact alone does not deny the fact that for many men such historical change may prove to be problematic.

Bibliography

Acker, S. (1981), No-Womans Land: British Sociology of Education 1960-1979, *Sociology* Review, Vol. 29, No.1, pp77-79.

Agassi, J.B. (1979), *Women on the Job: The Attitudes of Women and Men*, Lexington: USA.

Allatt, P., Keil, T., Bryman, A. and Bythway, B. (eds) (1987), *Women and the Life Cycle*, Macmillan: London.

Allen, I. (1988), *Any Room at The Top ? A study of Doctors and Their Careers*, Policy Studies Institute: London.

Allen, S. (1994), Review Article: Restructuring the World, *Work, Employment and Society*, Vol.8, No. 1, pp 113-126.

Allen, S., Truman, C. and Wolkowitz, C. (1992), Home-Based Work: Self-Employment and Small Business in Leighton, P. and Felstead, A. (1992), *The New Entrepenures*, Kogan Page: London.

Allen, S. and Wolkowitz, C. (1987), *Homeworking: Myths and Realities*, Macmillan: London.

Allport, G.W. and Odbert, H.S. (1935), Attitudes in Murchison. C. (1935), *Social Psychology*, Clark University Press.

Alwin, D. (1991), Aging Cohorts and Social Change: An Examination of the Generational Replacement model of Social Change, in Becker, H.A., (ed) (1991), *Dynamics of Cohort and Generational Research*, Amsterdam: Book Publishers.

Amato, P.R. and Booth, A. (1995), Changes in Gender Role Attitudes and Percieved Marital Quality, *American Sociological Review*, Vol.60, pp58-66.

Amos, V. and Parmer, P. (1984), Challenging Imperial Feminism, *Feminist Review*, Vol. 17, Autumn.

Anderson, M. (1980), *Sociology of the Family: Selected Readings 2nd ed,* Peguin: Harmondsworth

Andrews, A. and Bailyn, L. (1993), Segmentation and Synergy: Two Models of Linking Work and Family, in Hood, J, C. (ed) (1993), *Men, Work, and Family*, Sage Publications: Newbury Park.

Armstrong, P. and Armstrong, H. (1984), *The Double Ghetto: Canadian Women and their Segregated Work*, McClelland and Stewart: Toronto.

Ashton, D. and Green, F. (1996), *Education, Training and the Global Economy*, Edward Elgar, London.

Ashton, D. and Goodwin, J.D. (1996), Competence and the Professions: Reconciling the Irreconcilable?, Competent Decisions? *The Assessment of Competence in Management and the Professions*: Conference Proceedings, pp 1-11.

Ashton, D. and Sung, J. (1992), The Determinants of Labour Market Transitions: An Exploration of Contrasting Approaches, *Work, Employment and Society*, Vol.6, No.1, pp1-21.

Ashton, D. and Lowe, G. (1991), *Making Their Way: Education, Training and the Labour Market in Canada and Britain*, Open University Press, Buckingham.

Ashton, D. and Maguire, M. (1986), *Young Adults in the Labour Market*, Department of Employment Research Paper No.55.

Ashton, D. and Maguire, M. (1981), Dual Labour Market Theory and Organisation of the Local Labour Markets , *International Journal of Social Economics,* Vol.11, No.7.

Atkinson, M (1985), Manpower Strategies for Flexible Organisations. Personnel Management, August 28-31.

Attwood, M. (1982), Getting On, Gender Differences in Career Development: A Case Study in the Hairdressing Industry, in Gramarnikow, E., Morgan, D., Purvis, J. and Taylorson, D. (eds) (1983), *Gender Class and Work*, Heinemann: Aldershot.

Azjen, I. and Fishbein, M. (1977), Attitude-Behaviour Relations: A theoretical analysis and Review of Empirical Research, *Psychological Bulletin*, Vol. 84, pp 888-918.

Backett, K.C. (1987), The Negotiation of Fatherhood, in Lewis, C. and O'Brien, M. (eds) (1987), *Reassessing Fatherhood: New Observations on Fathers and the Modern Family*, Sage: London.

Backett, K.C. (1982), *Mothers and Fathers: A Study of the Development and Negotiation of Parental Behaviour*, Macmillan: Basingstoke.

Backett, K.C. (1980), Images of Parenthood, in Anderson, M. (1980), *Sociology of the Family: Selected Readings 2nd ed*, Peguin: Harmondsworth.

Backer, M. and Elias, P. (1991), Youth Unemployment and Work Histories, in Dex, S. (1991), *Life and Work History Analyses: Qualitative and Quantitative Developments*, Routledge, London.

Ballard, B. (1984), Women Part-time Workers: Evidence from the 1980 Women and Employment Survey, *Employment Gazette*, Vol.92, No.9, pp 409-416.

Barnett, R.C., Marshall, N.L. and Pleck, J. (1992), Men's Multiple Roles and Their Relationship to Men's Psychological Distress, *Journal of Marriage and the Family*, Vol.54, pp 358-367.

Barnett, R.C. and Baruch, G.K. (1988), Correlates of Fathers Participation in Family Work, in Bronstein, P. and Cowen, P.C. (eds) (1988), *Fatherhood Today: Mens Changing Role in the Family*, John Wiley: New York.

Barnett, R.C. and Baruch, G.K. (1987), Determinants of Fathers Participation in Family, *Work Journal of Marriage and the Family*, Vol 49, pp 29-40.

Beail, N. and McGuire, J. (1982), *Fathers: Psychological Perspectives*, Junction Books: London.

Beatson, M. (1995), Progress Towards a Flexible Labour Market, *Employment Gazette*, Feburary pp 55-66.

Becker, H.S. (1963), *Outsiders: Studies in the Sociology of Deviance*, The Free Press: New York.

Becker, W.H. (1993), Gender Race and the Tempation of Dualism, *The Journal of Mens Studies*, Vol.1, No.4, pp 403-425.

Bednarik, K. (1970), *The Male in Crisis*, Knopf: New York.

Beechey, V. (1979), Women and Production : A Critical Analysis of some Sociological Theories of Womens Work, in Beechey, V. (1987), *Unequal Work*, Verso: London.

Beechey, V. and Perkins, T. (1987), *Women, Part-time Work and the Labour Market*, Polity Press: Cambridge.

Beechey, V. (1987), *Unequal Work*, Verso: London.

Benjamin, O. (1996), The Importance of Difference: Conceptualising Increased Flexibility in Gender Relations at Home, *The Sociological Review*, Vol.44, No.4, pp 225-251.

Benjamin, O., (1992), Towards a Notion of Emotional Equality in Home-Life in Dunne, G.A., Blackburn, R.M. and Jarman, J.(eds) (1992), *Inequalities in Employment Inequalities in Home Life Conference Proceedings for the 20th Cambridge Social Stratification Seminar*, University of Cambridge 9th-10th September 1992.

Benn, T. (1985), *Arguments for Socialism*, Penguin: Harmondsworth.

Berardo, D.H., Shehan, C.L. and Leslie, G.R. (1987), A Residue of Tradition: Jobs, Careers, and Spouses' Time in Housework, *Journal of Marriage and the Family*, Vol. 49, pp381-390.

Berger, M., Wallis, B. and Watson, S. (1995), *Constructing Masculinity*, Routledge, London.

Berk, R. and Berk, S.F. (1979), *Labour and Leisure at Home*, Sage: USA.

Berk, S.F. (1985), *The Gender Factory: The Apportionment of Work in American Households*, Plenum, New York.

Berk, S.F. (ed) (1980), *Women and Household Labour,* Sage: USA.

Beskow, J. (1979), Suicide and Mental Disorder in Swedish Men, *Acta Psychiatrica Scandinavia*, Supplementum 277.

Beynon, H. (1973), *Working for Ford*, Allen Lane: Harmondsworth.

Bird, C.E. and Ross, C.E. (1993), Houseworkers and Paid Workers: Qualities of the Work and Effects on Personal Control, *Journal of Marriage and the Family*, Vol 55, No.3, pp913-925.

Blackburn, R.M. and Beynon, H. (1991), *Gender and Employment: Home Responsibilities and Involvement in Work*, Sociology Research Group, University Of Cambridge, Working Paper No.7.

Blair, S.L. and Johnson, M.P. (1992), Wives Perceptions of the Fairness of the Division of Household Labour, *Journal of Marriage and the Family*, Vol 54, 570-581.

Blair, S.L., Wenk, D. and Hardesty, C. (1993), Marital Quality and Paternal Involvement: Interconnections of Mens Spousal and Parental Roles, *The Journal of Mens Studies*, Vol.2, No.3, pp221-238.

Blair, S.L. and Johnson, M.P. (1992), Wives Perceptions of the Fairness of the Division of Household Labour, *Journal of Marriage and the Family*, Vol 54, 570-581.

Blanchflower, D. and Corry, B. (1986), Part-Time Employment in Britian: An Analysis Using Establishment Data, Department of Employment Research Paper.

Blauner, R. (1964), *Alienation and Freedom*, University of Chicago Press: Chicago.

Blee, K.M. and Tickamyer, A.R. (1995), Racial Differences in Men's Attitudes About Women's Gender Roles, *Journal of Marriage and the Family*, Vol 57, pp21-30.

Blood, R. and Wolf, D. (1960), *Husbands and Wives*, Free Press, New York.

Bly, J. (1992), *Iron John: A Book About Men*, Vintage: New York.

Bogardus, E.S. (1925), Measuring Social Distance, *Journal of Applied Sociology*, Vol. 9, pp 299-308.

Bögenhold, D. and Staber, U. (1991), Self-Employment Dynamics: A Reply to Meager, *Work, Employment and Society*, Vol. 7, No. 3, pp 465-472.

Bögenhold, D. and Staber, U. (1991), The Decline and Rise of Self-Employment, *Work, Employment and Society*, Vol. 5, No. 2, pp 223-239.

Bonney, N., Stockman, N. and Xuewen, S. (1994), Shifting Spheres: The Work and Family Life of Japanese Female Graduates, *Work Employment and Society*, Vol.8, No.3, pp387-406.

Bonney, N. and Reinach, E. (1993), Housework Reconsidered: The Oakley Book Twenty One Years Later, *Work Employment and Society*, Vol.7, No.4, pp615-627.

Booth, A. and Amato, P. (1994), Parental Gender Role Nontraditionalism and Offspring Outcomes, *Journal of Marriage and the Family*, Vol.56, No.4, pp 865-877.

Bose, C. (1980), Social Status of the Homemaker, in Berk, S.F. (ed) (1980), *Women and Household Labour*, Sage: USA.

Bott, E. (1957), *Family and Social Networks*, London: Tavistock.

Bowden, N. (1995), Who Manages Training? A Paper on the Potential for Employee Development in a Police Internal Labour Market, MSc in Training Residential Paper, 8th 9th April 1995.

Bowlby, J. (1946), *Forty-Four Juvenile Thieves*, London Balliere, Tindall and Cox.

Boyd, S.B. (1993), On Listening and Speaking: Men, Masculinity and Christianity, *The Journal of Mens Studies*, Vol.1, No.4, pp323-345.

Bozett, F.W. (1985), Gay Men as Fathers, in Hanson, S.M.H. and Bozett, F.W. (eds) (1985), *Dimensions of Fatherhood*, California: Sage

Bozett, F.W. (1988), Gay Fatherhood in Bronstein, P. and Cowan, C.P. (1988), *Fatherhood Today: Mens Changing Role in the Family*, New York: Wiley.

Bradley, H. (1989), *Mens Work, Womens Work*, Polity Press, Cambridge.

Brah, A. and Shaw, S. (1992), *Working Choices: South Asian Young Muslim Women and the Labour Market*, Department of Employment Research Paper No.91.

Brannen, J., Mészáros, G., Moss, P. and Poland, G. (1994), *Employment and Family Life: A Review of Research in the UK (1980-1994)*, Employment Department, Research Series No.41.

Brannen, J. and Moss, P. (1991), *Managing Mothers: Dual Earner Households After Maternity Leave*, Unwin Hyman: London.

Brannen, J. and Wilson, G. (1987), *Give and Take in Families: Studies in Resources Distribution*, Allen and Unwin: London.

Brannen, J. and Moss, P. (1987a), Dual Earner Households: Womens Financial Contributions After the Birth of the First Child, in Brannen, J. and Wilson, G. (1987), *Give and Take in Families: Studies in Resource Distribution*, Allen and Unwin: London.

Brannen, J. and Moss, P. (1987b), Fathers in Dual Earner Households - Through Mothers Eyes, in Lewis, C. and O'Brien, M (eds), *Reassessing Fatherhood*, Sage: London.

Brannen, J. (1986), The Resumption of Work After Childbirth: A Turning Point Within a Life Course Perspective, in Allatt, P., Keil, T., Bryman, A. and Bythway, B. (eds) (1987), *Women and the Life Cycle*, Macmillan: London.

Bravermann, H. (1974), *Labour and Monopoly Capital*, Monthly Review Press, New York.

Bray, M. and Littler, C. (1988), The Labour Process and Industrial Relations: Review of the Literature, *Labour and Industry*, Vol.1, No.2, pp 551-587.

Brayfield, A. (1995), Juggling Jobs and Kids: The Impact of Employment Schedules on Fathers Caring For Children, *Journal of Marriage and the Family*, Vol.57, No.2, pp321-332.

Brod, H. and Kaufman, M. (1994), *Theorising Masculinities*, London Sage.

Brod, H. (1987), A Case For Mens Studies, in Kimmel, M. (ed) (1987), *Changing Men: New Directions in Research on Men and Masculinity*, Sage: London.

Brod, H. (1987), A Case for Mens Studies, in Brod, H. (1987), *The Making of Masculinities*, Allen and Unwin: London.

Brod, H. (1987), Introduction: Themes and Theses of Mens Studies, in Brod, H., (1987), *The Making of Masculinities*, Allen and Unwin: London.

Brod, H. (1987), *The Making of Masculinities*, Allen and Unwin: Boston.

Bronstein, P. and Cowen, P.C. (eds) (1988), *Fatherhood Today: Men's Changing Role in the Family*, John Wiley: New York.

Brown, R.K. (1974), The Attitues to Work, Expectations and Social Perspectives of Shipbuilding Apprentices, in Leggatt, T. (1974), *Sociological Theory and Survey Research*, London: Sage.

Bruegel, I. (1979), Women as a Reserve Army of Labour: A Note on Recent British Experience , *Feminist Review*, No. 3, pp12-33.

Bryson, A. and White, M. (1996a), *From Unemployment to Self-Employment*, PSI paper, Policy Studies Institute, London.

Bryson, A. and White, M. (1996b), *Movements in and out of Self-Employment: Descriptive Analysis of Matched Labour Force Survey Data, 1992-1993*, Draft report to Employment Department.

Burchell, B. and Rubery, J. (1992), Catergorising Self-Employment: Some Evidence from SCELI in the UK, in Leighton, P. and Felstead, A. (1992), *The New Entrepenures* Kogan Page: London, pp 101-121.

Burchell, B. (1990), *The Effects of Labour Market Position, Job Insecurity and Unemployment on Psychological Health*, ESRC Working Paper 19.

Burris, B. H. (1996), Technocracy, Patriarchy and Management in Collinson, D.L. and Hearn, J. (eds) (1996), *Men as Managers, Managers as Men: Critical Perspectives on Men, Masculinities and Managements*, Sage: London.

Butler, N.R. and Golding, J. (eds) (1986), *From Birth to Five: A Study of the Health and Behaviour Of Britains Five Year Olds*, Pergamon: Oxford.

Bynner, J. and Fogelman, K. (1993), Makimg the Grade: Education and Training Experiences, in Ferri, E. (ed) (1993), *Life at 33*, NCB.

Campbell, R. (1747), The London Tradesman, T. Gardiner, London. Reprinted by David & Charles, 1969.

Campbell, A. (1995), Representations, repertoires and Power: Mother-Child Conflict, *The Journal for the Theory of Social Behaviour*, Vol.25, No.1 pp 35-58.

Campbell, M. and Daly, M. (1992), Self-Employment in the 1990s *Employment Gazette*, June, pp 269-292.

Canaan, J.E. (1996), One Thing Leads To Another: Drinking, Fighting and Working Class Masculinities in MaCanGhaill, Máirtín. (ed) (1996), *Understanding Masculinity: Social Relations and Cultural Arenas*, Open University Press, Buckingham.

Canetto, S.S. (1995), Men Who Survive a Suicidal Act, in Sabo, D. and Frederick-Gordon, D. (1995), *Men's Health and Illness: Gender, Power and the Body*, Sage, London.

Carrigan, T., Connell, B. and Lee, J. (1987), Towards a New Sociology of Masculinity, *Theory and Society*, Vo. 14, No.5, 551-604.

Carrigan, T., Connell, B. and Lee, J. (1985), Towards a New Sociology of Masculinity in Brod, H. (1987), *The Making of Masculinities*, Allen and Unwin: London.

Carter, R. and Kirkup, G. (1990), *Women in Engineering: A Good Place To Be?*, Macmillan: London.

Casey, B., Dragendorf, R., Heering, W. and John, G. (1989), Temporary Employment in Great Britain and the Federal Republic of Germany, *International Labour Review*, Vol.128, pp 449-466.

Casey, B. (1988), *Temporary Employment: Practice and Policy in Britain*, Policy Studies Institute, Oxford.

Casey, B. and Creigh, S. (1988), Self-Employment in Great Britain, *Work, Employment and Society*, Vol.2, No.3, pp 381-391.

Central Statistical Office (1996), *Regional Trends*, HMSO, London.

Central Statistical Office (1996), *Social Trends*, HMSO, London.

Central Statistical Office (1989), *Social Trends*, HMSO, London.

Chandler, H. (1991), *Women Without Husbands*, Macmillan: London.

Chapman, R. and Rutherford, J. (eds) (1988), *Male Order: Unwrapping Masculinity*, Lawrence and Wishart: London.

Charles, N. and Kerr, M. (1987), Just the Way it is: Gender and Age Differences in Family Food Consumption, in Brannen, J. and Wilson, G. (1987), *Give and Take in Families: Studies in Resource Distribution*, Allen and Unwin: London.

Charmaz, K. (1995), Identity Dilemas of Chronically Ill Men in Sabo, D., and Frederick-Gordon, D., (1995) *Men's Health and Illness: Gender, Power and the Body*, Sage, London.

Chestermann, C. (1979), *Women and Part-time Employment*, Unpublished M.A. book, University of Warwick.

Christian, H. (1994), *The Making of Anti-Sexist Men*, Routledge: London.

Chusmir, L.H. (1990), Men Who Make Non-Traditional Career Choices, *Journal of Counselling and Development*, pp 11-16.

Clark, J.M. (1994), The Third Gender: Implications for Mens Studies and Eco-Theology, *The Journal of Mens Studies*, Vol.2, No.3, pp 239-252.

Clark, J.M. (1993), From Gay Mens' Lives: Toward a More Inclusive, Ecological Vision, *The Journal of Mens Studies*, Vol.1, No.4 pp 347-358.

Clark, J.M. (1992), Mens Studies, Feminist Theology and Gay Sexuality, *The Journal of Mens Studies*, Vol.1, No.2, pp 125-155.

Cockburn, C. (1991), In The Way of Women: Men's Resistance to Sex Equality in Organisations, London, Macmillan.

Cockburn, C. (1987), *Computers: Hands On, Hands Off Two Track Training*, Macmillan.

Cohen, T. (1993), What do Fathers Provide? Reconsidering the Economic and Nurturant Dimensions of Men as Parents, in Hood, J, C. (ed) (1993), *Men, Work, and Family*, Sage Publications: Newbury Park.

Cohen, T.F. (1988), Gender, Work and Family: The Impact and Meaning of Work in Men's Family Roles, *Family Perspective*, Vol. 22, pp 293-308.

Cohen, T.F. (1987), Remaking Men: Men's Expereinces Becoming Husbands and Fathers and their Implications for Reconceptualizing Men's Lives, *Journal of Family Issues*, Vol. 8, pp 57-77.

Collinson, D. and Hearn, J. (1996), Men at Work: Multiple Masculinities/Multiple Workplaces, in MaCanGhaill, Máirtín. (ed) (1996), *Understanding Masculinity: Social Relations and Cultural Arenas*, Open University Press, Buckingham.

Collinson, D. and Hearn J. (1994), Naming Men as Men: Implications for Work, Organization and Management, *Gender Work and Organisation*, Vol.1, No.1, pp 2-22.

Collinson, D.L. (1988), *Barriers to Fair Selection: A Multi-Sector Study of Recruitment Practices*, EOC: HMSO.

Coltrane, S. and Ishii-Kuntz, M. (1992), Mens Housework: A Life Course Perspective, *Journal of Marriage and the Family*, Vol 54, pp 43-57.

Coltrane, S. and Valdez, E. (1993), Reluctant Compliance: Work-Family Role Allocation in Dual-Earner Chicano Families, in Hood, J, C. (ed) (1993), *Men, Work, and Family*, Sage Publications: Newbury Park.

Connell, R.W. (1995), *Masculinities*, Polity Press, Cambridge.

Connelly, P. and MacDonald, M. (1983), Womens Work: Domestic Labour in a Nova Scotia Community, *Socialist Review*, Vol. 10, pp 45-72.

Costich, N., Feinstein, J., Kidder, L., Marreck, J. and Pascale, L.K. (1975), When Stereotypes Hurt: Three Studies of Penalties for Sex-Role Reversals, *Journal of Experimental Psychology*, Vol. 11, pp 520-530.

Cousins, C. (1994), A Comparison of the Labour Market Position of Women in Spain and the UK with Reference to the Flexible Labour Debate, *Work, Employment and Society*, Vol. 8, No. 1, pp. 45-67.

Coverman, S. (1985), Explaining Husbands Participation in Domestic Labour, *The Sociological Quaterly*, Vol.26, No.1, pp 81-97.

Coyle, A. (1984), *Redundant Women*, The Womens Press: London.

Coyle, A. and Skinner, J. (eds) (1988), *Women and Work*, Macmillan: London.

Cragg, A. and Dawson, T. (1984), *Unemployed Women: A Study of Attitudes and Experiences*, Department of Employment Research Paper No.47.

Craig, S. (ed) (1992), *Men, Masculinity and the Media*, Sage, London.

Crompton, R. (1987), Gender, Status and Professionalism, *Sociology*, Vol.21, No.2, pp 413-428.

Crompton, R. and Saunderson, K. (1990), *Gendered Jobs and Social Change*, Unwin and Hyman: London.

Cunnison, S. (1987), Womens Three Working Lives and Trade Union Participation in Allatt, P., Keil, T., Bryman, A. and Bythway, B. (eds) (1987), *Women and the Life Cycle*, Macmillan: London.

Cunnison, S. (1982), Participation in Local Union Organisation, School Meals Staff: A Case Study, in Gramarnikow, E., Morgan, D., Purvis, J. and Taylorson, D. (eds) (1983), *Gender Class and Work*, Heinemann, Aldershot.

Curran, M. (1988), Gender and Recruitment: People and Places in the Labour Market, *Work Employment and Society*, Vol.2, No.3, pp 335-351.

Curran, M. (1985), *Stereotypes and Selection: Gender and Family in the Recruitment Process*, EOC: HMSO.

Curthoys, A. (1988), *For and Against Feminism: A Personal Journey into Feminist Theory and History*, Allen Unwin: London.

Curtin, C., Jackson, P. and O'Connor, B. (1987), *Gender in Irish Society*, Galway University Press, Galway.

Curtis, B. (1992), William Graham Sumner: A Chivalric Skull and Bones Man Faces Sexuality and the Breadwinner Ethic, *The Journal of Mens Studies*, Vol.1, No.1, pp 47-70.

Dale, A. and Glover, J. (1990), *An Analysis of Womens Employment Patterns in the UK, France and the USA: The Value of Survey Based Comparisons*, Department of Employment Research Paper, No.75.

Dale, A. and Bamford, C. (1988), Temporary Workers: Cause for Concern or Complacency? *Work, Employment and Society*, Vol.2, No.2, pp191-209.

Dale, A. (1987), Occupational Inequality, Gender and Life-Cycle, *Work Employment and Society*, Vol.1, No.3, pp. 326-351.

Dale, A., Arber, S. and Procter, M. (1988), *Doing Secondary Analysis*, Unwin Hyman, London.

211

Daly, M. (1994), A Matter of Dependency: Gender Provision in British Income Maintanance Provision, *Sociology*, Vol.28, No.3, pp 779-797.

Daniels, P. and Weingarten, K. (1982), *Sooner or Later: The Timing of Parenthood in Adult Lives*, New York, Norton.

Dart, B. and Clarke, J. (1988), Sexism in Schools: A New Look, *Educational Review*, Vol. 40, No.1, pp 41-49.

David, D.S. and Brannon, R. (1976), *The Forty Nine Percent Majority*, Addison-Wesley.

Davidoff, L. (1979), The Seperation of Home and Work: Landladies and Lodgers in 19th and 20th Century England, in Burman, S. (ed), *Fit Work for Women*, Groom Helm: London.

Davie, R., Butler, N.R. and Goldstein, H. (1972), *From Bith to Seven: A report of the National Child Development Study*, Longman: London.

Davis, N.J. and Robinson, R.V. (1991), Men and Women's Consciousness of Gender Inequality: Austria, West Germany, Great Britain and the United States, *American Sociological Review*, Vol. 56, pp72-84.

Dawes, L. (1993), *Long-Term Unemployment and Labour Market Flexibility*, Centre For Labour Market Studies, Leicester University.

Deem, R. (1978), *Women and Schooling*, Routlegde and Kegen Paul: London.

Deem, R. (ed) (1980), *Schooling for Womens Work*, Routledge and Kegen Paul: London.

Delphy, C. (1984), *Close to Home: A Materialist Analysis of Womens Oppression*, Huthcinson: London.

DeMarris, A. and Longmore, M.A. (1996), Ideology, Power and Equity: Testing Competing Explanations For the Perception of Fairness in Household Labour, *Social Forces*, Vol.74, No.3, pp 1043-1071.

Dench, G. (1994), *The Frog, The Prince and the Problem of Men*, Neanderthal Books: London.

Dennehy, K. and Mortimer, J. (1993), Work and Damily Orientations of Contemporary Adolescent Boys and Girls, in Hood, J, C. (ed) (1993), *Men, Work, and Family*, Sage Publications: Newbury Park.

Dex, S. (1988), *Womens Attitudes Towards Work*, Macmillan: London.

Dex, S. (1984), Womens Work Histories: An Analysis of the Women and Employment Survey, Department of Employment Research Paper, No.33.

Dex, S. (ed) (1991), *Life and Work History Analyses: Qualitative and Quantitative Developments*, Routledge: London.

Dimond, M.J. (1992), Creativity Needs in Becoming a Father, *The Journal of Mens Studies*, Vol. 1, No.1, pp41-45.

Doty, W.G. (1993), Companionship, Thick as Thieves: Our Myths of Friendship, *The Journal of Mens Studies*, Vol.1, No.4, pp 359-382.

Doucet, A. (1992), What Difference Does Difference Make? Towards and Understanding of Gender Ineqality and Difference in the Household Division of Labour, in Dunne, G.A., Blackburn, R.M. and Jarman, J.(eds) (1992), *Inequalities in Employment Inequalities in Home Life Conference Proceedings for the 20th Cambridge Social Stratification Seminar*, University of Cambridge 9th-10th September 1992.

Doucet, A. (1991), *Striking the Balance: Gender Divisions of Labour in Housework, Childcare and Employment*, Sociology Research Group, University Of Cambridge, Working Paper No.6.

Doyle, J. (1989), *The Male Expereince*, Brown and Benchmark, USA.

Duncombe, J. and Marsden, D. (1992), Workaholics and Whingeing Women: Gender Inequalities in the Performance of Emotion Work in the Private Sphere, in Dunne, G.A., Blackburn, R.M. and Jarman, J. (eds) (1992), *Inequalities in Employment Inequalities in Home Life Conference Proceedings for the 20th Cambridge Social Stratification Seminar*, University of Cambridge 9th-10th September 1992.

Dunne, G.A., Blackburn, R.M. and Jarman, J. (eds) (1992), *Inequalities in Employment Inequalities in Home Life Conference Proceedings for the 20th Cambridge Social Stratification Seminar*, University of Cambridge 9th-10th September 1992.

Dunning, E. (1986), Sport as a Male Preserve: Notes on the Social Sources of Masculine Identity and its Transformations, in Elias, N. and Dunning, E. (1986), *Quest for Excitement: Sport and Leisure in the Civilising Process*, Blackwell: Oxford.

Durkhiem, E. (1933), *The Division of Labour In Society*, Free Press: New York.

Durkhiem, E. (1984), *The Division of Labour In Society*, Macmillan: London.

Durkheim, E. (1961), Incest: The Nature and Origin of the Taboo, in Durkheim, E. and Ellis, A. (1963), *Incest*, Lyle Stuart: New York.

Easthope, A. (1990), *What a Mans Gotta Do: The Masculine Myth in Popluar Culture*, Unwin Hyman: Boston.

Edley, N. and Wetherell, M. (1996), Masculinity, Power and Identity in MaCanghaill, Máirtín. (ed) (1996), *Understanding Masculinity: Social Relations and Cultural Arenas*, Open University Press: Buckingham.

Edley, N. and Wetherell, M. (1995), *Men in Perspective: Practice, Power and Identity*, Prentice Hall, London.

Edwards, T. (1993), *Erotic Politics*, Routledege: London.

Eichler, M. (1980), *The Double Standard: A Feminist Critique of Social Science*, Croom Healm.

Eisenstein, Z. (ed) (1979), *Capitalist Patriarchy and the Case for Socialist Feminism*, New York, Monthly Review Press.

213

Eisenstein, H. (1963), *Contemporary Feminist Thought*, G.K. Hall: Boston.

Elias, N. (1991), *The Symbol Theory*, Sage: London.

Elias, N. (1987), The Changing Balance of Power Between the Sexes - A Process Sociological Study: The Example of the Ancient Roman Empire, *Theory Culture and Society*, Vol.4, pp 287-316.

Elias, N. (1987b), The Retreat of Sociologists into the Present, *Theory Culture and Society*, Vol.4, pp 223-247.

Elias, N. (1970), *What is Sociology?*, Hutchinson: London.

Elias, P. (1991), *Recruitment in Local Labour Markets: Employer and Employee Perspectives*, Department of Employment Research Paper No.86.

Elias P. and Balnchflower. D. (1989), *The Occupations, Earnings And Work Histories Of Young Adults: Who Gets The Good Jobs*, Department Of Employment Research Paper No. 68, London, HMSO.

Elias, P. and Main, B. (1982), *Women's Working Lives: Evidence from the National Training Survey*, University of Warwick: Institute for Employment Research.

Elliot, F.R. (1986), *The Family: Chnage or Continuity?*, Humanities Press International: USA.

Elshtain. (1981), in Tong. R. (1989), *Feminist Thought*, Unwin Hyman: London.

Employment Gazette, Feburary 1995, Vol. 103, No. 2.

Employment Gazette, December 1994, Vol. 102, No. 12.

Employment Gazette, January 1992, Part-Timers with Potential, pp19-26.

Employment Gazette, April 1992, Results of the 1991 Labour Force Survey, pp153-172.

Employment Gazette, May 1992, Employers and the flexible workforce, pp225-234.

Employment Gazette, June 1992, Self-Employment into the 1990s, pp269-292.

Employment Gazette, September 1992, Women and the Labour Market: results form the 1991 Labour Force Survey, pp433-459.

Engels, F. (1845), *The Condition of the Working Class in England*, Penguin, Harmondsworth.

Essen, J. (1979), Living In One-Parent Families: Attainment At School, *Child: Care, Health And Development*, Vol 5, No 3, pp. 83-93.

Essen, J. and Lambert, L. (1977), Living in One-Parent Families: Relationships and Attitudes of Sixteen-Year-Olds, *Child: Care, Health And Development*, Vol. 3, No. 5, pp 301-318.

Essen, J. and Parrinder, D. (1975), Housing For Children: Further Findings From the National Child Development Study, *Housing Review*, Vol. 24 No. 4, pp. 112-114.

214

ESRC (1993), SN:2011 National Child Development Study Fifth Follow Up, 1991, *USER GUIDE ESRC*, Data Archive, Clochester, Essex.

ESRC (1981), SN:3030 National Child Development Study Fouth Follow Up, 1981, *USER GUIDE ESRC*, Data Archive, Clochester, Essex.

ESRC (1974), SN:1407 National Child Development Study Third Follow Up, 1974, *USER GUIDE ESRC*, Data Archive, Clochester, Essex.

Evetts, J. (1988), Managing Childcare and Work Responsibilities: The Strategies of Married Women: Primary and Infant Teachers The *Sociological Review*, Vol.36, No.3, pp503-31.

Farkas, G. (1976), Education, Wage Rates, and the Division of Labour Between Husband and Wife, *Journal of Marriage and the Family*, Vol.38, pp473-483.

Fassinger, P. (1993), Meanings of Housework for Single Fathers and Mothers: Insights into Gender Inequality, in Hood, J, C. (ed) (1993), *Men, Work, and Family*, Sage Publications: Newbury Park.

Felstead, A. and Powell, M. (1996), *Contrasting Fortunes in Time and Space: Non-Standard Work in Canada and the United Kingdom*, CLMS, Leciester University and University of Alberta Canada, Mimeo.

Felstead, A. (1996), Homeworking in Britain: The National Picture in the Mid-1990's, *Industrial Relations Journal*, Vol.27, pp225-238.

Felstead, A., Jewson, N. with Goodwin J. (1996), *Homeworkers in Britain*, Department for Education and Employment: Research Studies RS1P, HMSO, London.

Felstead, A. and Jewson, N.(1995), Working at Home: Estimates from the 1991 Census, *Employment Gazette*, March 1995, p95.

Felstead, A., Goodwin, J. and Green, F. (1995), *Measuring Up To the National Training Targets: Womens Attainment of Vocational Qualifications*, Centre for Labour Market Studies, Leicester University.

Felstead, A. (1995), *Vocational Qualifications: Gender Barriers to the Certification of Work Related Skills*, Working Paper No.9, Centre for Labour Market Studies, Leicester University.

Felstead, A., Jewson, N. and Goodwin J. (1994), *Homeworkers in Britain: An Analysis of Large Scale Data Sets*, Interim Report to the Employment Department, Caxton House, London.

Felstead, A., Goodwin, J. and Green, F. (1994), *Womens Achievement of Vocational Qualifications National Advisory Council for Education and Training Targets,* Centre for Labour Market Studies.

Felstead, A. (1994), *The Gender Implications of Creating a Training Market: Alleviating or Reinforcing Inequality of Access*, Working Paper No.5 Centre for Labour Market Studies, Leicester University.

Felstead, A. and Green, F. (1993), *Cycles of Training ? Evidence from The British Recession of the Early 1990s*, University of Leicester, Department of Economics Working Paper, Vol. 93, No.3, pp1-23.

Felstead, A., Green, F. and Maguire, M. (1993), *Training in the Recession*, Centre for Labour Market Studies.

Felstead, A., Maguire, S. and Goodwin, J. (1993), *Evaluating the Funding for Training: A Training Cost Excercise*, Centre for Labour Market Studies.

Felstead, A. (1993), *The Corporate Paradox: Power and Control in the Business Franschise*, Routledge: London.

Felstead, A. and Leighton, P. (1992), Issues, Themes and Reflections on the Enterprise Culture, in Leighton, P. and Felstead, A. (1992), *The New Entrepenures*, pp 15-38 Kogan Page: London.

Femiano, S. (1992), The Function of Affect in Therapy With Men, *The Journal of Mens Studies*, Vol.1, No.2, pp 117-124.

Ferree, M.M. (1987), The View from Below: Womens Employment and Gender Equality in Working Class Families, in Hess, B.B. and Sussman, M.B. (eds), *Women and the Family: Two Decades of Change*, Haworth Press: New York.

Ferri, E. (1993), Partnerships and Parenthood, in Ferri, E. (1993), *Life at 33*, NCB, London.

Ferri, E. (1993), *Life at 33*, National Children's Bureau, London.

Fevre, R. (1987), Subcontracting in Steel, *Work, Employment and Society*, Vol. 1, No.4.

Finch, J. (1983), *Married to the Job*, Allen and Unwin: London.

Finch, J. (1980), Devising Conventional Performances: The Case of the Clergymens Wives, *Sociological Review*, Vol. 28, pp 851-870.

Fiske. S.T. and Taylor, S.E. (1984), Social Cognition, Addison Wesley.

Fitzgerald, L.F. and Cherpes, C.C. (1985), On the Reciprocal Relationship Between Gender and Occupation: Rethinking the Assumption Concerning Masculine Career Development, *Journal of Vocational Behaviour*, Vol. 27, pp 109-122.

Fogelman, K. (1986), *After School: The Education And Training Experiences Of The 1958 Cohort*, London, Further Education Unit.

Fogelman, K. (1986), The British Experience: The 1946, 1958 And 1970 National Cohorts, Paper Pesented To American Educational Research Association Annual Meeting, 1986, Reproduced By Edrs, US Office Of Education (Ref No Ed 271 863).

Fogelman, K. (ed) (1983) *Growing up in Great Britain: Papers from the National Child Development Study*, Macmillan: London.

Fogelman, K. (ed) (1976), *Britains Sixteen-Year-Olds*, London: National Childrens Bureau.

Ford, D. and Hearn, J. (1991), *Studying Masculinity*, Bradford University, Department of Applied Social Studies.

Fout, J.C. (1992), The Moral Purity Movement in Wilhelmine Germany and the attempt to Regulate Male Behaviour, *The Journal of Mens Studies*, Vol.1, No. 1, pp 5-31.

Fout, J.C. (1992), Sexual Politics in Wilhelmine Germany: The Male Gender Crisis, Moral Purity and Homophobia, *Journal of the History of Sexuality*, No.2, pp 388-421.

Franklin, C. (1984), *The Changing Definition of Masculinity*, New York: Plenum.

Freidan, B. (1974), *The Feminine Mystique*, Dell: New York.

Freidan, B. (1981), *The Second Stage*, Summit: New York.

Frese, M. (1985), Stress at Work and Psychosomatic Complaints, A Causal interpretation, *Journal of Applied Psychology*, Vol. 70, pp314-328.

Freud, S. (1905), Three Essays On Sexuality, in Freud, S. (1986), *The Essentials of Psychoanalysis*, Penguin: Harmondsworth.

Fromm, E. (1962), *Beyond The Chains of Illusion: My Encounter with Marx and Freud*, Abacus: UK.

Fryer, D. and Payne, R. (1983), Proactivity in Unemployment: Findings and Implications, *Leisure Studies*, Vol.3, pp 273-295.

Furlong, A. (1992), Growing up in a Classles Society, Edinburgh University Press: Edinburgh.

Galambos, N.L. and Silberesien, R.K. (1989), Role-Strain in West German Dual-Earner Households, *Journal of Marriage and the Family*, Vol.5 No.2, pp 385-389.

Gallie, D. and White, M. (1993), *Employee Commitment and the Skills Revolution: First Findings From the Employment in Britain Survey*, PSI, London.

Gane, M. (1983a), Durkheim: The Sacred Language, *Economy and Society*, Vol.12, No.2.

Gane, M. (1983b), Durkheim: Women as Outsider, *Economy and Society*, Vol.12, No.2.

Gane, M. (1984), Institutional Socialism and the Sociological Critique of Communism, *Economy and Society*, Vol.13.

Gavron, H. (1966), *The Captive Wife*, Pelican: Harmondsworth.

Gardiner, J. (1976), Women and Unemployment, *Red Rag*, No.10.

Gibbins, C. (1994), Women and Training: Data form the Labour Force Survey, *Employment Gazette*, November, pp391-402.

Giddens, A. (1971), *Capitalism and Modern Social Theory*, CTP: Cambridge.

Gill, D.S. and Mathews, B. (1995), Changes in the Breadwinner Role: Punjabi Families in Transition, *Journal of Comparative Family Studies*, Vol.26, No.2, pp 255-263.

Glasner, A. (1987), Gender, Class and the Workplace, *Sociology*, Vol.21, No.2, pp 294-303.

Glass, J. (1992), Housewives and Employed Wives: Demographic and Attitudinal Change 1972-1986, *Journal of Marriage and the Family*, Vol. 54, pp 559-569.

Glass, J. and Fujimoto, T. (1994), Housework, Persoanl Work and Depression, *Journal of Health and Social Behaviour*, Vol.35, pp 179-191.

Glover, J. (1994), Women Teachers and White Collar Workers: Domestic Circumstances and Paid Work, *Work Employment and Society*, Vol.8, No.1, p 87.

Gluksmann, M. (1986), In a Class of Their Own? Women Workers in the New Industries in Inter-War Britain, *Feminist Review*, No.24 (October).

Goldscheider, F.K. and Waite, L.J. (1991), *New Families, No Families ? Transformation of the American Home.* University of California, Berkely.

Goldthorpe, J.H., Lockwood, D., Bechhofer, F. and Platt, J. (1968), *The Affluent Worker: Industrial Attitudes and Behaviour*, CUP, Cambridge.

Goodnow, J. (1989), Work in Households: An Overview and Three Studies, in Ironmonger, D. (ed), *Households Work*, Allen and Unwin: Sydney.

Goodwin, J.D. (1995), Men and Non-Standard Work in NCDS5 SSRU Cohort Studies.

Goodwin, J.D. (1993), *Gender Studies and the Critique of Men*, University of Leicester Discussion Papers in Sociology, Vol. S93, No.6 - July, Leicester.

Gould, R. (1976), Measuring Masculinity by the Size of a Paycheck, in David, D. and Brannon, R. (eds), *The Forty-Nine Percent Majority:The Male Sex-Role*, Addison-Wesley, Reading, MA.

Gove, W.R. and Hughes, M. (1980), Reexamining the Ecological Fallacy: A Study in Which Aggregate Data are Critical in Investigating the Pathological Effects of Living Alone, *Social Forces*, Vol.57, pp 1157-1177.

Gover, M.R. (1992), Men as Primary Love Objects: On Mahler, Seperatness and Father Roles, *The Journal of Mens Studies*, Vol.1, No.2, pp 105-115.

Greenhalgh, L. (1984), Job Insecurity: Towards a Conceptual Strategy, *Academy of Management Review*, Vol.9, pp 438-448.

Graham, H. (1987), Being Poor: Perceptions and Coping Strategies of Lone Mothers, in Brannen, J. and Wilson, G. (1987), *Give and Take in Families: Studies in Resource Distribution*, Allen and Unwin: London.

Graham, H. (1983), *Do Her Answers Fit His Questions? Women and the Survey Method*, in Gamarnikow, E. *et al* (1983), The Public and the Private, Heinemann: London.

Gramarnikow, E., Morgan, D., Purvis, J. and Taylorson, D. (eds) (1983), *Gender Class and Work*, Heinemann: Aldershot.

Greer, G. (1971), *The Female Eunuch*, Paladin: London.

Greer, G. (1976), *Sex and Destiny*, Paladin: London.

Green, F. (1994), The Determinants of Training Male and Female Employees, and Some Measures of Discrimination, in McNabb, R., and Whitfield, K. (1994), The Market For Training, Aldershot: Avebury

Green, F., Krahn, H. and Sung, J. (1992), *Non-Standard Work in Canada and the United Kingdom*, Population Research Laboratory, University of Alberta Research Discussion Paper 91, April 1992.

Green, F. and Ashton, D. (1992), Skill Shortage and Skill Deficiency: A Critique, *Work, Employment and Society*, Vol.6, No.2, pp287-301.

Gregson, N. and Lowe, M. (1994), Waged Labour and the Renegotiation of the Domestic Division of Labour within Dual Career Households *Sociology*, Vol.28, No. 1, pp 55-79.

Gregson, N. and Lowe, M. (1993), Renegotiating the Domestic Division of Labour? A Study of Dual Career Households in North East and South East England, *The Sociological Review*, Vol.41, No.3, pp 475-505.

Greif, G., DeMaris, A. and Hood, J. (1993), Balancing Work and Single Fatherhood, in Hood, J, C. (ed) (1993), *Men, Work, and Family*, Sage Publications: Newbury Park.

Greenstein, T.N. (1996), Gender Ideology and Perceptions of Fairness of the Division of Household Labour: Effects on Marital Quality, *Social Forces*, Vol.73, No.2, pp 1029-1042.

Greeken, M. and Gove, W. (1983), *At Home and at Work: The Family Allocation of Labour*, Sage, Beverly Hills.

Gross, R.D. (1992), *Psychology: Science of Mind and Behaviour*, Hodder and Stoughton.

Hacker, M.H. (1957), The New Burdens of Masculinity, *Marriage and Family Living*, No. 19, pp 229.

Hagan, K. L. (ed) (1992), *Women Respond to the Mens Movement*, Pandora: San Fransico.

Hakim, C. (1996), *Key Issues in Women's Work: Female Heterogeneity and the Polarisation of Women's Employment*, Athlone Press, London.

Hakim, C. (1988), Self-Employment in Britain: Recent Trends and Current Issues, *Work, Employment and Society*, Vol.2, No.4, pp421-450.

Hakim, C. and Dennis, R. (1982), *Homeworking in Wages Council Industries: A Study based on Wages Insepctorate Records of Pay and Earnings*, Department of Employment Research Paper No.37.

Hakim, C. (1979), *Occupational Segregation*, Department of Employment Research Paper No.9.

Hakim, C. (1985), *Employers Use Of Outwork*, Department of Employment Research paper No.44.

Hakim, C. (1987), *Home-Based Work In Great Britain*, Department of Employment Research Paper No.60.

Hallaire, J. (1968), *Part-time Employment, Its Extent and Problems*, OECD, Paris.

Hammersley, M. (1992), On Feminist Methodology, *Sociology*, Vol.26, No.2, pp 187-206.

Hanson, S.M.H. and Bozett, F.W. (1985), *Dimesnions of Fatherhood*, Sage: London.

Harding, S. (1986), Is there a Feminist Method?, in Harding, S. (1986), *Feminism and Methodology*, Bloomington, USA, pp 1-14.

Harris, C.C. (1983), *The Family and Industrial Society*, Allen and Unwin: London.

Harris, C.C. (1969), *The Family*, Allen and Unwin: London.

Harris, E., Lea, S. and Foster, D. (1995), The Construction of Gender: An Analysis of Men's Talk on Gender, *South African Journal of Psychology*, Vol.25, No.3, pp 175-183.

Hartley, R.E. (1959), Sex Role Pressures in the Socialisation of the Male Child, *Psychological Reports* Vol.5, pp 458.

Hartmann, H. (1979), in Tong, R. (1989), *Feminist Thought*, Unwin Hyman: London.

Hartmann, H. (1979), The Unhappy Marriage of Marxism and Feminism: Towards a More Progressive Union, in Eisenstein, Z.R. (1979), *Capitalist Patriachy and the Case for Socialist Feminsim*, Monthly Review Press, London.

Hartmann, H. (1976), *The Historical Roots of Occupational Segregation: Capitalism, Patricarchy and Job Segregation by Sex*, Signs, Vol.1, No.3 pp 137-69.

Hass, L. (1993), Nurturing Fathers and Working Mothers:Changing Gender Roles in Sweden, in Hood, J, C. (ed) (1993), *Men, Work, and Family*, Sage Publications: Newbury Park.

Haywood, C. and MaCanghaill, Máirtín. (1996), Schooling Masculinities in MaCanghaill, Máirtín. (ed) (1996), *Understanding Masculinity: Social Relations and Cultural Arenas*, Open University Press, Buckingham.

Hearn, J. (1996), Is Masculinity Dead? A Critique of the Concept of Masculinity/Masculinities, in MaCanGhaill, Máirtín. (ed) (1996), *Understanding Masculinity: Social Relations and Cultural Arenas*, Open University Press, Buckingham.

Hearn, J. (1994), Research in Men and Masculinities: Some Sociological Issues and Possibilities, *The ANZJS*, Vol.30, No.1, pp 47-70.

Hearn, J. (1989), *Some Sociological Issues in Researching Men and Masculinities*, Hallsworth Research Fellowship, University of Manchester Working Paper No.2.

Hearn, J. (1988), *The Critique of Men: Current Lessons for the Theory and Practice of Men*, Hallsworth Research Fellowship, University of Manchester Working Paper No.1.

Hearn, J. (1987), *The Gender of Oppression: Men, Masculinity and the Critique of Marxism*, Wheatsheaf: Brighton.

Hearn, J. (1987), Changing Men's Studies: Studying Men and Masculinity, *Achilles Heel*, No. 8, pp18-22

Heather, P., Rick, J., Atkinson, J. and Morris, S. (1996) Employers' Use of Temporary Workers, in *Labour Market Trends*, September, pp 403-411, CSO, London.

Helgeson, V.S. (1995), Masculinity, Men's Roles, and Coronary Heart Disease, in Sabo, D. and Frederick-Gordon, D. (1995), *Men's Health and Illness: Gender, Power and the Body*, Sage, London.

Heward, C. (1996), Masculinities and Families, in MaCanGhaill, Máirtín. (ed) (1996), *Understanding Masculinity: Social Relations and Cultural Arenas*, Open University Press, Buckingham.

Hibbett, A. and Fogelman, K. (1990), Future Lives Of Truants: Family Formation and Health- Related Behaviour, *British Journal Of Educational Psychology*, Vol.60, pp 171-179.

Hibbett, A., Fogelman, K. and Manor O. (1990), Occupational Outcomes Of Truancy, *British Journal Of Educational Psychology*, Vol. 60, pp 23-36.

Hill, S. (1991), How do you Manage a Flexible Firm? The Total Quality Model, *Work, Employment and Society*, Vol.5, No.3, pp 397-415.

Hills, K. (1995), *The Development of Women Managers Careers: A Comparative Study of Hong Kong and the UK*, Centre for Labour Market Studies, Leicester University, Working Paper No. 10.

Hochschild, A. and Machung, A. (1989), *The Second Shift: Working Parents and the Revolution at Home*, Viking, New York.

Hochschild, A. (1989), *The Second Shift*, Avon Books: New York.

Hoffman, L.W. and Nye, F.I. (eds) (1974), *Working Mother*, Jossey-Bass: San Fransisco.

Hofstede, G. (1984), *Cultures Consequences: International Differences in Work-Related Values*, Sage: London.

Hooks, B. (1984), *Feminist Theory: From Margin to Centre*, South End Press, Boston.

Hooks, B. (1982), *Ain't I a Woman*, Pluto Press, London.

Hood, J, C. (ed) (1993), *Men, Work, and Family*, Sage Publications: Newbury Park.

Horrell, S. and Rubery, J. (1991), *Employers Working-Time Policies and Womens Employment*, EOC, HMSO.

Huber, J. and Spitze, G. (1983), *Sex Stratification: Children, Housework and Jobs*, Academic Press, New York.

Hughes, J. (1994), *Philosophy of the Social Sciences and Empirical Research: Critical Observations from a Process-Sociological Perspective*, University of Leicester Discussion Papers in Sociology, S94/2 - December.

Hughes, K.D. (1991), *Developments in the Non-Traditional Employment of Women and Men in Canada 1971-1986*, Sociology Research Group, University Of Cambridge, Working Paper No.1.

Humm. M. (ed) (1992), *Feminsim: A Reader*, Harvester Wheatsheaf, London.

Hunt, E.H. (1981), British Labour History II 1815-1914, cited in Roberts, E. (1988), *Women's Work 1840-1940*, Macmillan, London.

Hunter, L.C. and Macinnes, J. (1991), *Employers Labour Use Strategies*, Department of Employment Research Paper No.87.

Ireson, C. and Gill, S. (1988), Girls Socialization for Work, in Helton, A. (1988), *Women Working: Theories and Facts in Perspective*, Maffield: California.

Ishii-Kuntz, M. (1993), Japanese Fathers: Work Demands and Family Roles, in Hood, J, C. (ed) (1993), *Men, Work, and Family*, Sage Publications, Newbury Park.

Jackson, B. (1984), *Fatherhood*, Allen and Unwin: London.

Jackson, D. (1990), *Unmasking Masculinity: A Critical Autobiography*, Unwin Hyman: London.

Jacobson, D. (1987), A Personological Study of Job Insecurity Expereince, *Social Behaviour*, No.2, pp143-155.

Jansson, S. (1995), Food Parctices and the Divison of Labour: A Comparison Between British and Swedish Households, *The Sociological Review*, Vol.43, No.3, pp462-477.

Jenkins, R. (1983), *Lads, Citizens and Ordinary Kids: Working-Class Youth Life-Styles in Belfast*, Routledge and Kegan Paul: London.

Joeman (1994), *Homeworking in Britain: Findings from the Spring 1992 LFS*, Employment Deprtament Mimeo.

Johansson, S. and Åhlfeldt, J. (1996), Stress Expereinced by Informal Caregivers: On Confliciting Demands in Everyday Life, *Scandanavian Journal of Social Welfare*, Vol.5, No.2, pp83-96.

Johnson, T. (1972), *Professions and Power*, Macmillan, London.

Joshi, H. (1987), The Cost of Caring, in Glendinning, C. and Millar, J. (eds), *Women and Poverty in Britain*, Wheastsheaf Books: London.

Joshi, H. (1984), *Womens Participation in Paid Work*, Department of Employment Research Paper No.45.

Kasel, S.V. and Cobb, S. (1982), Variability of stress effects amongts young men experiencing job loss, in Goldgerger, L. *et al* (1982), *Handbook of Stress: Theoretical Perspectives*, The Free Press, New York.

Kennedy, M. (1993), Clothing, Gender and Ritual Transvestisim: The Bissu of Sulawesi, *The Journal of Mens Studies*, Vol.2, No.1, pp 1-14.

Kerr, C., Dunlop, J.T., Harbison, F. and Myers, C.A. (1973), *Industrialism and Industial Man*, Pelican: Harmondsworth.

Kilgore, J. (1984), *The Intimate Man: Intimacy and Masculinity in the 1980s*, Abingdon, Nashville.

Kimmel, M. (1990), After Fifteen Years:The Impact of the Sociology of Masculinity on the Masculinity of Sociology, in Hearn, J. and Morgan, D. (eds) (1990), *Men, Masculinities and Social Theory*, Unwin Hyman: London.

Kimmel, M. (ed) (1987), *Changing Men: New Directions in Research on Men and Masculinity*, Sage: London.

Kimmel, M. (1986), Toward Men's Studies, *American Behavioural Scientist*, Vol.29, No.5, pp517-529

Kimmel, M. and Messener, M. (ed) (1989), *Mens Lives*, New York, Macmillan.

Kingston, P.W. and Nock S.L. (1985), Consequences of the Family Work Day, *Journal of Marriage and the Family*, Vol. 47, No 3, pp619-630.

Klumas A.L. and Marchant, T. (1994), Images of Men in Popular Sitcoms, *The Journal of Mens Studies*, Vol.2, No.3, pp269-285.

Klien, A.M. (1995), Life's Too Short to Die Small, in Sabo, D. and Frederick-Gordon, D. (1995), *Men's Health and Illness: Gender, Power and the Body*, Sage, London.

Klien, V. (1965), *Britains Married Women Workers*, London.

Kohn, M.L. and Schooler, C. (1983), *Working and Personality: An Inquiry into the Impact of Social Stratification*, Norrwod, New Jersey.

Komarvosky, M. (1964), *Blue Collar Marriage*, Vintage: NY.

Komarvosky, M. (1946), Cultural Contradictions and Sex Roles, *American Journal of Sociology*, Vol.52, Nov.

Kposowa, A.J., Breault, K.D. and Gopal, S.K. (1995), White Male Suicide in the United States: A Multivariate Individual Level Analysis, *Social Forces*, Vol.74, No.1, pp315-323.

Krondorfer, B. (1994), Our Soul has Not Suffered, *The Journal of Mens Studies*, Vol.2, No.3, pp 209-220.

Kruk, E. (1992), Child Custody Determination: An Analysis of the Litigation Model, Legal Practices and Mens Experiences in the Process, *The Journal of Mens Studies*, Vol.1, No.2, pp 163-185.

Labour Force Survey (1994), *Rapid Release No.1*, August.

Labour Force Survey (1994), *Quartely Bulletin No.9*, September.

Labour Force Survey (1993), *Historical Supplement*, April.

Lai, G. (1995), Work and Family Roles and Psychological Well-Being in Urban China, *Journal of Health and Social Science*, Vol.36, No.1, pp 11-37.

Lamphere, L. (1987), *From Working Daughters to Working Mothers: Immigrant Women in a New England Community*, Cornell University Press: London.

Lanis, K. and Cowell, K. (1995), Images of Women in Avertisements: Effects on Attitudes Related to Agression, *Sex Roles*, Vol.32, Nos9-10, pp 639-649.

LaPiere, R.T. (1934), Attitudes Versus Action, *Social Forces*, Vol. 13, pp 230-7.

LaRocco, J.M. (1983), Attitudes , Intentions, and Turnover: An Analysis of Effects Using Latent Variables, *Human Relations*, Vol.36, No.9, pp 813-26.

LaRossa, R. (1988), Fatherhood and Social Change, *Family Relations*, Vol. 37, pp 451-457.

LaRossa, R. and LaRossa, M.M. (1987), *Transition to Parenthood: How Infants Change Families*, Sage: Beverly Hills, California.

Laurie, H. and Taylor, M. (1992), *Homeworkers in Britain*, Report Commissioned by Employment Department from ESRC Research Centre on Micro-Social Change, University of Essex.

LeeBlair, S., Wenk, D. and Hardesty, C. (1994), Marital Quality and Parental Involvement: Interconnections of Mens Spousal and Parental Roles, *The Journal of Mens Studies*, Vol.2, No.3, pp 221-237.

Leighton, P. and Felstead, A. (1992), *The New Entrepenures*, Kogan Page: London.

Leighton, P. (1983), *Contractual Arrangements in Selected Industries: A study of Employment Relationships in Industries with Outwork*, Department of Employment Research Paper No.39.

Leighton, G. (1992), Wive's Paid and Unpaid Work and Husband's Unemployment, *Sociology Review*, Vol.1, No.3, pp 11-17.

Leman, S. and Williams, Y. (1995), Apprentices and Other Long-Term Trainees: Data form the LFS and other surveys, *Employment Gazette*, Feburary, pp 67-73.

224

Lennon, M.C. and Rosenfield, S. (1994), Relative Fairness in the Division of Housework: The Importance of Options, *American Journal of Sociology*, Vol.100, pp 506-31.

Lenski, G.E. (1966), *Power and Privilege: A Theory of Social Stratification*, McGraw-Hill: New York.

Levy, G. and Carter, D. (1989), Gender Schema, Gender Constancy and Gender-role Knowledge: The Roles of Cognitive Factors in Pre-schoolers Gender-role Stereotype Attributions, *Development Psychology*, Vol.25, No.3, pp444-449.

Lewis, R.A. and Salt, R.E. (eds) (1986), *Men and Families*, Sage, Beverly Hills.

Lewis, C. and OBrien, M. (eds) (1987), *Reassessing Fatherhood: New Observations on Fathers and the Modern Family*, Sage: London.

Lewis, C. (1986), *Becoming a Father*, OUP: Milton Keynes.

Lewis, J., Porter, M. and Shrimpton, M. (eds) (1988), *Women, Work and the Family in the British, Canadian and Norwegian Offshore Oil Fields*, MacMillan: London.

Lieulfsrud, H. and Woodward, A. (1987), Women at Class Crossroads: Reupdating Conventional Theories of Family Class, *Sociology*, Vol.21, No.2, pp393-412.

Likert, R. (1932), A Technique for the Measurement of Attitudes, *Archives of Psychology*.

Llewellyn, M. (1980), Studying Girls At School, in Deem, R. (ed) (1980), *Schooling for Womens Work*, Routledge and Kegan Paul.

Lowe, G.S. and Nirthcott, H.C. (1988), The Impact of Working Conditions, Social Roles and Personal Characteristics on Gender Differences in Distress, *Work and Occupations*, Vol. 15, pp 55-77.

Lukes, S. (1973), *Emile Durkheim: His Life and Work*, Allen Lane: London.

Lysonski, S. (1985), Role Portrayals in British Magazine Advertisements, *European Journal of Marketing*, Vol.19, No.7, pp 37-55.

MaCanGhaill, Máirtín. (ed) (1996), *Understanding Masculinity: Social Relations and Cultural Arenas*, Open University Press, Buckingham.

MacInnes, J. (1997), Why Capitalism is not Patriarchal and Gender Doesn't Exist, paper from, MacInnes, J. (1997), *The End of Masculinity*, Open University Press, Forthcoming.

MacInnes, J. (1996), Analysing Men, *Gender Work and Organization*, Vol.3, No.1, pp 51-63.

Managan, J.A. and Walvin, J. (1987), *Manliness and Morality: Middle-Class Masculinity in Britain and America 1800-1940*, Manchester University Press: Manchester.

Manke, B., Seery, B.L., Crouter, A.C and McHale, S.M. (1994), The Three Corners of Domestic Labour: Mothers, Fathers, and Childrens Weekday and Weekend Housework, *Journal of Marriage and the Family*, Vol.56, pp657-668

Mansfield, B. (1997), *Mystery, Rationalism and Democracy - The Journey of A Concept*, Unpublished paper presnetd at the Competency Network AGM, June 1997.

Marsh, C. (1989), *Exploring Data*, Polity.

Marsh, C. (1989), *Hours of Work of Men and Women in Britain*, EOC, HMSO.

Marshall, C.M., Heck, R., Hawkins, A.J. and Roberts, T.A. (1994), *Family Work and Fairness: Listening to Husbands in Dual-Earner Families*, Vol.3, No.1, pp 1-19.

Martin, C.L., Eisenbud, L. and Rose, H. (1995), Children's Gender-Based Reasoning About Toys, *Child Development*, Vol.66, No.5, pp1453-1471.

Martin, J. and Roberts, C. (1984), *Women and Employment: A Lifetime Perspective*, HMSO, London.

Marullo, S. (ed) (1995), *Comparisons of Regulations on Part-time and Temporary Employment in Europe: A briefing Paper*, Department of Employment Research Series, No.52

Marx, K. and Engels, F. (1845), *The Origin of the Family, Private Property and the State*, Lawrence Wishart: London.

Marx, K. and Engels, F. (1848), *The Communist Manifesto*, Lawrence Wishart: London.

Marx, K. (1867), *Capital Vol.1*, Everymans Library: New York.

Marx, K. (1986), *Selected Writings in Sociology and Social Philosophy*, Bottomore, T. and Rubel, M. (ed) (1986), *Selected Writings in Sociology and Social Philosophy*, Penguin: Harmondsworth.

Mason, K.O. and Yu-Hsia, Lu. (1988) Attitudes Towards Women's Familial Roles: Changes in the United States, 1977-1985, *Gender and Society*, Vol.2, pp39-57.

Maynard, M. (ed) (1994), *Researching Womens Lives from A Feminist Perspective*, Taylor and Francis, London.

Maynard, M. (1990), The Re-Shaping of Sociology? Trends in the Study of Gender, Sociology, Vol.24, No.2, pp 269-290.

McGivney, V. (1994), *Wasted Potential: Training and Career Progression for Part-Time and Temporary Workers*, Leicester: NIACE.

McHale, S. and Crouter, A.C. (1992), You Can't Always Get What You Want: Incongruence Between Sex-Role Attitudes and Family Work Roles and Its Implications for Marriage, *Journal of Marriage and the Family*, Vol.54, No.3, pp 537-547.

McHale, S., Baartko, W., Crouter, A. and Perry-Jenkins, M. (1990), Childrens Housework and Psychosocial Functioning: The Mediating Effects of Parents Sex-role Behaviours and Attitudes, *Child Development*, Vol. 61, pp1413-1426.

McKay, J. (1993), Marked Men and Wanton Women: The Politics of Naming Sexual Deviance in Sport, *The Journal of Mens Studies*, Vol.2 No.1, pp 69-87.

McRae, S. (1986), *Cross-Class Families: A Study of Wives Occupational Superiority*, Clarendon Press: Oxford.

McKee, L. and Bell, C. (1986), His Unemployment, Her Problem, in Allen, S., Waton, A., Purcell, K. and Wood, S. (eds) (1986), *The Experience of Unemployment*, MacMillan: London.

Meager, N. and Court, G. (1994), *Self Employment and the Distribution of Income*, Brighton: IMS Report 270.

Meager, N. (1992a), The Characteristics of the Self-Employed: Some Anglo-German Comparisons, in Leighton, P. and Felstead, A. (1992), *The New Entrepenures*, Kogan Page: London, pp 69-99.

Meager, N. (1992b), The Fall and Rise of Self-Employment (Again): A comment on Bögenhold and Staber, *Work, Employment and Society*, Vol. 6, No. 1, pp 127-134.

Mennell, S. (1992), *Norbert Elias: An Introduction*, Basil Blackwell, Oxford.

Messiner, M., Humpherys, S.M., Meis, M. and Scheu, W.J. (1975), No Exit for Wives, *Canadian Review of Sociology and Anthropology*, Vol. 12, No. 4, pp424-439.

Miller, D. and Swanson, G. (1958), *The Changing American Parent*, John Wiley, New York.

Miller, S. (1983), *Men and Friendship*, Boston: Houghton.

Millet, K. (1970), *Sexual Politics*, Doubleday: New York.

Mincer, J. (1962), *Labor Force Participation of Married Women: A Study of Labour Supply*, in National Bureau of Economic Research, Aspects of Labor Economics: A Conference of the Universities-National Bureau Committee for Economic Research, Princeton University Press, Princeton.

Miner, M.M. (1992), Documenting the Demise of Manly Love: The Virginian, *The Journal of Mens Studies*, Vol.1, No. 1, pp 33-39.

Mitchell, J. and Oakley, A. (1986), *What is Feminism*, Basil Blackwell. Oxford.

Mitchell, J. (1971), *Womens Estate*, Penguin: Harmondsworth.

Mitchell, J. (1975), *Psychoanalysis and Feminism*, Penguin: Harmondsworth.

Mitchell, J. and Anderson, K. (1989), Mental Health and the Labour Force Participation of Older Workers, *Inquiry*, Vol.26, p262.

Morgan, D.H.J. (1992), *Discovering Men*, Routledge: London.

Morgan, D. (1981), Men, Masculinity and the Process of Sociological Enquiry, in Roberts, H. (1981), *Doing Feminist Research*,. Routledge and Keegan Paul, London.

Morra, N. and Smith, M.D. (1993), Men in Feminsim: Theorizing Sexual Violence, *The Journal of Mens Studies*, Vol.2, No.1, pp 15-28.

Morris, L. (1993), Household Finance Management and the Labour Market: A Case Study of Hartlepool, *The Sociological Review*, Vol.41, No.3, pp506-536.

Morris, L. (1990), *The Workings of the Households*, Polity Press, Cambridge.

Morris, L. (1988), Employment, the Household and Social Networks in Duncan, G. (ed), *Employment in Britain*, Basil Blackwell: Oxford.

Morris, L. (1985), Renegotiation of the Domestic Division of Labour, in Roberts, B. *et al* (eds) (1985), *New Approaches to Economic Life*, MUP: Manchester.

Morris, L. (1983), Renegotiation of the Domestic Division of Labour in the Context of Male Redundancy, in Newby, H. *et al* (1983), *Restructuring Capital: Recession and Reorganization in Industrial Society*, Macmillan Press: London.

Morrow, V. (1991), *Family Values*, Cambridge University, 16th May 1991.

Mortimer, J.T. and Simmons, R.G. (1978), Adult Socialisation, *Annual Review of Sociology*, Vol.4 pp 421-545.

Mort, F. (1988), Boys Own: Masculinity, Style and Popular Culture, in Chapmand, R. and Rutherford, J. (eds) (1988), *Male Order: Unwrapping Masculinity*, Lawrence and Wishart, London.

Moss, P. and Fonda, N. (eds) (1980), *Work and Family*, Temple Smith: London.

Murrcot, A. (1983), Its a Pleasure to Cook For Him: Food, Mealtimes and Gender in some South Wales Households, in Gamarnikow, E. *et al* (1983), *The Public and the Private*, Heinemann, London.

Myers, D.G. (1988), *Social Psychology*, McGraw Hill, New York.

Myrdal, A. and Klien, V. (1956), *Womens Two Roles*, Routledge and Kegan Paul: London.

Nardi, P. (1992), *Mens Freindships*, Sage: Newbury Park.

Nätti, J. (1993), Temporary Employment in the Nordic Countries: A 'Trap' or a 'Bridge'? *Work Employment and Society*, Vol.7, No.3, pp 451-464.

Nelson, J.B. (1988), *The Intimate Connection: Male Sexuality, Masculine Spirituality*, Westminster Press, USA.

Newell, S. (1993), The Superwoman Syndrome: Gender Differences in Attitudes Towards Equal Oppotunities at Work and Towards Domestic Responsibilities at Home, *Work Employment and Society*, Vol.7, No.2, pp275-289.

Nichols, T. and Beynon, H. (1977), *Living With Capitalism*, RKP: London.

Nicholson, J. (1980), *What Society Does to Girls*, Virago: Oxford.

Nielsen, F. and Alderson, A.S. (1997), The Kvinets Curve and the Great U-Turn: Income Inequality in U.S Counties, 1970-1990. *American Sociological Review*, Vol.62, Feb, pp 12-33.

Norman, P., Collins, S., Lonner, M., Martin, R. and Rance, J. (1995), Attributions, Cognitions and Coping Styles: Teleworkers Reactions to Work-Related Problems, *Journal of Applied Social Psychology*, Vol.25, No.2, pp 117-128.

Oakley, A. (1989), Womens Studies in British Sociology, *British Journal of Sociology*, Vol. 40, No.3.

Oakley, A. (1987), *Housewife*, Pelican: Harmondsworth.

Oakley, A. (1974), *The Sociology of Housework*, Basil Blackwell: Oxford.

Oakley, A. (1972), *Sex, Gender and Society*, Temple Smith: London.

O'Brien, M. (1995), Allocation of resources in Households: Children's Perspectives, *The Sociological Review*, Vol.43, No.3, pp501-517.

O'Connell-Davidson, J. (1994), What do Franchisors Do? Control and Commercialisation in Milk Distribution, *Work, Employment and Society*, Vol. 8, No. 1, pp 23-44.

O'Connell-Davidson, J. (1991), Subcontract, Flexibility and Changing Employment Relations in the Water Industry, in Blyton, P. and Morris, J. (eds) (1991), *A Flexible Future?: Prospects for Employment and Organization*, Berlin: Walter de Gruyter.

O'Neil, R. and Greenberger, E. (1994), Patterns of Commitment to Work and Parenting: Implications for Role Strain, *Journal of Marriage and the Family*, Vol.56, No.1, pp 101-108

OECD (1996), *Employment Outlook*, OECD Paris.

OECD (1991), *Employment Outlook*, OECD Paris.

Orwell, G. (1937), *The Road to Wigan Pier*, Victor Gollancz: London.

Osgood, C.E. *et al* (1957), *The Measurement of Meaning*, University of Illinios Press.

Pahl, J. (1993), Money, Marriage and Ideology: Holding the Purse Strings *Sociology Review*, pp7-10.

Pahl, J. (1989), *Money and Marriage*, Macmillian, Basingstoke.

Pahl, R.E. (1984), *Divisions of Labour*, Basil Blackwell, Oxford.

Pahl, R.E. and Wallace, C. (1985), Household Work Strategies in Economic Recession, in Redclift, N. and Minigione, E. (eds), *Beyond Employment: Household, Gender and Subsistence*, Basil Blackwell: Oxford.

Parsons, T. and Bales, R. (1956), *Family, Socialization and the Interaction Process*, Routledge: London.

Parsons, T. (1951), *The Social System*, Routledge & Kegan Paul: London.

Patel, N., Power, T.G. and Baunagri, N.P. (1996), Socialisation Values and Practices of Indian Immigrant Parents: Correlates of Modernity and Acculturation, *Child Development*, Vol.67, No.2, pp 302-313.

Payne, J. (1987), *Early Parenthood and Mens Unemployment: Is there a Causal Link ?* Unpublished Paper, December 1987.

Payne, J. (1984), *Work Histories and Employment Outcomes at Age 23*, National Children's Bureau Working Paper No.21.

Peace, H. (1993), *The Pretended Family: A Study of The Divison of Labour in Lesbian Families*, Leciester University Discussion Papers in Sociology S93/3.

Pearce, F. (1989), *The Radical Durkheim*, Unwin Hyman, London.

Pearson, K. (1997), *A Study of Men in a Changing Patriarchal Trade Union Culture*, Unpublished M.Sc Dissertation, University of Leicester.

Pearson, R. and Lambert, L. (1977), Sex Education, Preparation For Parenthood and The Adolescent, *Community Health*, Vol.9, No.2, pp 84-90.

Pearson, R. and Peckham, C. (1977), Handicapped Children In Secondary Schools From The National Child Development Study (1958 Cohort). *Public Health*, Vol.91, pp 296-304.

Peet, R. (1991), *Global Capitalism: Theories of Societal Development*, Routledge, London.

Pennington, S. and Westover, B. (1989), *A Hidden Workforce*, Macmillan, London.

Perrucci, C.C., Potter, H.R. and Roulds, D.L. (1978), Determinants of Male Family-Role Performance. *Psychology of Women Quarterly*, Vol. 3, No.1, pp 53-66.

Pettegrew, J. (1993), The Return of Primal Man: The Psychology of Primitivism in Turn of the Cebtury Naturalist Fiction and College Football, *The Journal of Mens Studies*, Vol.2, No.1, pp 29-52.

Pheonix, A. (1988), *The Afro-Caribben Myth*, New Society, March.

Phizacklea, A. and Wolkowitz, C. (1995), *Homeworking Women: Gender, Racism and Class at Work*, London, Sage.

Phizacklea, A. (1990), *Unpacking the Fashion Industry*, London, Routledge.

Piña, D.L. and Bengtson, V.L. (1993), The Household Division of Labour and Wives Happiness: Ideology, Employment, and Perceptiuons of Support *Journal of Marriage and the Family*, Vol.55, pp 901-912.

Pinder, R. (1995), Bringing Back the Body Without Balme? The Expereince of Ill and Diabled People at Work, *Sociology of Health and Illness*, Vol.17, No.5, pp 605-631.

Pleck, J. (1993), Are "Family-Supportive" Employer Policies relevant to Men? in Hood, J.C. (ed) (1993), *Men, Work, and Family*, Sage Publications, Newbury Park.

Pleck, E.H. and Pleck, J. (1980), *The American Man*, Englewood, USA.

Pleck, J. (1985), *Working Wives, Working Husbands*, Sage, Beverly Hills, California.

Pleck, J. (1983), Husbands Paid Work and Family Roles: Current research Issues, in Lopata, H. and Pleck, J. (eds) (1983), *Research into the Interweave of Social Roles: Families and Jobs*, Vol. 3, pp 251-333, Grenwich, CT.

Pleck, J. (1981), *The Myth of Masculinity*, MIT, Cambridge.

Pleck, J. (1979), Men's Family Work: Three Perspectives and Some New Data, *Family Co-Ordinator*, Vol. 28, pp 473-480.

Pleck, J. (1976), The Male Sex Role: Definitions, Problems and Sources of Change, *Journal of Social Issues*, No. 32, pp 155-164.

Pollert, A. (1982), Women, Gender relations and Wage Labour, in Gramanikow, E. *et al* (ed), *Gender, Class and Work*, Heinemann, Aldershot.

Pollert, A. (1982), *Girls Wives and Factory Lives*, Macmillan, London.

Polych, C. and Sabo, D. (1995), Gender Politics, Pain and Illness, in Sabo, D. and Frederick-Gordon, D. (1995), *Men's Health and Illness: Gender, Power and the Body*, Sage, London.

Poster, M. (1978), *Critical Theory of the Family*, Pluto Press, London.

Presser, H.B. (1994), Employment Schedules Among Dual-Earner Spouses and Division of Labour by Gender, *American Sociological Review*, Vol.59, No.3, pp 348-364.

Pringle, K. (1995), *Men, Masculinities and Social Welfare*, London, UCL Press.

Pringle, R. (1989), *Secretaries Talk*, London, Verso.

Procter, S., Rowlinson, M., McArdle, L., Hassard, J. and Forrester, P. (1994), Flexibility, Politics and Strategy: In Defence of the Model of the Flexible Firm, *Work, Employment and Society*, Vol.8, No.2, pp 221-242.

Radin, N. (1988), Primary Caregiving Fathers of Long Duration, in Bronstein, P. and Cowen, C.P. (eds), *Fatherhood Today: Mens Changing Role in the Family*, John Wiley, New York.

Radin, N. and Russell, G. (1983), Increased Father Paticipation and Childcare Development Outcomes, in Lamb, M.E. and Sagi, A. (eds) (1983), *Fatherhood and Family Policy*, Erlbaum, USA.

Radin, N. (1982), Primary Caregiving and Role Sharing Fathers, in Lamb, M.E. (1982), Non-Traditional Families: Parenting and Child Development, Erlbaum, USA.

Raphael, B. (1984), *The Anatomy of Bereavement*, London Hutchinson.

Raj, K. (1995), Relationships Between Sex Role Attitudes and Self-Esteem to Fear of Success Among College Women, *Psychological Studies*, Vol.40, No.2, pp 82-86.

Rapping, E. (1994), *Mediations: Forays into the Culture and Gender Wars*, South End Press, Bostson, MA.

Rees, T. (1994), *Women and Access to Training: Feminising the European Unions Training Programmes Delivery of Effective Training*, Sheffield, March 1994.

Reisman, D. (1953), *The Lonely Crowd*, New York.

Rexroat, C. and Shehan, C. (1987), The Family Life Cycle and Spouses' Time in Housework, *Journal of Marriage and the Family*, Vol. 49, No. 4 pp737-750.

Rindfuss, R.R., Liao, T.F. and Tsuya, N.O. (1992), Contact with Parents in Japan: Effects on opinions Toward Gender and Intergenerational Roles, *Journal of Marriage and the Family*, Vol 54, No.4, pp 812 - 822.

Roberts, E. (1988), *Womens Work 1840 - 1940*, Macmillan, London.

Roberts, E. (1984), *A Womans Place: An Oral Histroy of Working Class Women: 1890-1940*, Basil Blackwell, London.

Roberts, K. (1994), Flexibility and Individualism: A Comparison of Transitions into Employment in England and Germany, *Sociology*, Vol.28, No.1, pp 31-54.

Roberts, H. (ed) (1981), *Doing Feminist Research*, Routledge, London.

Robertson, J.M. and Verschelden, C. (1993), Voluntary Male Homemakers and Female Providers: Reported Experiences and Percieved Social Reactions, *The Journal of Mens Studies*, Vol.1, No.4, pp 382-402.

Robinson, O. and Wallace, J. (1984), Growth and Utilisation of Part-Time Employment in Great Britain, *Employment Gazette*, Vol. 92, No.9, pp 391-397.

Robins, L.N., West, P.A. and Murphy, G.E. (1977), The High Rate of Suicide in Older White Men: A Study Testing Ten Hypotheses, *Social Psychiatry*, No.12, pp 1-20.

Rodgers, G. and Rodgers, J. (eds) (1989), *Precarious Jobs in Labour Maeket Regulation: The Growth of Atypical Employment in Western Europe*, International Institute for Labour Studies, Free University of Brussels.

Rogoff, B., Mistry, J., *et al* (1983), Guided Participation in Cultural Activity by Toddlers and Caregivers, *Monographs of the Society for research in Childhood*, No.58.

Rokeach, M. (1968), *Beliefs, Attitudes and Values,* Jossey-Bass, San-Fransico.

Roper, M. (1994), *Masculinity and the British Organisation Man Since 1945*, Oxford, OUP.

Ross, C.E. and Wu, C.L. (1995),The Links Between Education and Health, *American Sociological Review*, Vol.60, No.5, pp 719-745.

Ross, C.E. (1987), The Divisions of Labour at Home *Social Forces*, Vol. 65, pp 816-833.

Rotunda, E.A. (1987), Learning About Manhood: Gender Ideals and the Middle-Class Family in Nineteenth-Century America, in Managan, J.A and Walvin, J. (1987), *Manliness and Morality: Middle-Class Masculinity in Britain and America 1800-1940*, Manchester University Press, Manchester.

Rowbotham, S. (1989), *The Past is Before Us: Feminsim in Action Since the 1960's*, Penguin, Harmondsworth.

Rubin, L. (1983), *Intimate Strangers: Men as Women Together*, Harper and Row, New York

Russell, G. (1987), Problems in Role Reversed Families, in Lewis, C. and OBrien, M. (1987), *Reassessing Fatherhood*, Sage, London.

Russell, G. (1983), *The Changing Roles of Fathers*, UQP, London.

Sabo, D. and Frederick-Gordon, D. (1995), *Men's Health and Illness: Gender, Power and the Body*, Sage, London.

Scott, J., Alwin, D.L. and Braun, M. (1996), Generational Changes in Gender-Role Attitudes: Britain in a Cross-National Perspective, *Sociology*, Vol.30, No.3, pp 471-492.

Secord, P.F. and Backman, C.W. (1964), *Social Psychology*, McGraw-Hill, NY.

Segal, L. (1990), *Slow Motion: Changing Men, Chaging Masculinities*, Virago Press, London.

Segal, L. (1983), Smash the Family, in Segal, L. (ed), *What is to be Done about the Family?*, Penguin, Harmondsworth.

Seidler, V.J. (1994), *Unreasonable Men: Masculinity and Social Theory*, Routledge, London.

Seidler, V.J. (1991), *Achilles Heel Reader: Men, Sexual Politics and Socialism*, London, Routledge.

Seymour, J. (1992), Not a Manly Thing To Do ? Gender Accountability and the Divison of Domestic Labour, in Dunne, G.A. Blackburn, R.M. and Jarman, J.(eds) (1992), *Inequalities in Employment Inequalities in Home Life Conference Proceedings for the 20th Cambridge Social Stratification Seminar*, University of Cambridge, 9th-10th September 1992.

Sexton, P. (1969), *The Feminized Male*, Random House, NY.

Sharpe, S. (1976), *Just Like a Girl: How Girls Learn to be Women*, Pelican, Harmondsworth.

Sharma, U. (1986), *Womens Work: Class and the Urban Household: A Study of Shimala, North India*, Tavistock: London.

Shelton, C. and John, D. (1993), Ethnicity, Race and Difference: A Comparison of White, Black and Hispanic Mens Household Labour Time, in Hood, J, C. (ed) (1993), *Men, Work, and Family* Sage Publications, Newbury Park.

Simons, R.L., Beaman, J., Conger, R.D. and Chao, W. (1992), Gender Differences in the Intergenerational Transmission of Parenting Beliefs, *Journal of Marriage and the Family*, Vol.54, No.4, pp 823-836.

Simon, R. (1995), Gender, Multiple Roles, Role Meanining and Mental Health, *Journal of health and Social Behaviour*, Vol.36, No.2, pp 182-194.

Simpson, M. (1994), *Male Impersonators*, Cassell, London.

Skills and Enterprise Network (1993), *Labour Market and Skill Trends SEN*, Nottingham.

Smith, D. (1988), *The Everyday World as a Problematic: A Feminist Sociology*, OUP, Milton Keynes.

Smith, R.M. and Smith, C.W. (1981), Child Rearing and Single Parent Fathers *Family Relation*, Vol.30, No.3, pp 411-417.

Social Attitudes (1997), HMSO: London

South, S.J. and Spitz, G. (1994), Housework in Marital and Non-Marital Households, *American Sociological Review*, Vol. 59, No.3, pp 327-347.

Spender, D. (1982), *Invisible Women: The Schooling Scandal*, Writers and Readers Publishing Co-operative, London.

Spender, D. (ed) (1981), *Men's Studies Modified: The Impact of Feminism on the Academic Discipline*, Pergamon, New York.

Spitz, G. and Ward, R. (1995), Household Labour in Intergenerational Households, *Journal of Marriage and the Family*, Vol.57, No.2, pp355-361.

Stacey, M. (1983), Social Sciences and the State: Fighting Like a Woman, in Gramarnikow, E. (1983), *The Public and the Private*, Heinemann, London.

Stanworth, M. (1981), *The Significance of Gender in Teachers Views of Their Pupils Gender and Schooling*, Hutchinson: London

Stanworth, M. (1984), Women and Class Analysis: A Reply to John Goldthorpe, *Sociology*, Vol.18, No.1, pp59-81.

Starkey, K. and McKinlay, A. (1994), Managing for Ford, *Sociology*, Vol.28, No.4, pp 975-990.

Steakley, J.D. (1975), *The Homosexual Emancipation Movement in Germany*, Adorno, New York.

Stier, H. and Tienda, M. (1993), Are Men Marginal to the Family? Insights from Chicagos Inner City, in Hood, J, C. (ed) (1993), *Men, Work, and Family*, Sage Publications, Newbury Park.

Stillion, J.M. (1995), Premature Death Among Males, in Sabo, D. and Frederick-Gordon, D. (1995), *Men's Health and Illness: Gender, Power and the Body*, Sage, London.

Stockman, N. (1994), Gender Inequality and Social Structure in Urban China, *Sociology*, Vol.28, No.3 pp 759-777.

Stomquist, N. (1990), Gender Inequality in Education: Accounting For Womens Subordination, *British Journal of the Sociology of Education*, Vol. 11, No.2, pp137-153.

Stuart, J. (1994), Patriarchy Reconsidered, *The Journal of Mens Studies*, Vol.2, No. 4, pp 309-324.

Stümke, H.G. (1989), *Homosexuelle in Deutschland: Eine Politishce*, Geschiete Beck, Muncih.

Syrett, M. (1985), *Temporary Work Today*, FRES, London.

Szasz, T. (1961), *The Myth of Mental Illness*, Paul Hesher, New York.

Tewksbury, R. (1993), Peep Shows and Perverts, *The Journal of Mens Studies*, Vol.2, No.1, pp 53-67.

Tiger, L. (1969). *Men in Groups*, Nelson, London.

Tilly, L.A. and Scott, J.W. (1987), *Women, Work and Family*, 2nd ed, Holt, Rinehart and Winston, New York.

Thrasher, F.M. (1927), *The Gang*, University of Chicago Press, Chicago.

Thorne, B. and Yalom, M. (eds) (1982), *Rethinking the Family: Some Feminist Questions*, Longman, London.

Thurstone, L.L. and Chave, E.J. (1929), *Primary Mental Attitudes*, Chicago University Press.

Tolson, A. (1987), *The Limits of Masculinity*, Routledge, London.

Tong, R. (1989), *Feminist Thought*, Unwin Hyman, London.

Trent, K. and South S.J. (1992), Sociodemongraphic Status, Parental Background, Childhood Family Structure an Attitudes towards Family Formation, *Journal of Marriage and the Family*, Vol.54, No.2, pp427-439.

Turbin, J. (1987), *State Intervention Into Labour Market For Youth: The Implementation of the Youth Training Scheme in Three Local Labour Markets*, Unpublished Ph.D. , University of Leicester.

Ungerson, C. (1987), *Policy is Personal:Sex, Gender and Informal Care*, Tavistock, London.

Vance, C.S. (1995), Social Construction Theory and Sexuality, in Berger, M., Wallis, B. and Watson, S. (1995), *Constructing Masculinity*, Routledge, London.

VanSoes, T.A. (1995), Structural Models of Family Labour Supply, *Journal of Human Relations*, Vol.30, No.1, pp 63-88.

Vogler, C. and Pahl, J. (1994), Money, Power and Inequality Within Marriage, *The Sociological Review*, Vol. 42, No.2, pp 263-288.

Walby, S. (1986), *Patriarchy at Work*, Polity Press, Cambridge.
Walby, S. (1989), Theorising Patriarchy, *Sociology*, Vol.23, No.2, pp213-234.
Walby, S. (1990), *Theorising Patriarchy*, Basil Blackwell, Cambridge.
Walby, S. and Bagguley, P. (1990), Sex Segregation in Local Labour Markets, *Work Employment and Society*, Vol. 4, No.1, pp59-81.
Waldron, I. (1995), Contributions of Changing Gender Differences in Behaviour and Social Roles to Changing Gender Differences in Mortality, in Sabo, D. and Frederick-Gordon, D. (1995), *Men's Health and Illness: Gender, Power and the Body*, Sage, London.
Walker, K.E. and Woods, M.E. (1976), *Time Use: A Measure of Household Production of Family Goods and Services*, American Home Economics Association, Washington.
Walker, A. and Lewis, P. (1977), Careers Advice and Employment Experiences Of A Small Group Of Handicapped School-Leavers, *Careers Quarterly*, Vol. 29, No. 1, pp5-14.
Wallman, S. (1984), *Eight London Households*, Tavistock, London.
Warren, S. and Jahoda, M. (eds)(1973), *Attitudes*, Penguin: Harmondsworth.
Wasserman, I. (1984), A Longtitudinal Analysis of the linkage Between Suicide, Unemployment and Marital dissolution, *Journal of Marriage and the Family*, Vol.46, pp 858-859.
Ward, C., Dale, A. and Joshi, H. (1993), Participation in the Labour Market, in Ferri, E. (ed) (1993), *Life at 33*, National Children's Bureau.
Warr, P. (1987), *Work Unemployment and Mental Health*, OUP, Oxford.
Weber, M. (1948), *The Protestant Ethic and the Spirit of Capitalism*, Butler and Tanner, London.
Wedderburn, D. and Crompton, R. (1972), *Workers Attitudes and Technology*, CUP, Cambridge.
Weiss, R.S. (1990), *Staying on Course: The Emotional and Social Lives of Men Who do well at Work*, Free Press: New York.
Westwood, S. (1996), Feckless Fathers: Masculinities and the British State, in MaCanGhaill, Máirtín. (ed) (1996), *Understanding Masculinity: Social Relations and Cultural Arenas*, Open University Press, Buckingham.
Westwood, S. and Bhachu, P. (1988), Images and Realities, *New Society*, May.
Wheelock, J. (1990), *Husbands at Home Routledge*, London.
Whelehan, I. (1995), *Modern Feminist Thought: From Second Wave to 'Post-Feminism'*, Edinburgh University Press, Edinburgh.
Whyte, W.F. (1943), *Street Corner Society*, University of Chicago Press, Chicago.
Wicker, A.W. (1969), Attitudes Versus Actions. *Journal of Social Issues*, Vol. 25, 41-78.

Wickham, A. (1986), *Women and Training*, Milton Keynes: Open University.

Wiggins, R.D. and Bynner, J. (1993), Social Attitudes, in Ferri, E. (1993), *Life at 33*, NCB.

Williams, N. (1993), Elderly Mexican American Men: Work and Family Patterns, in Hood, J. C. (ed) (1993), *Men, Work, and Family*, Sage Publications, Newbury Park.

Williams, W.L. (1992), From Samurai to Capitalist: Male Love, Mens Roles, and the Rise of Homophobia, in Japan, *The Journal of Mens Studies*, Vol.1, No.1, pp 71-74.

Willinger, B. (1993), Resistence to Change: College Mens Attitudes Toward Family and Work in the 1980s, in Hood, J. C. (ed) (1993), *Men, Work, and Family*, Sage Publications, Newbury Park.

Willot, S. and Griffin, C. (1996), Men, Masculinity and the Challenge of Long-Term Unemployment, in MaCanGhaill, Máirtín. (ed) (1996), *Understanding Masculinity: Social Relations and Cultural Arenas*, Open University Press, Buckingham

Wilkie, J.R. (1991), The Decline in Mens Labour Force Participation and Income and the Changing Structure of Family Economic Support, *Journal of Marriage and the Family*, Vol.53, pp 111-122.

Willis, P. (1977), *Learning to Labour*, Saxon House, Farnborough.

Wimbush, E. (1987), Transitions: Changing Work, Leisure and Health Experiences Among Mothers with Young Children, in Allatt, P., Keil, T., Bryman, A. and Bythway, B. (eds) (1987), *Women and the Life Cycle*, Macmillan, London.

Witz, A. (1992), *Professions and Patrairchy*, Routledge, London.

Wollstonecraft, M. (1985), *A Vindication of The Rights of Women* (1792), Penguin Classics, Harmondsworth.

Wray, K. (1985), *The Demand for Labour in a Local Labour Market with Particular Reference to Twilight Workers and Homeworkers*, Unpublished Ph.D, Loughbrough University of Technology.

Yelin, E., Maithais, S.D., Buesching, D.P., Clayton, R., Calucin, R. and Fifer, S. (1996), The Impact of Employment as an Intervention to increase the Recognition of Previously Untreated Anxiety Among Primary Physicians, *Social Science and Medicine*, Vol.42, No.7, pp 1069-1075.

Yogman, M.W., Vooley, J. and Kindlon, D. (1988), Fathers, Infants and Toddlers: A Developing Relationship, in Bronstein, P. and Cowan, C.P. (eds), *Fatherhood Today: Mens Changing Role in the Family*, Wiley Sons, New York.

Yudkin, S. and Holme, A. (1969), *Working Mothers and their Children*, London.

Zavella, R. (1987), *Womens Work and Chicano Families: Cannery Workers of the Santa Clarra Valley*, CUP, Cornell.

Zimmerman, M.A., Salem, D.A. and Maton, K.I (1995), Family Structure and Psychosocial Correlates among urban African-American Adolescent Males, *Child Development*, Vol.66, No.6, pp 1598-1613.

Index

158, 159, 160, 162, 168, 169, 170, 173, 174, 175, 176, 177, 179, 183, 186, 187, 190, 192, 193, 194, 195, 196, 197, 198, 199, 200, 201